DELIVERING DESTRUCTION

STUDIES IN MARINE CORPS HISTORY AND AMPHIBIOUS WARFARE

WILLIAM A. TAYLOR, EDITOR

This series advances understanding of Marine Corps history and amphibious warfare by publishing original scholarship across a broad spectrum of innovative studies. The series analyzes an extensive array of vital aspects of the Marine Corps, amphibious warfare, and their collective role in global security, including battles, leaders, strategy, operations, tactics, doctrine, technology, personnel, organization, and culture. Incorporating both historical and contemporary perspectives, this series publishes important literature about the Marine Corps and significant works relevant to amphibious warfare that span the globe, feature diverse methodologies, and reach general audiences. As a result, the series provides a professional home, central venue, and premier destination for the best and newest research on Marine Corps history and amphibious warfare.

DELIVERING DESTRUCTION

AMERICAN FIREPOWER AND AMPHIBIOUS ASSAULT FROM TARAWA TO IWO JIMA

CHRIS K. HEMLER

Naval Institute Press

Annapolis, Maryland

Naval Institute Press
291 Wood Road
Annapolis, MD 21402

Library of Congress Cataloging-in-Publication Data
Names: Hemler, Chris K., author.
Title: Delivering destruction : American firepower and amphibious assault from Tarawa to Iwo Jima / Chris K. Hemler.
Description: Annapolis, Maryland : Naval Institute Press, [2023] | Series: Studies in Marine Corps history and amphibious warfare | Includes bibliographical references and index.
Identifiers: LCCN 2023013518 (print) | LCCN 2023013519 (ebook) | ISBN 9781682471340 (hardcover) | ISBN 9781682471357 (ebook)
Subjects: LCSH: World War, 1939–1945—Naval operations, American. | World War, 1939–1945—Amphibious operations. | World War, 1939–1945—Campaigns—Pacific Area. | BISAC: HISTORY / Wars & Conflicts / World War II / Pacific Theater | HISTORY / Military / United States
Classification: LCC D769.45 .H46 2023 (print) | LCC D769.45 (ebook) | DDC 940.54/26—dc23/eng/20230501
LC record available at https://lccn.loc.gov/2023013518
LC ebook record available at https://lccn.loc.gov/2023013519

♾ Print editions meet the requirements of ANSI/NISO z39.48–1992 (Permanence of Paper).
Printed in the United States of America.

31 30 29 28 27 26 25 24 23 9 8 7 6 5 4 3 2 1
First printing

To Dylan and Lincoln

That whatever their future passions, they might remain forever students.

CONTENTS

MAPS

ACRONYMS

AAG	air, artillery, and (naval) gunfire
ALP	air liaison party
ANGLICO	air-naval gunfire liaison company
CSA	commander support aircraft
FLEX	fleet landing exercise
JASCO	joint assault signal company
LFASCU	landing force air support control unit
LCI	landing craft, infantry
LCVP	landing craft, vehicle, personnel
LST	landing ship, tank
LVT	amphibious vehicle, tracked
NGLO	naval gunfire liaison officer
SFCP	shore fire control party

FOREWORD
GETTING ASHORE

All of the major belligerents of World War II recognized a requirement to transport major land combat forces across water barriers, ranging from oceans to rivers, to seize important terrain defended by stationary and mobile enemy air and ground forces. The accumulated wisdom on opposed landings since Roman times suggested that the best place to land was a sandy beach that extended for miles, relatively free of destructive reefs and rocks, and punctuated by exit roads. The immediate strategic objective was to seize and secure a defensive landing site or a port to allow extended operations ashore (e.g., the occupation of Anglo-Danish Wessex in 1066). The history of such operations produced three results: the operations were too risky and not tried; over time and with heavy costs, the operations were stopped and any forces still ashore were withdrawn or abandoned; and the landings succeeded, at least in part.

Studying World War I landings, several national armed forces that faced strategic naval contingencies found the requirements for a permanent landing quite daunting. The British Commonwealth operations on Turkey's Gallipoli peninsula, 1915–16, provided lessons by the brigade, most of them negative. Recognizing some need for amphibious (ship-to-shore) operations, the naval forces of Great Britain, Japan, the United States, the Soviet Union, France, the Netherlands, Italy, and Spain created landing forces before World War II. Amphibious landings were most often thought of as raids upon port facilities, canal locks, bridges, communications sites, and other high-value naval warfare assets. The probability of landings of successful strategic significance seemed slight.

The ability to defend potential amphibious objectives—ports or extended beaches—seemed possible and likely to remain so for the future. Site defense plans included combat aircraft, heavy naval guns inside concrete casemates, protected howitzers, mortars, and anti-armor guns, heavy rapid fire (40- and 75-millimeter) cannon, and machine guns, all protected by bunkered infantry. Inland, a defender could hide tanks, assault guns, and mechanized infantry. The defender would have mines, traps, barriers, barbed wires, and smoke/gas generators. The German Atlantic Wall, 1940–44, was a laboratory for coast and port defenders.

The best amphibious option seemed to be a raid on key coastal facilities, conducted by elite troops equipped with the most advanced technology. The speed and special weapons might provide fleeting advantages: tactical surprises, enhanced by bombing and assaults by airborne infantry. The common factor was that the attackers would leave—an admission of limited missions mounted from the sea. In World War II, British forces mounted many such missions with varied success, as did the Soviet Union, Italy, and Spain.

The U.S. Marine Corps had little more capability for landing operations than any other nation's "marines," but it had organizational advantages that other forces did not have. It was a separate service (since 1834) in the Department of the Navy. It had good relations with Congress. Its "foreign service" since the 1880s had given it an image of combat competence and frugal service. The record of the Marine brigade in France, 1918, gave it a national reputation for professionalism, especially when General John J. Pershing assigned senior Marine officers to command Army units. In the postwar review of U.S. contingency plans and force structure, the Marine Corps received the missions of amphibious warfare, at least the role of planning and force development. Despite deployments to Nicaragua and China that stopped amphibious training, a cadre of sophisticated Marine officers especially dedicated to the amphibious missions inherent in War Plan Orange (i.e., war with Japan) worked out many of the requirements for successful landings against defended beaches.

Two major challenges faced the prewar amphibious planners. First was carrying ground forces ashore adequate to hold positions (inside the force beachhead line) so defended to allow mass logistical and troop offloading without enemy disruption. The second requirement came from the first. No likely enemy, especially Japan, would leave an appealing landing site undefended. When it came to Pacific islands—from coral atolls to the large Marianas identified as essential advanced air and naval bases—landing sites were obvious. The chances for surprise options of sites were limited.

All studies and war games at the Naval War College and the Marine Corps Schools–Quantico led to an unavoidable conclusion: cannon and machine guns mounted on landing ships (the Landing Ship, Tank [LST] and smaller beaching craft) and tracked amphibious vehicles (the Landing Vehicle, Tank 1–4 and Assault) could not silence well-built beach defense fortifications. To destroy or neutralize casemated coast artillery required accurate, high-velocity, flat trajectory naval guns mounted in the turrets of battleships, cruisers, and destroyers. Ships carrying the landing forces, ranging from large beaching ships like the LST to the landing craft and amphibian tractors carrying troops to the beach, faced rapid-fire cannon up to 40 millimeters and heavy machine guns. Heavy anti-armor cannon could ravage landing craft and amphibian vehicles. Such defenses could be placed in fortifications in defilade that allowed firing along the long axis of a beach, immune to naval gunfire. A defender could weaken and slow any landing forces with mines, barriers, traps, barbed wire, and clouds of gas and smoke. A defender could deploy infantry in field fortifications to protect his guns as well as position armored task forces for counterattacks out of naval gunfire range.

Thanks to the limited testing and a great deal of theorizing, the small cadre of Navy and Marine Corps officers who had become amphibious warfare experts (really, theorists) concluded by 1941 that to destroy beachport defense would require the heaviest shells any battleship could fire with perfect accuracy. With accuracy the determining factor, the 5- to 8-inch guns on destroyers and cruisers might be better options for penetrating gunports and apertures. Naval gunfire alone might not neutralize beach defenses. The only other off-shore source of destruction was an aerial bomb, carried by a carrier aircraft. In 1941–42 the two standard carrier aircraft for carrying a bomb could only carry one 500-pound bomb each.

This book gives a detailed account of how a small group of Navy and Marine Corps officers created the doctrine, techniques, communications technology, and skilled personnel that made naval gunfire and close air support (NGF-CAS) an essential ingredient in amphibious warfare.

The author provides the organizational framework that explains how the NGF-CAS pioneers worked through the service and operational barriers that slowed an essential reform that ensured the success of amphibious landings. The Japanese provided the final validation of NGF-CAS operations in 1944–45. Their defense of Peleliu and Iwo Jima demonstrated the lethality of Japanese cave and tunnel defense, but it did not prevent four Marine divisions from destroying the Japanese defenders. The Japanese paid the Marine Corps–Navy NGF-CAS spotters, fire directors, and naval gunfire and air crews the ultimate compliment on April 1, 1945, when the U.S. 10th Army landed two Marine and two U.S. Army divisions on the beaches of Okinawa. The Japanese garrison, more than 100,000 in numbers and as well armed as any other army, did not oppose the landing.

Allan R. Millett
Colonel, USMCR (Ret.)
Author, *Semper Fidelis: The History of the United States Marine Corps*

ACKNOWLEDGMENTS

My debts run deep. Only with the selfless and enduring support of friends, family, colleagues, and mentors did I complete this project. This work would not have been possible without the generous assistance—both personal and financial—of several individuals and organizations. John Lyles, Chris Ellis, Dominic Amaral, Alisa Whitley, Michael Westermeier, and Tyler Reed (all of or formerly of the Marine Corps History Division) provided patient and expert assistance at the Corps' archives in Quantico, Virginia. Annette Amerman, formerly with the History Division, made for a warm and selfless colleague along the way. I thank her for her wonderful and personal support.

Though the Quantico archives provided the preponderance of my sources, I also found evidence even closer to home. The U.S. Naval Academy's Special Collections and Archives Branch offered an essential source base. I thank Jennifer Bryan and her team, especially for the impressive digitized collection available online. Michael Macan at the Naval Academy's Nimitz Library was quick to provide research expertise as well. Chris McDougal with the National Museum of the Pacific War in Fredericksburg, Texas, also provided skillful assistance.

My research benefited from two substantial fellowships in 2019. The Marine Corps Heritage Foundation's General Lemuel C. Shepherd Jr. Memorial Dissertation Fellowship and the Naval History and Heritage Command's Rear Admiral Samuel Eliot Morison Supplemental Scholarship provided critical funding at an early juncture. I thank both organizations for their support, which allowed me to execute research early and often during my journey.

While tackling my dissertation, which later became this book, I spent three years teaching as a military instructor with the History Department at the U.S. Naval Academy. I could not have been more fortunate. In Annapolis, I was surrounded by a dedicated and encouraging cadre of scholars. Nearly every one of them contributed to my project in some form or fashion. Some directly guided my work and commented on my chapters. Others shared sources and shaped my research through conversation. Still others gave a heartening word when it was needed most. Though I will doubtlessly miss someone worthy of recognition, the following historians provided welcome guidance, critique, or encouragement: B. J. Armstrong, Mary DeCredico, Matthew Dziennik, Joe Eanett, Stan Fisher, Mark Folse, Bill Fouse, John Freymann, Fred Harrod, Jeff Hobbs, Wayne Hsieh, Marcus Jones, Molly Lester, Joe Moretz, Lee Pennington, Rick Ruth, Ernie Tucker, Don Wallace, and Kathy Williams. To the entire History Department at the Naval Academy: thank you. Similarly, I must offer my sincere appreciation to the many students I had the privilege to teach at Annapolis. Not only did their thoughts influence my scholarship, but they also inspired me to be a better Marine, historian, and person.

My graduate committee could have easily been confused with a list of award recipients at a prestigious academic banquet, yet somehow I stumbled into their collective presence at Texas A&M. I cannot adequately express my gratitude for professors Brian Linn, Lorien Foote, Lisa Cobbs, and Jasen Castillo. Together, they shaped my work, challenged my assumptions, encouraged my progress, and guided my interpretations. I thank each of them for their patience and generosity. To Brian Linn in particular, I must declare my unqualified thanks. He is the ideal graduate advisor—firm but patient, professional but approachable, demanding but pragmatic. It is only fitting that as this book approached the printing press, the Society for Military History righteously awarded Brian the 2023 Samuel Eliot Morison Prize for his remarkable service and achievements. Without his committed attention, I could not have succeeded.

My good sense to pursue graduate work at Texas A&M University gave me more than a top-tier committee. In College Station, I was surrounded by bright and engaged peers who influenced my work and guided my writing. Even after transitioning to my post at the Naval Academy, many of my Aggie colleagues continued to provide both critique and encouragement. I thank the members of the TAMU Summer Project, which provided an excellent space for critique, conversation, and fellowship. Under the charge of the ever-gracious Lisa Cobbs, the group endured well into the fall and winter seasons. I consider our longevity an accomplishment in itself. In particular, I must thank Mike Morris and Ryan Abt for their personal and engaged support in College Station and beyond.

As I moved the project from a dissertation to a manuscript, yet another team of scholars and professionals supported my efforts. I thank Padraic (Pat) Carlin, Bill Taylor, Allan Millett, Chris Robinson, Deborah Patton, Lisa Yambrick, Ashley Baird, Adam Kane, and two peer reviewers arranged through the Naval Institute Press. Each provided generous assistance in their respective roles; my words and ideas could never have transitioned into print without them.

While moving from a military to civilian career and completing this manuscript, a number of mentors provided steadfast support. For their patient and selfless encouragement—as well as their critical influence on my spiritual life—I thank Kyle Sponaugle and Aaron Hixson. Other mentors shaped my journey by guiding my professional growth beyond the military and the academic classroom. In particular, I thank Alexa Courtney, Steve Sheamer, and the remarkable band of humans at Frontier Design Group.

To my family—both extended and immediate—I owe unconditional thanks. My parents, in different ways, provided me with a foundation that enabled my boldest dreams. My father, Jody, and brother, Jon, gave constant encouragement. Their sheer curiosity about American history as well as our energetic conversations continue to inspire me.

Though hardly conscious of my endeavor, my daughter Dylan and son Lincoln provided inspiration just the same. In a twist of irony, sleepless nights attending to one child or another supplied unanticipated blocks of time to write. Finally, thank you to my wife, Paige, for her steadfast love and support. She cheered when I needed it most, and her confidence often carried me. I look forward to our days ahead.

Despite these Herculean efforts from family, friends, and colleagues, perfection continues to elude me. All remaining errors are my own.

MAP 1. CENTRAL PACIFIC OVERVIEW

Prepared by Chris Robinson

INTRODUCTION

In the morning hours of February 23, 1945, forty U.S. Marines scaled the 550-foot peak of Mount Suribachi on the volcanic island of Iwo Jima in the Western Pacific. Moments after cresting the height, the Marines discovered a nearby iron pipe, lashed an American ensign along its end, and raised their national colors over the battlefield below. Unsatisfied with the size of the initial flag, the detachment called for a larger ensign. As this second, grander flag went up, Associated Press photographer Joe Rosenthal snapped his iconic photograph. The picture quickly became a symbol of the Marines' unwavering courage and the fighting spirit of the American infantryman in the Pacific. Through heroic resolve, the image seemed to say, the Marines had overcome a tenacious Japanese enemy. Quite likely, Fleet Admiral Chester Nimitz had Rosenthal's image in mind when he declared that for the Marines on Iwo Jima, "uncommon valor was a common virtue."[1]

Heartening and patriotic as it may seem, the "uncommon valor" narrative fails to capture the full story of American triumph in the Pacific. Courageous infantrymen—though indispensable to final victory—did not win the conflict alone. Élan could hardly overwhelm the skilled Japanese defenders by itself. Rather, it took the full weight of American triphibious forces—those of land, sea, and air—to overwhelm the enemy. Behind the bayonet and nerve of the Marine rifleman on Iwo Jima was a sophisticated and highly evolved network of what this study terms triphibious firepower—an assault that encompassed heaven and earth. On D-day alone at Iwo Jima, more than 1,900 16-inch shells, 1,500 14-inch shells, and 30,000 5-inch shells came from American ships at sea. Simultaneously, hundreds of American aircraft rained ordnance from above. As men with rifles fought their way onto land, F4U Corsairs and F6F Hellcats screamed overhead at speeds exceeding four hundred miles per hour. Some planes strafed the beaches with .50-caliber machine gun fire while others dropped 100- and 1,000-pound bombs on stubborn defensive positions. Dozens more aircraft observed the chaos from above, communicating target adjustments to the ships offshore. As the landing force touched down on the beaches and surged its units ashore, 105-millimeter (mm) howitzer shells, 81-mm mortar rounds, and 75-mm pack howitzer rounds joined the orchestra.[2] Simply put, the landing force moved ashore behind a carefully choreographed symphony of devastation. In fact, the Americans' apparatus of firepower permitted the infantry's advance. In the struggle for Iwo Jima—as elsewhere in the Central Pacific—the progress of the Marine infantryman was both augmented by, and utterly dependent upon, robust and continuous fire support from the sea and sky.

Triphibious coordination did not come naturally to American forces in World War II. Indeed, the synchronization displayed at Iwo Jima required painstaking development and adaptation during the early years of the conflagration. In order to apply the tremendous firepower necessary to support the infantry's advance and to seize heavily fortified beaches, American task forces had to synchronize the efforts of their aggregate components. Throughout the battles of 1943 and 1944 on islands in the Gilbert, Marshall, and Mariana chains, the Marines refined their coordination of supporting fires, developed more reliable and effective means of fire control, and fostered stronger integration among the disparate components of the amphibious task forces. American troops learned that to achieve its fullest effect, firepower had to be coordinated, integrated, and properly managed.

Between 1943 and 1945, in direct response to the early combat lessons of the Pacific War, the U.S. Marine Corps' V (Amphibious) Corps embarked on a path of deliberate wartime adaptation to address the pressing tactical challenges of the amphibious assault. By war's end, the unit had adopted numerous changes in doctrine, training, organization, and battlefield tactics. Chief among those changes, the Marine Corps—with the assistance of the U.S. Navy—developed solutions in the control and coordination of triphibious firepower. Through both innovation and adaptation, a small, specialized service produced a dynamic system to effectively channel and orchestrate American firepower in the amphibious arena.

This study in fire control and supporting arms coordination spans several important academic fields. First, it expands the historiography of World War II. Although there are thousands of books on military operations in the Pacific theater, the organizations, concepts, technologies, and tactics that solved the challenges of triphibious firepower have gone largely unstudied. Instead, primary works on the Pacific War focus on strategy, generals and admirals, campaigns, and domestic support for the war.[3] More recent accounts highlight the international context of the war, recognize the U.S. Army's underappreciated role, or attempt a comprehensive, riveting narrative of the conflict.[4] But neither the classic studies nor the latest books address in any great detail how American forces in the Pacific solved the tactical problems of the amphibious assault and adapted their way to victory over Japan. Indeed, Phillips O'Brien's recent *How the War Was Won*—a volume that specifically accentuates the role of air and sea power in Allied victory—does not even list "amphibious warfare" or "U.S. Marine Corps" in its index.[5]

This study also addresses scholarship that attributes the Allies' victory in World War II to their industrial advantage or technological superiority.[6] While quantitative and technological advantages do matter, such narratives underplay the human contribution. This project contends that people, ideas, and decisions mattered. The mere presence of massive armies and superior weapons does not win battles. Individual judgment, calculation, and learning play decisive roles as well. In the case of the Pacific War, the Allies were forced to solve daunting tactical problems in applying firepower ashore. Although the weapons of war—Allied ships, aircraft, tanks, and howitzers— were indeed important, the effective and efficient application of those tools mattered even more. And that application depended upon a dynamic and proficient system of human experts. To leverage the weapons of triphibious war, the V Corps had to continuously apply technical skill, critical thinking, and reflective analysis. In other words, the Allies' "brute force" had to not only be present; it also had to be effectively prescribed, coordinated, and executed.

Additionally, the study expands scholars' understanding of Marine Corps history. The service's five-volume "official" account of the war—*History of U.S. Marine Corps Operations in World War II*—did not carefully track the Corps' wartime adaptation. Moreover, the series' final volume was published nearly half a century ago. Other primary works on Marine Corps history explore prewar innovation but do not examine the changes that occurred during the Central Pacific campaigns of 1943 to 1945.[7] The book that most closely approximates this study is Jeter Isely and Philip Crowl's *The U.S. Marines and Amphibious Warfare*, published in 1951. These historians argued that the Marine Corps created effective amphibious doctrine during the interwar period and gradually evolved its approach to the amphibious assault throughout the war. With a triumphalist tone, the authors presented a decades-long story of evolving doctrine and operations. They advanced such a well-supported thesis that over the course of seven decades, the book has achieved canonical status. Yet their landmark account did not analyze in detail the tactical components of the Marines' success—in particular, the critical role of firepower. This study will reexamine Isely and Crowl's enduring thesis by concentrating on the V Corps' development of fire control and the nascent units, training initiatives, and organizational changes that made triphibious firepower work in the Pacific.[8]

Other scholars have addressed the Marines' wartime adaptation but have not delivered a comprehensive account of triphibious warfare. Sharon Tosi Lacey's 2013 *Pacific Blitzkrieg* focused on "ground forces learning to work together" and emphasized the battlefield intersection between U.S. Army and Marine Corps units.[9] While underlining the lessons-learned approach and tactical adaptation that appears in this book, Lacey's study investigated infantry tactics, equipment, weapons, and vehicles. Naturally, then, *Pacific Blitzkrieg* gave minimal attention to the integration of the air and sea domains.

By telling the Marines' story of triphibious fire control and coordination in World War II, this work challenges the "uncommon valor" narrative of the Pacific War. Several historians have highlighted the Marines' tenacity and aggressive spirit throughout the island-hopping campaigns of the conflict.[10] Similarly, popular American films have glorified the Marine rifleman and his battlefield courage.[11] But this popular interpretation betrays the combat support behind the infantryman. Through painstaking development and committed staff work, the Marine Corps learned the necessity of effective and sustained firepower in the amphibious assault. Accordingly, this project decenters the well-recognized infantryman and sheds crucial light on the combat support and expertise that enabled Allied victory.

In recent decades, scholars have also highlighted the brutality and savagery of combat in the Pacific, with some blaming the war's horrific nature on racist attitudes, particularly among American troops.[12] However provocative, supporters of this thesis have failed to establish a direct connection between overtly racist attitudes and the conduct of combat soldiers. This book argues that the transformation of the battlefield in the Pacific lent itself to particular tactics, most notably the Americans' extensive use of firepower. By 1944 Japanese techniques had matured into a highly effective, and increasingly costly, defensive approach that extracted greater and greater human costs from the attacker. As enemy troops closed in on the Home Islands, Japanese forces increased their zeal—already at a remarkable level—in defense of the empire. To further complicate their tactical missions, the Marines' island assaults left little room for maneuver, and the costly frontal attack often became the Americans' only tactical option. To seize their assigned objectives, Allied forces required more firepower—and consequently more destruction. In short, each side dug into its entrenched mission and aggravated the already savage nature of combat in the Pacific. Although the ferocity of the war continues to trouble contemporary observers, this work argues that it was the nature of combat and the transformation of the Pacific War battlefield—not racism—that explain the conflict's ferocious emphasis on firepower.[13]

In a broader context, this book contributes to the study of military innovation and adaptation by exploring the V Corps' development of fire control and coordination. Although recent scholarship has highlighted these themes in the study of war, most historians have turned their focus to the U.S. Army and the European theater. In addition, contemporary theories on military innovation continue to neglect ground-level tactical improvisation, the very catalyst that drove the Marines' evolution.[14] To address these gaps, this book will study the Marine Corps' adaptation on the battlefield and at the grassroots level. Consequently, it will minimize the perspective of senior leaders and service hierarchies while elevating the experiences of those engaged directly in the field—those carrying the ammunition, handling the radios, and advancing into the sights of enemy guns. Through this perspective, the book will explore the conditions required for intrawar, bottom-up change on the front lines. By broadening the scope to include the Pacific War and the specialists behind the rifleman, this work breaks new ground and uncovers a fresh account of wartime adaptation.

Though a topic of increasing attention in the twenty-first century, military adaptation remains understudied in relation to its significance. Past generations of scholars—most notably in the 1990s—turned to peacetime innovation, technological achievement, and other precombat ingredients to explain victory on the battlefield. Triumph, for these authors, was in the preliminary arrangements.[15] But as military historian Frank G. Hoffman persuasively argues in his 2021 book *Mars Adapting*, "the ultimate test of military preparation and effectiveness does not end once a war begins. On the contrary, history strongly reflects the enduring phenomena of learning and implementing change during war as well."[16] Hoffman's conclusion is welcome, but it is not a revelation. As the great nineteenth-century military theorist Carl von Clausewitz inherently understood, war demanded flexibility and learning. For the Prussian general, combat experience was the only reliable means of introducing and then habituating an army to war. Adaptation was natural, necessary, and ultimately decisive.[17] This project joins a contemporary cadre of scholars focused not on prewar actions and predictive formulas but rather on the decisive role of adaptation during war.[18]

The book also sheds critical light on security studies and existing debates over the evolution of twentieth-century warfare. Historians have argued convincingly that a "modern" form of combat emerged in World War I. As the belligerents came to blows in the early years of the conflict, armies struggled to deal with the new technologies and devastating firepower of the twentieth century. Faced with machine guns, trenches, and the rising dominance of artillery fire, military leaders were forced to work out the tactical solutions of modern war. Without question, the Great War had ushered in a new era of conflict—one in which firepower was king. The message of 1918 was straightforward and unchallenged: in battle, artillery conquers, and infantry occupies. One need only coordinate artillery fire with the movement of the riflemen to achieve unity—and success—in combat.[19]

But the story of "modern" warfare is much richer and more complicated than the immediate realizations of the Great War. Those who recognize the dominance of artillery in that conflict are correct, but their investigation is incomplete. Despite the conflict's fundamental restructuring of firepower and ground operations, the war left several tactical problems unsolved—or, more appropriately, unacknowledged. Most notably, the challenge of applying modern firepower in amphibious warfare remained unaddressed, as the British-led attack at Gallipoli so clearly demonstrated through its insufficient fire support, inaccurate intelligence, and inadequate logistics.

The great European conflict made firepower king, but that conclusion alone did not resolve all operational issues. Indeed, the technology that enabled such destruction and bloodshed in World War I also advanced the complexity and inherent challenges of combined military operations, a term for which (despite its utility and pervasiveness) historian Jeremy Black concludes "there remains no agreed definition."[20] To fill the void, Black argues that combined operations revolve around varying blends of firepower ("combined arms"), unit types (such as naval and land forces), and even national allegiances (typically in the form of alliances).

This study will primarily investigate the first two components of Black's comprehensive definition: the combination of firepower and disparate units operating in battle. As will become clear in the experience of the V Corps—and in Black's own words—"by their very nature [these] combined operations face major issues in cooperation between institutions, groups, and individuals who have different backgrounds, cultures, training, fighting practices, weaponry platforms, and often interests."[21] The V Corps' challenges in the Pacific included these hurdles and more, as the American services labored to draw together nascent technology, disparate unit cultures, and untested tactics while operating under the incredible institutional and human pressures of war.

Given its focus on the U.S. Marine Corps' V Corps, this study highlights the role of triphibious operations, a type of warfare that both originated and reached a rapid zenith in the massive battles of the Pacific War. It was in the South and Central Pacific where the unresolved prewar issue of applying and coordinating triphibious firepower found acute relevance.

And it was here where the Americans would come to lead the Allied war effort. Accordingly, the dilemma of triphibious operations and the questions it produced fell primarily to the United States. When fighting across the world's oceans, how would units apply newfound military power? How did the "modern system" of twentieth-century conflict fit into the amphibious space? How would naval gunfire and aviation support factor in? And with more developed ships, aircraft, tanks, and guns, how would armed forces manage and coordinate their efforts across even greater geographical space and altitude without blowing up the wrong men?

World War II, then, initiated a second wave of development in modern warfare. Added to the fundamental coordination of infantry, artillery, and tanks was the integration of naval gunfire and air support. Inherent in this new brand of combat were the challenges of radio communication, impending sea states, and increased mobility on the oceans, in the skies, and ashore. If the engagements of the Great War might be compared to an "age of sail" frigate, with its rather basic designs and capabilities, World War II introduced the ironclad *Monitor*, with its steam-powered propeller, revolving turret, and 11-inch guns. The problem was far more complex, and the product was far more destructive.

This book broadens our understanding of Marine Corps history, World War II, and the study of military innovation and adaptation at both the tactical and operational levels. As the weapons of war have changed, armed forces have continued to wrestle with the successful integration of firepower on the battlefield. Building upon the lessons of artillery employment and infantry maneuver from World War I, the Marine Corps learned how to apply modern weapons and methods on the bloody beachheads of the twentieth century's second great conflict.

CHAPTER 1

"GETTING THE SHELLS TO FALL WHERE YOU WANT THEM"

COORDINATING NAVAL GUNFIRE AND AIR SUPPORT IN THE INTERWAR PERIOD

Traditional accounts maintain that the United States Marine Corps deserves near-unqualified praise for its pioneering work in amphibious warfare during the years of peace between the world wars. Though some challenges remained, these authors reason, the Marines had resolved every predictable hurdle of the amphibious assault. Led by visionaries such as George Barnett, Earl "Pete" Ellis, John Lejeune, and John Russell, the Marines grappled with the intricacies of amphibious combat and emerged with established principles and reliable doctrine by which they would defeat their enemy. In these widely accepted interpretations, the fighting itself was predetermined; the battles were decided even before they began.[1]

Despite this rousing narrative, it is clear that Navy and Marine Corps planners failed to sufficiently address several problems that would confront U.S. forces in the looming conflict. Of these omissions, one of the greatest concerned the application of naval and aerial fires in support of an amphibious landing.[2] Though American officers recognized and resolved concerns over landing craft, logistics, casualty evacuation procedures, communications, and much more, planners failed to solve the difficulties of controlling and coordinating supporting firepower in a triphibious operation.[3]

This revision does not discredit the significant progress the Navy and Marine Corps made in amphibious warfare between 1918 and 1941. Throughout the 1920s the Americans advanced their war plans for the Pacific, improved the technology and techniques required to move a landing force from ship to shore, and developed promising models for future landing craft and amphibian tractors. Building on this foundation, throughout the 1930s, U.S. naval officers considered more carefully the problems of both getting to and staying on the beach. Leaders dedicated increasing attention to firepower considerations, both on- and offshore. But their efforts were often constrained by an independent approach to naval, aerial, and ground-based fires. When war began, the critical challenge of integrating and coordinating triphibious firepower in an amphibious assault remained.

A TASK TOO TALL: THE AMPHIBIOUS ASSAULT IN THE EARLY TWENTIETH CENTURY

In the nineteenth and early twentieth centuries, conventional military wisdom ruled that assaulting an enemy-held shore was an irrational, impractical, even idiotic proposition. Contemporary technology seemed to grant almost every advantage to the defender. Inherently, land-based guns benefitted from a more stable firing platform, larger shells, and more reliable targeting methods. These characteristics promised increased range, improved accuracy, and more destructive power over shipboard ordnance. To seize a defended shore—in the face of machine guns, entrenched artillery, and preregistered mortars—amphibious troops would need to overcome suicidal disadvantages. For the attentive student, the task seemed all but impossible. As British Admiral John Fisher put it during World War I: "Any naval officer who engages a fort worthy of the name deserves to be shot."[4]

Indeed, the Allied disaster at the Dardanelles in 1915 confirmed the death of the amphibious assault as a sensible military operation.[5] In their attempt to land on the Gallipoli peninsula and expel the Ottoman empire from World War I, British and French forces experienced stunning failure. Although the troops got ashore, the operation suffered from poorly trained, underequipped units unprepared for the full challenge. These shortcomings were multiplied by tactical errors of the highest degree. Several units landed on the wrong beaches, touching down on territory that did not even appear on their maps. In the opening moments, British and French commanders acted with indecision and failed to create any momentum along the tenuous beachhead. Air support, naval gunfire, and artillery all proved insufficient. Amid the chaos, Ottoman counterattacks stole any semblance of initiative from the floundering assault. By January 1916 Allied forces had abandoned the landing and retreated from the theater.[6] Though the lesson would take time to crystallize, Gallipoli suggested just how difficult it could be to surge combat power ashore in the face of a capable and entrenched defensive force. Not just getting ashore, but remaining ashore, would prove a significant challenge for any future landing force.

In the aftermath of the bungled Gallipoli attack, military officers and advisors alike had renewed reason to retire the amphibious assault. For most military theorists, the mere name Gallipoli became "synonymous with incompetence and failure."[7] Even the chief of staff of the Royal Navy squadron during the Dardanelles operation, Commodore Roger Keyes, declared that "[one of] the most valuable lessons we learnt from the original landings was the folly of attempting to storm a defended beach in daylight."[8] The twentieth-century amphibious assault, it seemed, was suited for none but a martial madman.

Such deep-seated doubts over offensive landing operations were hardly unique to British officers. Skepticism ran deep in the U.S. Army as well, where officers were quick to point out the inherent advantages of the defender. In a focused piece on coastal defense procedures, Army Major General William G. Haan summarized the attacker's precarious situation: "An enemy landing from boats on an open beach will consist largely of infantry without transportation, with limited ammunition and with no artillery except the smallest portable guns."[9] In Haan's mind, the outcome was predetermined—the inadequate firepower of the landing force would be no match for a mobile defense with artillery, obstacles, and modern machine guns at its disposal. In nearly every consideration, the amphibious assault was an onerous—perhaps even futile—endeavor.

Against this stern and well-founded resistance, however, the Marine Corps began to plot the complexities, challenges, and potential solutions of the modern amphibious assault. Alerted by Japan's growing ambitions in China and already serving the twentieth-century Navy as an "advance-base force," the Corps embarked on an energized search for purpose. Hopeful that the amphibious mission would bolster and confirm the Corps' contribution within the American armed forces, several key leaders embarked on a tumultuous transformation of the Marines' capabilities, structure, and commission.[10] The decades ahead promised change for the Corps, but few could have predicted just how fundamental, and ultimately decisive, that change would be.

SETTING A NEW COURSE: THE MARINES AS AMPHIBIOUS PIONEERS

The Marine Corps emerged from World War I with newfound credibility, combat experience, and, most importantly, public support. Throughout their service in General John Pershing's American Expeditionary Forces—and most notably at Belleau Wood—the Marines displayed remarkable courage, grit, and resiliency. Enjoying more autonomy and higher quality recruits because of their service's relatively small size, the Marines used their wartime exploits to cultivate their identity as an elite, specialized force. A dash of embellishment on top—aided by the American press corps—further solidified the Marines' image. Even before the belligerent nations made their peace at Versailles in 1919, the Marine Corps had bolstered its reputation as a distinct and unparalleled American fighting force.[11] Yet even in light of a reinforced image, Marines and outsiders alike continued to disagree over the Corps' proper role in the American military apparatus. Should it continue a trend of expeditionary service on land, act as a colonial police force, or reassert its naval roots and purpose?[12] Though the service had strengthened its standing, World War I further compromised the existential purpose of the Marine Corps.

In the aftermath of the war, then, the Marines pivoted back to their prewar function as an advance-base force of the U.S. Navy. Under this vision (which found both its roots and its strength in the ideas of the indomitable naval theorist Alfred Thayer Mahan), the Marines were to act as a maritime force capable of securing and defending overseas bases that would, in turn, sustain American warships anywhere in the world. By seizing an expanding web of coaling stations for the U.S. fleet, the Marine Corps would play a fundamental role in any future naval conflict.

Yet this early concept still pictured the Marines as a reactive, defensive force rather than a robust team built for offensive landing operations. The Marines were to seize territory and fortify it for battle. At most, they anticipated nominal resistance. More likely, they would land unopposed and claim the bases as their own. As two notable Marine historians revealed, "In practice all of the training concentrated on the defense. . . . [The] advance-base force was in actuality little more than an embryo coastal artillery unit."[13]

Two Marines in particular deserve credit for gradually shifting the Corps' attention from the defense of unoccupied shores to the rapid, offensive seizure of strengthened enemy posts. The first, John A. Lejeune, became Marine commandant in 1920 and set the service on a progressive, patient path toward aggressive amphibious operations. Unsettled by growing Japanese aggression in the Pacific and alarmed by the significant territorial concessions made to Japan at Versailles, Lejeune began to connect American security in the Pacific with the U.S. ability to launch offensive landing operations across the region. Pursuing his vision for a modern Marine Corps, Lejeune slowly refined and buttressed the service's purpose in light of contemporary security concerns.[14]

Lejeune was hardly the first to detect the growing rift in the Pacific. Indeed, by the early 1920s the Navy Department identified Japan as its most likely future enemy and began deliberate preparations for the looming contest. The resultant plan—famously labeled War Plan Orange—went through a series of revisions in the succeeding decades, each of which centered on defending the Philippines and waging a prolonged naval campaign to capture Japanese bases across the Pacific. Here, Lejeune's shift toward offensive amphibious operations neatly paralleled—indeed, reflected—the Navy's intention to turn back Japanese expansion. War with Japan would compel a succession of amphibious assaults across the Central and Western Pacific. Lejeune, and Marine leaders that followed, were determined to position the Marine Corps for that exact task. Of course, shifting the Marines' focus to offensive landing operations not only helped solve the operational problems of a future Pacific war, it also delivered an existential purpose for the post–World War I Corps.

To study the growing problem in the Pacific, Lejeune appointed a young staff officer named Earl "Pete" Ellis. Though Ellis was known as a heavy drinker with a fiery temper, he also carried an equally established reputation as one of the Corps' most talented strategic thinkers. Even for the disciplined and professional Lejeune, Ellis' brilliance outweighed his dangerous penchant for a stiff drink. When Lejeune, as commanding general of the 2d Division during World War I, was alerted that Ellis appeared "indisposed," he snapped a confident reply: "Ellis drunk is better than anyone else around here sober."[15]

Having established a personal rapport with Lejeune, Ellis emerged from the Great War ready to tackle the general's next great task: that of confronting the Japanese in the Pacific. Alongside the Navy Department's broader development of War Plan Orange, Ellis quickly acknowledged the disturbing but unavoidable work that awaited the Corps. In order to win a contest in the Pacific, the Marines would have to prepare for a succession of concentrated amphibious assaults. As the prescient Ellis well knew, such attacks would be met by fierce and organized Japanese resistance from hardened island positions. In words that would become prophecy, Ellis declared: "The landing will entirely succeed or fail practically on the beach."[16]

Fatefully, Ellis would not live to see the theoretical battles that he studied with such vigor and diligence. In 1923 he died on Palau Island while on a self-appointed reconnaissance mission to study existing Japanese defenses. Though the circumstances remained mysterious for decades, recent evidence shows that Ellis drank himself to death, allowing his personal vice to get the best of him.[17] Nonetheless, his capstone research, eventually christened "Operation Plan 712: Advanced Base Operations in Micronesia," formed the Corps' interwar foundation of amphibious strategy and doctrine. In part, Ellis' pioneering work helped advance the rising stature and expectations of the Marines. By 1927 a Navy Department directive specifically assigned amphibious landing operations to the Marine Corps, and in 1933 Navy General Order 241 reorganized the Corps as a "Fleet Marine Force." Through these bold bureaucratic moves—and in large part thanks to the energetic leadership and vision of John Lejeune and Pete Ellis—the service found itself explicitly structured for its budding amphibious mission.[18]

PAINFUL FITS AND STARTS: EARLY AMPHIBIOUS EXERCISES AND DOCTRINAL PROGRESS

Administrative change was one thing, but if the Marines were to embrace and develop their nascent mission, they would need practical, hands-on experience. In 1922—just months after Ellis completed his landmark Operation Plan 712—the Corps formed a provisional battalion and dispatched it to Guantanamo Bay and Culebra (in Cuba) for a series of landing exercises. The following year a detachment of Marines practiced amphibious landings at Cape Cod. By early 1924 the Marine Corps had solicited participation from the Navy's Atlantic Fleet and several nearby Army contingents for a further sequence of exercises at Culebra.

These early amphibious maneuvers—or fleet problems, as they were titled—presented the Marines with a number of obvious challenges, perhaps too many to address at once. The 1924 operations at Culebra revealed embarkation difficulties, poor timeline coordination across the force, inefficient loading procedures, and inadequate transport shipping (in both amount and quality). The most pressing concern exposed in the Caribbean maneuvers, however, concerned the Navy Department's landing craft. Navy and Marine officers alike found the attack craft too few in quantity and generally unsuited for the task. Although the inadequacy of the boats became clear at this early stage of the interwar period, it would take years before the Corps settled on a permanent model.[19]

After their Caribbean ventures, the Marines completed one final landing exercise (based on the historical example of Gallipoli) on the Hawaiian island of Oahu in the spring of 1925 before tabling their practical amphibious training for more than five years.[20] Sidelined by events abroad, Marine expeditionary service in China and Nicaragua siphoned both valuable troops and senior leaders' attention from the amphibious mission. Accordingly, not until the mid-1930s would the service resume its exercises and refocus its full attention on the seizure of enemy-held islands.

To their credit, senior Marine leaders quickly reasserted the Marines' amphibious role in the aftermath of the Chinese and Nicaraguan expeditions. Under Commandant Ben H. Fuller and Assistant Commandant John H. Russell, the Corps set out to develop the requisite doctrine for the task in front of them; indeed, as the years passed, conflict in the Pacific seemed only more likely. Beginning in 1931 Fuller and Russell took increasing advantage of the resident faculty, staff, and students at the Marine Corps Schools in Quantico, Virginia, and assigned them to study amphibious landing operations. By November 1933 Fuller had ordered that Quantico discontinue all ongoing classes, form specialized committees to study particular aspects of the task, and otherwise dedicate complete focus to the creation of a suitable manual.[21]

The resulting doctrine, codified as the *Tentative Manual for Landing Operations* in 1934, became the Marines' interwar roadmap. In the words of Jeter Isely and Philip Crowl, the manual represented "pioneer work of the most daring and imaginative sort."[22] The study, later adopted and rebranded as the Navy's Fleet Training Publication 167, addressed command relationships, transportation, logistics, and preparatory training as it related to offensive landing operations. Spurred by visionary leaders such as Lejeune, Ellis, Fuller, and Russell, the impromptu committees tackled their commission with vigor and, within a few years, provided a firm theoretical foundation for the Corps' future niche.[23]

On top of its more general guidance, the *Tentative Manual* acknowledged the essential roles of naval gunfire and air support during offensive landing operations. Lacking artillery in the opening minutes (perhaps even hours) of the assault, the landing force was compelled to rely upon alternative forms of supporting firepower. As the manual flatly stated: "A landing operation against opposition is, in effect, an assault on [a] defensive position modified by substituting initially ships' gunfire for that of light, medium, and heavy field artillery, and frequently, carrier-based aviation for land-based air units until the latter can be operated from shore."[24]

Though the manual recognized the significance of sea-based fire support, naval gunfire presented a number of practical challenges for U.S. forces at the time. While the landed artilleryman fired from a stable position, Sailors at sea fired from a moving platform amid rolling waves and threatening swells. Further, naval guns were designed for combat at sea, lacking the high muzzle angles and resulting trajectories of land-based fire support. While artillery ashore operated in close proximity to the infantry units they supported (especially in the condensed beachhead of an amphibious assault), ships at sea fought from dedicated "firing stations" typically between six and eleven miles offshore. At such distances, the ships depended upon remote "observers"—either ashore or airborne—to assist in targeting, record effects, and make spotting adjustments during battle. To add even more complexity, ships steamed at speeds approaching if not exceeding twenty knots while they maneuvered and perhaps even evaded enemy threats within the coordinates of their assigned firing station. Inherently, radio communications became more difficult across sand, surf, and sea. In short, projecting a single, accurately placed naval shell on a land target under the chaotic circumstances of amphibious combat was no simple task.[25]

If controlling naval gunfire was difficult, coordinating it within the broader efforts of an American task force was an even more formidable chore during the interwar period. Yet alongside a Navy culture committed to conventional surface operations and the emergence of the aircraft carrier, the challenge of cross-community coordination became all the more acute. Perhaps for this reason, the *Tentative Manual* focused on the distinct and independent execution of naval gunfire, and the Marines' treatise largely neglected the indispensable coordination of firepower.[26] Although the manual devoted twenty-eight pages to the "Employment of Naval Supporting Groups" in amphibious operations, not even one full page went to the section on "coordination of ships' gunfire."[27] Instead, most of the chapter's ink went to the organization of the naval task force, the positioning of the vessels, and the most effective fuze-shell combinations for targets ashore. Yet as the U.S. Navy and Marine Corps were destined to learn on the future battlefields of the Pacific, amphibious assaults required close and committed cooperation. Even one component out of tune with the larger scheme could spell disaster for the entire endeavor.

The *Tentative Manual* also addressed aerial support with unfettered confidence but offered little advice on how to synchronize aircraft within the larger scheme of the battle. While assigning pilots tasks such as reconnaissance and close support of the landing force, the authors of the manual failed to adequately address coordination between sea-based and aerial fires.

The treatise discussed aerial spotting—by then an established mission for aviators—but did not delve into the intricacies of air-ground coordination or communication.[28] In these ways, the 1934 manual continued to highlight the individual roles of naval gunfire and air support without confronting the more general coordination of land, sea, and air efforts.

The *Tentative Manual* also minimized the importance of flexibility and continuous coverage in amphibious fire support. Here, the authors valued centralization over responsiveness, dictating that fire support should be "carefully regulated by a firing schedule" rather than remain sensitive to the actual progress of the landing force.[29] Instead of demanding a continuous umbrella of firepower to protect and enable the attacking infantry, the manual accepted that "the time gap between the lift of beach fire of off-shore supporting ships and the landing of the first assault wave is inherently large."[30] By conceding a significant hiatus in fire support just as the landing force approached the beach and choosing centralization over flexibility, the Marines' prewar theory failed to deal with the dynamic conditions of an amphibious assault. Such formulaic firepower would hardly be enough to put a landing force ashore.

The manual's noticeable omissions concerning naval gunfire may perplex the present-day observer, but they appear representative of broader Marine distrust in naval gunfire at the time. Just as Commandant Russell had begun arranging the initial development of the *Tentative Manual* in 1931, the Marine Corps chartered a special board of three Marine officers at Quantico to investigate the capabilities and limitations of naval gunfire in support of amphibious operations. The committee's eventual report, "Naval Gunfire in Support of Landings," though nominally confident, revealed more skepticism and concern than the final version of the *Tentative Manual* admitted several years later.

Although the committee displayed apparent confidence in its opening and concluding remarks, the details of the report exposed several alarming issues upon closer inspection. Rather prophetically, the report recognized one of the great unknowns that would plague the U.S. Navy and Marine Corps in the opening battles of the Pacific more than a decade later: the amount of naval gunfire support required to aid an amphibious assault. As the committee concluded on this matter, naval artillery could do the job, but it was difficult "to state in general terms what constitutes adequate artillery support, that is, the number of guns required to successfully attack on a given front."[31] Devoid of practical experience, few Navy or Marine officers had even a notion of the number of naval guns that would be sufficient—and more importantly, insufficient—to support a landing operation.

If uncertain about the exact number of naval vessels and guns required to send the landing force ashore, the 1931 Quantico board did recognize the importance of continuous fire support as the Marines approached the beach. Unlike the Corps' later manual, the special board discussed the dilemma between firepower coverage and the Marines' arrival on the beach with transparency and candor. If the assault was to succeed, the committee reasoned, the task force must "reduce to a minimum the interval between the lifting of the artillery fire from the hostile position and the arrival of the attacking infantry in that position."[32] But although they acknowledged what the *Tentative Manual* later refused to take on, the board members still stopped short of proposing a solution to the intractable issue: just how were Navy and Marine units to choreograph this delicate balance between effective fire support and the very safety of the men making their way ashore? The 1931 committee seemed satisfied to have recognized the problem without rectifying it.

Despite these underlying concerns, the general conclusions and recommendations of the board displayed steadfast confidence, just as the *Tentative Manual* would do three years later. Though accepting the complexity and inherent challenges of the modern amphibious assault, the 1931 committee touted that specialized equipment, diligent practice, and advanced training would all ensure success. In a display of confidence that future Marines were sure to take issue with, the board decreed that "with boats in sufficient numbers, of the proper type, speed and equipment, and with properly trained crews, the advance over water offers no particular disadvantage in itself."[33] At another point in their comments, the board judged that "the yearly target practices of the fleet demonstrate clearly that if the enemy positions were visible on the ground, and the form of the terrain and visibility permitted direct laying on the target, ships' guns could deliver an accurate, effective fire on hostile positions, so concentrated that attacking infantry could advance within reasonable assaulting distance before the fire would have been lifted."[34] Despite being aware that these conditions for success were more exceptional than typical, the board failed to investigate what might happen when enemy positions were not visible on the ground and enemy forces deliberately camouflaged, misled, and confused American plans. Of course, Japanese units were to take unforgiving advantage of such oversights.

While the special board's 1931 report included concerning details, neither the committee's formal conclusions nor the Marines' *Tentative Manual* that followed seemed willing to engage with the messy, difficult, perhaps even hopeless dilemma of appropriate naval gunfire coverage and the advance of the landing force. Looking past the official sources and into a personal conversation within the Marine Corps, however, it seems that frustration and skepticism ruled the day. Following his participation on the special board, Major Charles Barrett penned a biting letter to a fellow officer that revealed deep-seated doubt. In the context of a personal letter, Barrett seemed much more willing to discuss the inherent and perhaps insurmountable difficulties of the job. Given Barrett's familiarity with the topic and his participation on the 1931 special board, his analysis deserves to be quoted at length: "If the [enemy] machine guns open fire at a range as great as 1500 yards and the fire was immediately observed by the ships, they could only shell the beach for two or three minutes at the most, with [friendly] boats traveling at eight knots. It is more than likely that an alert enemy would hold his machine guns' fire until the disembarkation from the boats actually began, when help from the ships would be absolutely impossible."[35]

Once the landing force reached the beach, Barrett continued, the problem became even more acute:

> Theoretically, aero planes should be able to call for panels and thus keep you advised of the location of your front lines, but practically this does not work out so well. Panel men get killed; troops rushing forward cannot watch every plane for signals; troops in woods do not see the panels; planes get shot down. . . .

> The question then arises as to how to insert artillery fire into this melee and at what stage in the game; that is, from the artillery or ships which previously have not been firing. It seems absolutely impossible while the troops are still moving forward. If you wait until a battalion is stopped, the artillery fire will come too late as the damage will have been done. If you tell the front-line troops to stop and call for artillery fire as soon as fired upon, the result manifestly would be a halting hesitating attack and not the energetic operation pushed home to the limit which must be expected from troops that are to succeed.
>
> The foregoing discussion deals primarily with the question of where and when to put the fire, and does not consider the mechanical difficulties of *getting the shells to fall where you want them* [emphasis added]. Communications manifestly offer some troublesome problems. Then there is the question of getting the shells to fall on the enemy without doing damage to your own troops. We know that we can rarely succeed without artillery fire. If the fire falls on your own troops, it is not simply a question of killing some men, but the result is worse than not having any artillery at all, because the morale of the troops will be destroyed.[36]

Having established his reservations, Barrett offered a concluding admission that would appear almost verbatim in the Marines' *Tentative Manual* three years later. Unable to remedy the delicate balance between naval gunfire and the mobile landing force, Barrett conceded that on-call fire support was simply too dangerous, too difficult, and impossible for the amphibious assault. Accordingly, "[naval gunfire] support of infantry will have to be, in the future as in the past, according to some prearranged plan."[37]

TURNING INTO THE FOG: THE 1930S FLEET LANDING EXERCISES

With their doubts in hand, Navy and Marine officers alike knew that they had to turn their efforts to practical fleet training in order to make tangible progress with the amphibious assault. For all its groundbreaking theory, the *Tentative Manual* remained little more than an intellectual appraisal in 1934. As General James Breckinridge, then in command of the Marine Corps Schools in Quantico, put it, the authors of the manual had been "largely groping in the dark."[38] The head of the *Tentative Manual*'s aviation committee expressed a similar conviction, stating that his team had tackled its assigned tasks "with a lantern in one hand and a candle in the other."[39] Having wrestled with theory, it was time for practical learning.

Even as a few diligent leaders labored to turn the Navy and Marine Corps' attention toward amphibious training, they encountered a series of hurdles. First and foremost, a shift toward amphibious warfare faced opposition within the Navy Department itself. As historian Craig C. Felker has shown, many senior Navy leaders remained averse to amphibious operations throughout the 1930s. Primarily, their disapproval reflected concern that an amphibious pivot would necessarily dilute other training initiatives and compromise the identity of the fleet. Enchanted with Alfred Thayer Mahan, traditionalists clung to conventional naval warfare and the great theorist's vision of "decisive" battle. From this perspective, amphibious operations were nothing more than "a distraction from sea control."[40] As Mahanian disciples saw it, battleships were designed to fight the enemy at sea, not play second fiddle to a landing force laboring its way ashore. In this view, amphibious operations not only degraded but also endangered American battleships by tethering them to specific terrain—the landing beach. Restricted to nearby waters, the fleet remained under constant threat from enemy airfields and shore batteries. Mahan's adherants could not abide.[41]

In addition to the Navy's cultural aversion, a shortage in manpower plagued the Marines' ability to develop their amphibious efforts. As early as 1932, Commandant Ben H. Fuller wrote, "The reduction of the enlisted strength of the Marine Corps from 18,000 to 15,343 has made it impossible for the corps to carry out its primary mission of supporting the United States Fleet by maintaining a force in readiness to operate with the fleet. On the present strength only weakly skeletonized organizations of such arms that are essential to a modern military force can be maintained."[42]

At the time of Fuller's words, the Great Depression helped to cap the Herbert Hoover–era Marine Corps. But as the interwar years ticked by—and war became more likely—the Marines' manpower problem persisted. Five years later, in 1937, the enlisted force had grown by only 1,100 men. By 1939 total enlisted manpower reached just 17,500. Convinced that offensive naval forces had helped precipitate World War I, and equally certain that the Marine Corps represented an aggressive, interventionist tool, Congress embraced isolationist policies and strict caps that kept the service modest in size.[43]

On top of its general manpower constraints, a litany of military duties helped to further dilute the Marine Corps' interwar focus on amphibious training. As late as 1937, just 24 percent of the service's enlisted manpower served in Fleet Marine Force units. The remainder of the Corps filled shipboard duties, domestic and foreign guard duties, and expeditionary units (particularly in China). By 1939—and even as the international crises in Asia and Europe became more acute—the proportion of Marines in the Fleet Marine Force actually dropped to 20 percent, just 3,422 of the service's 17,500 enlisted troops. Not until 1940 did the Fleet Marine Force's proportion of manpower begin to surge, when 42 percent of the Corps served in such a capacity.[44]

Despite the personnel challenges of the 1930s and the powerful influence of Mahanian theory, the Navy and Marine Corps began to shift some attention toward the amphibious mission. After a hasty 1934 fleet maneuver in the Caribbean, the two services initiated a series of large-scale amphibious exercises meant to test American doctrine and procedures between 1935 and 1941. Appropriately titled fleet landing exercises (FLEXs), the annual drills drew together landing troops, naval gunfire platforms, and aviation sections for common training. Within the exercises, the Navy and Marine Corps made notable progress in particular elements of the amphibious assault. The design of landing craft improved reliably, with Andrew Higgins' "Eureka" prototype (eventually the famed Higgins boat) and the lesser-known Donald Roebling's amphibian tractor both emerging from the FLEX continuum. In addition, casualty evacuation procedures, beach organization practices, and the logistics behind the assault all matured.[45]

In spite of these humble strides and a genuine desire for realistic training conditions, the services' annual maneuvers suffered from debilitating artificialities. To reduce confusion on the beaches and maximize safety, the exercise umpires used stationary flags to represent enemy units and wooden targets to signify enemy pillboxes and bunkers. Consequently, the drills looked more like target practice than realistic maneuvers. Gunfire officers embraced area bombing over point-targeting, confident that a broad sweep of naval fires could do the job for the landing force. The umpires often prohibited naval gunfire training while friendly troops were ashore and instead directed the naval guns to fire on separate beaches and islands. Safe from each other's fires, the detached American forces failed to appreciate the tremendous complexity and onerous burden of coordinating naval gunfire under the chaotic and dynamic circumstances of an amphibious attack.[46]

Artificialities hampered the integration of aviation units in a comparable manner. Following FLEX 3 in 1938, Marine Captain W. C. Lemly drafted a biting critique of the operation: "First of all I should like to speak of artificialities. The San Clemente Exercise was full of them. The realistic element was not stressed enough." Because of the limitations, Lemly charged, the exercise was "little more realistic than a map problem." In his piercing conclusion, the aviator professed that "the training and benefit the squadron received in carrying out this operation order, other than through a vigorous exercise of the imagination, was practically nil."[47]

Throughout the FLEXs, Marines training ashore complained that the aviators lacked familiarity with the ground situation and were therefore unable to provide effective air support. Mechanical problems and communication errors often delayed the aircraft, leaving troops to clamor for more flexibility and responsiveness from their brothers overhead. In most training runs, the naval pilots focused on internal capabilities and missions, with only peripheral concern for amphibious integration.[48] Almost universally, units valued training safely over training realistically. As historian Allan Millett summarized, "The aviation bombing and strafing practices were, like the shore bombardments, so restricted by safety precautions that their utility was limited."[49] Throughout the interwar exercises, and in part because of the maneuvers' limitations, timely and effective air support remained elusive.

FLEX planners tolerated artificialities in the annual drills for a number of understandable—if not entirely defensible—reasons. First and foremost, commanders prioritized the safety of their troops and the survival of their equipment over the authenticity of battlefield conditions. For most officers, the desire to preserve life and limb was simply too strong. Budget limitations and a desire for simplicity also pushed the exercises toward artificiality. Training in a separate and scripted manner meant that the naval gunners could focus on their task of delivering shells ashore while the landing force focused on its mission of attacking the beach. Each of these factors contributed, however innocently, to unrealistic training conditions in the 1930s.

In short, as the Navy and Marine Corps focused almost singularly on their own individual tasks, the FLEXs consistently avoided the messy but essential business of coordinating triphibious operations and, in particular, triphibious firepower. Efficient and safe as it was in peacetime drills, the isolated and careful approach left little room to practice the larger integration of the task force. Instead of refining communications procedures and cooperation techniques between shipboard gunners, attacking aircraft, and infantry units, most ships obsessed over proper shell and fuze combinations for the wooden targets they prosecuted. The utter weight of their guns, applied through their familiar focus on "area fire" targeting, was sure to do the job. The landing force was equally content to focus on their own journey from the transport ships to the beach, as well as the logistics and other internal support measures that would sustain them ashore. Absorbed in their own challenging tasks, few leaders were concerned over the delicate orchestration of land, sea, and air actions.

TASK IDENTIFIED, RESOLUTION DELAYED

Even while the Navy and Marine Corps resolved important issues related to logistics, prelanding bombardments, the use of reserve troops, and the employment of landing craft during the interwar period, they failed to rectify the uncomfortable realities of supporting arms coordination during an amphibious assault. While notable pioneers provided important advances, the Americans' prewar approach was incomplete. Throughout the 1920s and into the 1930s, the Marine Corps focused its amphibious training time and resources on transporting a landing force from the ship to the beach. This phase produced important theories and promising landing craft prototypes, but it did not effectively address the full challenge of landing and sustaining combat power ashore.[50]

In those interwar years, lonely voices of concern could be heard. These visionaries recognized that despite valuable advances in offloading techniques, amphibious shipping and equipment, and procedural efficiencies, serious hurdles remained. The Navy and Marine Corps could get troops to the shore, that was clear. But how might they stay on the beach? It was an issue, they reasoned, of supporting firepower.

One admiral, after observing FLEX 2, argued that the Americans' interwar landing force was understrength in both firepower and personnel. The exercise, he judged, had provided insufficient training on the integration and fire support necessary to seize the beach. He came to the depressing conclusion that "against any sort of determined and resourceful opposition it is believed that the strength of the Fleet Marine Force is totally inadequate, for the purpose designated."[51] Following the next annual drill in 1937, a Marine lieutenant colonel added to the admiral's skepticism, arguing that even "complete and detailed orders cannot make up for a lack of training in a composite organization consisting of units that have not previously trained together."[52] By 1938 yet another critic went so far as to offer a solution in his postexercise report: "Troops should be required to request naval gunfire support to give needed training in coordination." Dodging the task was foolish, he continued, since these exact types of bombardments seem "quite certain to be required of our battleships in case of war. It is an intricate problem for which we lack much preparation."[53]

The following year, Navy Commander C. G. Richardson reflected these same sentiments, petitioning that "[our] fire control must provide for great flexibility of fire . . . and gun groups must permit heavy fire to be laid down immediately on any target observed." Since the interwar theory and associated war plans called for landing operations, he continued, "it is squarely up to us who comprise the naval service to accept this decision and proceed to the solution of the problem, no matter now involved or how difficult it may be."[54] But the pleas of Richardson and his predecessors often fell on deaf ears, as the majority of the naval officer corps sustained its preference for conventional fleet engagements.

Put simply—and in spite of the lonely critics—the late 1930s exercises revealed that U.S. Navy officers expected the destructiveness of their guns to win the battle outright. They would fire on the enemy, offload the Marines, and return to their cherished purpose of fighting at sea. Naval aviation's mission, except for the most committed of carrier warfare proponents, was to support battleship gunnery and reconnoiter the battlefield. For the Marines' part, they appeared content that supporting firepower would knock down enemy defenses, get the landing force ashore safely, and adequately assist the attack.

Between the world wars, very few American officers—either Navy or Marine—anticipated the inherent complexity and difficulty of triphibious coordination, integration, and flexibility. None of these principles seemed worthy of their close attention or concern. Between 1935 and 1941, the Navy and Marine Corps' fleet landing exercises failed to sufficiently address the orchestration of land, sea, and air operations. If the landing force was to get ashore against a fortified, prepared, and equipped enemy, someone had to carefully synchronize troop movements with supporting munitions. To be certain, some leaders identified the challenge and expressed appropriate concern, but even those engaged with the problem struggled to imagine or advance sufficient solutions. Tragically, this combination of ignorance and insufficient attention left the Americans categorically unprepared, at the outbreak of war, to effectively coordinate and integrate firepower during a contested amphibious assault.

CHAPTER 2

THE FIRST TEST

TARAWA, 1943

On November 19, 1943, Marines of the V Corps landed on the beaches of the Tarawa atoll in the Central Pacific, capping a deliberate institutional journey of more than twenty years. The amphibious theory and doctrine that the Marine Corps had labored to produce since 1920 were approaching examination day. After an intellectually creative but untested interwar phase, the Marines initiated their first contested amphibious assault of World War II.

It was here—on Tarawa's Betio Island in particular—that the Marines displayed the limits of their prewar preparation for triphibious war. Against a dogged enemy and unaccommodating environment, the Marine landing force struggled to execute the ideas that appeared so unassailably correct in the Corps' *Tentative Manual for Landing Operations*. Several obstacles revealed in the interwar FLEXs resurfaced, now accentuated by the unforgiving conditions of combat. But many of the worst problems that emerged on Tarawa had not been anticipated. Partially in light of its alarming costs, the battle of Tarawa provided a myriad of lessons for American forces to carry forward in their drive across the Central Pacific. In particular, U.S. troops experienced first-hand the failures in controlling and coordinating supporting firepower as they fought their way ashore. Informed by combat itself, the U.S. naval service finally got serious about developing the modern amphibious assault.

THE ROAD FROM PEARL HARBOR: JAPAN TRIUMPHANT

The path toward war in the Pacific began long before Japan's surprise attack at Pearl Harbor on December 7, 1941. For most of the 1930s the two nations anticipated and planned for a future conflict. When Japan seized Manchuria, occupied additional portions of China, and shifted its sights south toward British Malaya and the Dutch East Indies, the United States turned increasing attention to defense of the Philippines (an effort some deemed futile from the start). Concurrently, the Franklin D. Roosevelt administration ratcheted up economic pressure on Japan, including embargos on aircraft parts, aviation fuel, lubricants, and, eventually, iron and steel of all types. Following Japan's breezy march into Indochina in the spring of 1941, President Roosevelt froze Japanese assets in the United States and prohibited Japanese vessels—even those in mid-drop—from offloading cargo in American ports.[1]

By the autumn of 1941 renewed diplomacy could do little to reconcile the differences between American and Japanese perspectives. Even as Japanese representatives entertained U.S. Secretary of State Cordell Hull's plea for a summit meeting in September, Japanese negotiations were to continue "hand in hand with military preparations."[2] On November 5 Prime Minister Tojo Hideki determined—and senior advisors quickly concurred—that if no promising agreement emerged within the month, Japan would move to war. Preparing for such a possibility, a Japanese naval strike force consisting of six carriers and dozens of supporting vessels and submarines departed the coast of Etorofu on November 26 and set course for the American naval base at Pearl Harbor, thousands of miles across the fog and foam of the Pacific Ocean.[3]

After nearly two weeks of transit in complete radio silence, just before 8 a.m. on December 7, 1941, Admiral Chuichi Nagumo's carrier force commenced a stunning attack against American targets on and around the Hawaiian island of Oahu. Tactically speaking, the assault was a brilliant success. Nagumo's 360 bomber and fighter aircraft flew with near impunity as they strafed and bombed sitting duck targets on Hickam Airfield and then turned their sights toward vulnerable warships moored on "Battleship Row." As if waking from a daze, U.S. troops scrambled to mount an effective resistance. Although shipboard crews provided nominal opposition, U.S. shore batteries had no ammunition prepared at their gun positions when the first wave of enemy aircraft arrived. In acts representative of the moment, munitions vehicles frantically conveyed ordnance to the gun positions while troops climbed aboard static aircraft and pointed the mounted machine guns toward the sky.[4] Bewildered—perhaps even incredulous—American forces found themselves at war.

Though President Roosevelt declared that December 7 would "live in infamy," the passing of that painful day brought little relief for the United States. Indeed, Japan's blitz at Pearl Harbor commenced a six-month nightmare for American troops, statesmen, and citizens. Although the Marines' defense of Wake Island later that month offered a stirring tale of heroism and valor, the outpost fell just the same. Seizing Guam, Japanese forces secured complete control of the Central Pacific. Two weeks later, Americans watched British and Canadian forces surrender Hong Kong on Christmas day. Triumphant Japanese units marched south toward Singapore. In the Philippines, U.S. and Filipino troops evacuated Manila, retreating first to Bataan and then to Corregidor Island. Words from the Marine Corps' official history of the war captured the tenor of the moment: "The Japanese seemed to be everywhere at once and everywhere successful."[5]

Even as winter turned to spring, the Allied war effort in the Pacific stirred little hope. Singapore fell to the Japanese, where an army of 130,000 British, Australian, and Indian soldiers surrendered to an enemy force just half that strength. According to British Prime Minister Winston Churchill, it was "the worst disaster and largest capitulation of British history."[6] The news got worse in March when the Allies conceded the Dutch East Indies. That same month in Burma, the Allies commenced a spring retreat. Meanwhile, the American situation in the Philippines turned from bad to desperate. On Bataan and Corregidor, U.S. and Filipino soldiers went to one-third and eventually one-quarter rations.[7] In early May, as the Americans surrendered their remaining forces in the Philippines, British troops retreated west from Burma into India, yielding yet another corner of Southeast Asia to Japan's rapidly expanding "Greater East Asia Co-Prosperity Sphere." In the Pacific at least, Americans wondered just what the summer of 1942 would bring. With the Allied position in disarray, Japan reigned over Southeast Asia as well as the South and Central Pacific.

A TURNING TIDE: THE AMERICAN RESPONSE

Dark as the hometown headlines were in the spring of 1942, Americans drew strength from a few examples of determined—albeit strategically insignificant—heroism. In the days following the attack on Pearl Harbor, the Marines on Wake Island, armed with just twelve antiaircraft guns and a dozen F4F-3 Wildcat fighter aircraft, successfully turned back a Japanese task force of 450 men, three light cruisers, and six destroyers. American newspapers celebrated the Marines' underdog victory and circulated tales of dogged resistance. Although Japanese forces seized the island two weeks later with a far superior invasion party of two thousand men buttressed by two aircraft carriers and four heavy cruisers, U.S. news outlets clung to the valor and resolve displayed by the Marines on Wake.[8]

In the Philippines, Americans took courage from the tenacity of their Allied troops despite troubling realities. Fighting from the Bataan Peninsula, joint U.S.-Filipino forces stubbornly resisted for nearly five months before succumbing to the Japanese invaders. Here again, in spite of a terrible rout, U.S. citizens clung to the courage of Allied servicemen, who had fought to the bitter end. Perhaps—as evidenced on Wake Island and the Bataan Peninsula—there was hope amid the ashes of defeat.

Finally, American fortunes began to shift in the Pacific in the early summer of 1942. That June, the commander in chief of the Japanese combined fleet, Admiral Isoroku Yamamoto, made a bold attempt on the American outpost at Midway Island, some 1,500 miles west of Hawaii. Yamamoto spared no means. Hoping for the decisive blow that eluded him at Pearl Harbor, Yamamoto committed four large carriers, two light carriers, two battleships, eight cruisers, and twenty-five destroyers in a simultaneous attack on the U.S. base at Midway and the American-held Aleutian Islands, with the latter serving as a diversion. Yet even Yamamoto's threatening task force could not overcome the Americans' distinct advantage. This time, they knew the plan.

Alerted by determined U.S. codebreakers, Admiral Chester Nimitz, the commander in chief of the U.S. Pacific Fleet, laid a trap for his aggressive Japanese counterpart. After sighting the enemy strike force early on June 4, Nimitz's carriers made haste to close on the enemy and coordinate an air strike. While the fleets jockeyed for position and searched for one another on the open seas, luck took its turn in determining the course of the battle. Just as the Japanese carriers rearmed and refueled their aircraft from an earlier morning raid against Midway Island, American dive bombers located the enemy force and attacked the vulnerable Japanese flattops littered with fuel lines, bombs, and attending crewmen. Within minutes, American pilots scored a sequence of hits and set the carriers ablaze. The Japanese *Soryu*, *Akagi*, and *Kaga* all settled at the ocean bottom by nightfall, and *Hiryu* the next morning. Early the following morning, Admiral Yamamoto ordered a general retreat of his fleet. At a disheartening cost of four large carriers, Yamamoto's bid for Midway Island ended in utter disaster.[9]

Victory spurred American confidence and focused the country's strategic vision in the summer of 1942. With the Japanese fleet thrown on its heels, Allied forces could—for the first time in the Pacific theater—seize the initiative. Although President Roosevelt remained committed to a "Germany First" strategy on the counsel of his strategists and the insistence of his allies, he sanctioned a modest offensive in the Solomon Islands for August 1942. If successful, such an operation would safeguard communication and supply lines between the United States and Australia against a Japanese advance. Furthermore, action in the Solomons would enable an Allied attack on Japan's vital anchorage and aviation base at Rabaul, some six hundred miles to the northwest.[10]

Time was of the essence. Each passing week allowed the Japanese to increase their numbers and reinforce their defenses in the Solomon Islands. Accordingly, on July 2 the joint chiefs of staff formally directed Operation Watchtower, ordering August 1 landings on Tulagi and Guadalcanal at the southern end of the island chain. Though well-reasoned, Watchtower's condensed timeline caught nearly everyone off guard. Indeed, the 1st Marine Division—the amphibious assault force tasked with the Guadalcanal landing—was still at sea en route to its training grounds in New Zealand. Its commander, Major General Alexander Archer Vandegrift, had not expected a combat assignment before January 1943 at the earliest.[11] With gallows humor, Vandegrift's men replaced the operation's official title with a more representative moniker: "Operation Shoestring." Though the skepticism of the troops was natural, reality demanded rapidity. As authors Isely and Crowl later acknowledged, any Allied offensive in the Pacific in the summer of 1942 "would have required improvisation as to means."[12]

Notwithstanding the need for haste, Vandegrift secured his Marines a one-week delay. On August 7, 1942, the men of the 1st Marine Division charged ashore on Guadalcanal and established a defensive perimeter around the island's crucial airfield. To the Marines' surprise, they encountered only nominal resistance. The island's Japanese detachment was almost entirely made up of construction workers who, to the Marines' hearty relief, failed to live up to the powerful mystique of the Imperial Japanese Army. Digging in to their defensive positions, the 1st Marine Division renamed the airstrip Henderson Field in memory of a fallen aviator at the battle of Midway and prepared for the counterattack that was sure to come.

Despite the relatively bloodless landing, the Japanese response to Watchtower in the next days and weeks matched the Marines' prebattle expectations. Japanese commanders funneled reinforcements south from their stronghold in Rabaul. By day, Japanese pilots flew to Guadalcanal and peppered the island with continuous air strikes. By night, surface ships delivered infantry troops ashore under cover of darkness. Although their resistance proved fierce and unrelenting, a lack of intelligence plagued the Japanese endeavor, just as at Midway. Unaware of the Americans' true troop strength ashore, and convinced that their steady pressure would ultimately prevail, Japanese ground commanders squandered their units in local, piecemeal attacks.[13]

As the Marines strengthened their defensive perimeter around Henderson Field, the effect of American naval gunfire support was uneven. Referencing one particular bombardment in a mid-October memorandum, Admiral William "Bull" Halsey—commanding U.S. land, sea, and air forces in the South Pacific—wrote that naval gunfire was "considered highly effective."[14] Other commanders praised American ships' gunfire for reaching targets that landed artillery could not destroy. Yet in some cases, naval fires were held back by procedural inefficiencies and errors. In the same bombardment that Halsey labeled "highly effective," commanding officers of the destroyers USS *Aaron Ward* and USS *Lardner* reported fundamental lapses in coordination. The ships waited for almost three hours for their aerial spotter planes to check in on the assigned radio frequency. After continual attempts to contact the planes themselves, the gunners received confirmation from troops ashore that there were indeed "no spotting planes in the air." Finally, an aircraft arrived overhead, just as the ships were ordered to cease fire. As the *Ward* and *Lardner*'s reports concluded with disappointment, "no spots were received prior to cessation of the bombardment."[15]

In the early battles on Guadalcanal, American air-ground fire support encountered a number of problems. Whether communicating with ship gunfire crews via radio or integrating themselves within the larger choreography of the battle, American pilots had much to learn. Task Group 67.5, which consisted of destroyers *Nicholas*, *De Haven*, *O'Bannon*, and *Radford*, criticized Marine and Navy pilots for their inexperience with amphibious operations and their lack of familiarity with standard procedures.[16] The pilots themselves had other explanations. Major John Smith, a Marine F4F Wildcat pilot and future flying ace, bluntly alleged that on Guadalcanal, "long wave [radio] communications weren't worth a damn. They were using a frequency band which is good over water, but it's been proved time and time again that it is no good where you have land around it."[17] Another officer lamented that communications were "too unreliable" and were known to "go out unexpectedly."[18]

Regardless of blame, as Smith later reflected, "We were learning as much about them [the enemy] every day as they were about us, and it was just about even."[19] Even when technology and proximity did allow for coordination, U.S. ground and air forces were not always able to work to maximum effectiveness. When the battle of the Tenaru River (a misnomer, for the battle was actually fought over Alligator Creek) broke out on the night of August 20–21, Smith complained that "we didn't know what was going on. We thought it was just a Fourth of July celebration about a mile and a half from us, and went on to sleep." The following morning, Smith's squadron awoke to realize that nearby infantrymen had killed more than eight hundred Japanese troops. Understandably, the assistant operations officer of the 1st Marine Division petitioned for closer coordination—via an air liaison officer—between pilots and the infantrymen they supported.[20] Although Marine aviation support would improve noticeably throughout the campaign, cooperation did not organically arise in the Solomons.

While naval gunfire and air support efforts developed throughout the months-long Guadalcanal campaign, field artillery—in the form of 75-mm, 105-mm, and eventually 155-mm howitzers—quickly emerged as reliable and effective fire support. In their defense of Alligator Creek, Marine artillerymen fired 375 rounds from their 75-mm pack howitzers and 30 rounds from their 105-mm howitzers. As more cannons and ammunition streamed ashore, the 1st Marine Division relied increasingly on its artillery support. In the two-day battle for Edson's Ridge in mid-September, the Marines fired 878 rounds from their pack howitzers and 1,992 rounds from their 105-mm howitzers. By late October, Lieutenant Colonel Thomas Hughes' Marine artillery battalion was averaging more than six hundred rounds of 75-mm and 105-mm shells per day in interdiction and harassing fires alone. When supporting a specific tactical operation, howitzers added several thousand rounds to the effort.[21]

Despite earlier problems, air-ground coordination improved rapidly, especially once Brigadier General Roy Geiger's "Cactus Air Force" contested and eclipsed Japanese air superiority. In true complementary warfare, the Marines defended the airfield, and the airfield defended the Marines. Vandegrift's combined arms approach proved too much for the enemy's disjointed attacks, and by November the 1st Marine Division was relieved by the U.S. Army's XIV Corps (comprised of the 2d Marine Division, the 25th Infantry Division, and the Americal Division).[22] Though the struggle continued another three months, the outcome became increasingly inevitable. In early February 1943 the Americans declared Guadalcanal secure.[23]

The Marines took many substantive lessons from their struggle in the Solomons, including several in firepower coordination and control. First, the infantry units and their supporting firepower needed common maps instead of their internally specific nautical charts, aerial overlays, or ground terrain maps. In several instances, divergent maps delayed or even precluded effective coordination on the battlefield. As Guadalcanal veterans attested, troops needed common maps and needed them in abundance.[24] Vandegrift's own postbattle report acknowledged, "The lack of adequate maps and photographs was a distinct handicap which continued throughout the entire period of our occupation of Guadalcanal."[25]

While some weaknesses appeared and received redress, others went unnoticed. The extended nature of the campaign allowed American troops to rely on personal rapport and direct experience rather than institutional procedures and established methods. Settled into their positions, enemy targets and units on Guadalcanal became familiar knowledge for American gunners offshore. Consequently, coordination between various U.S. units became first artificial and then unnecessary. As Vandegrift and his staff rightly concluded, "the [Guadalcanal] operation did not involve a real test of methods of controlling ship's gunfire by shore-based fire control parties."[26] Marine pilots bivouacked at Henderson Field could easily arrange and adjust air support efforts with land components throughout the campaign. Coordination for triphibious war was thus largely an informal, "unofficial" affair. Solutions were immediate and unique, not systematic and institutional. One postbattle analysis concluded that the success of Marine close air support on Guadalcanal "could not have been achieved without short-cutting command procedure to a point where the association of close support aviation and front line combat units has brought forth immediate and dependable cooperation."[27] Vandegrift and his staff also recognized the artificialities and recommended increased training for "regularly organized air support parties" that would "accompany ground forces for liaison and control purposes."[28]

Even the artillery arm, which had performed admirably across the campaign, had room to improve its liaison efforts.[29] Attentive observers knew that future battles in the Pacific would not promise the static arrangements and organic working relationships of Guadalcanal. Coordination had to improve. Lieutenant Colonel William Twining recommended that troops be trained in "actual close artillery support fires. Units in Guadalcanal, including Army, drew back hundreds of yards when the [friendly] artillery fires were being laid down, only to have to fight to regain the territory."[30] Brigadier General Pedro del Valle, the division artillery officer, agreed wholeheartedly: "[Our] troops have developed a fear of being fired into by our own artillery . . . [and] don't follow closely behind our barrages."[31]

Victory on Guadalcanal was a long-awaited and energizing triumph for the Allies in the Pacific. For the first time, U.S. forces had punctured the myth of Japanese invincibility. After advancing at will from 1936 thorough early 1942, Japanese forces tasted defeat and yielded important territory. As is so often the case, the stirring victory did not come without a price. Though the Marines lost just over one thousand combat dead to Japan's twenty-two thousand killed or missing, the noncombat toll ran far deeper. Heat exhaustion, infections, malaria, and other tropical diseases took far more casualties than did enemy bullets. To these less conspicuous threats, the Allies lost several thousand dead and more than four thousand wounded. On average, American servicemen fighting on Guadalcanal lost thirty pounds before earning relief from a replacement outfit.[32] The Pacific War, it seemed, had far more to offer than a dogged Japanese opponent.

In many ways, the Guadalcanal campaign set the tone for the campaigns of the southern Pacific. Japanese troops learned—contrary to their assumptions—that the Americans intended to stand and fight. Furthermore, Americans brought to the battlefield an overwhelming industrial capacity. Allied aircraft, munitions, and equipment flowed steadily into Guadalcanal throughout the campaign. Even more alarming to the Japanese, the U.S. manufacturing machine was still realizing its potential as the Japanese began their withdrawal. In the Solomons as in the subsequent contests, a battle of attrition favored the United States.

If Guadalcanal introduced the Japanese to a committed and capable enemy, the island also familiarized U.S. forces with a zealous and determined opponent. The Imperial Japanese Army had been proven mortal, but it was no accommodating enemy. With equal measures of horror and incredulity, U.S. Marines observed the harrowing banzai tactics of the Japanese. As one officer described a nighttime fight for Guadalcanal's "Bloody Ridge," "The [Japanese] chanting became a mad religious rite, which heralded a series of frenzied banzai charges through the pouring rain. . . . when one wave was mowed down—and I mean mowed down—another followed it into death."[33] Though few could have anticipated them, the ferocious combat methods later seen on Saipan, Iwo Jima, and Okinawa were born on the Solomons.

For the many new experiences that Guadalcanal offered in late 1942 and early 1943, the operation commenced with an uncontested main landing. Despite the Corps' interwar focus on the beachhead, Vandegrift's

MAP 2. TARAWA

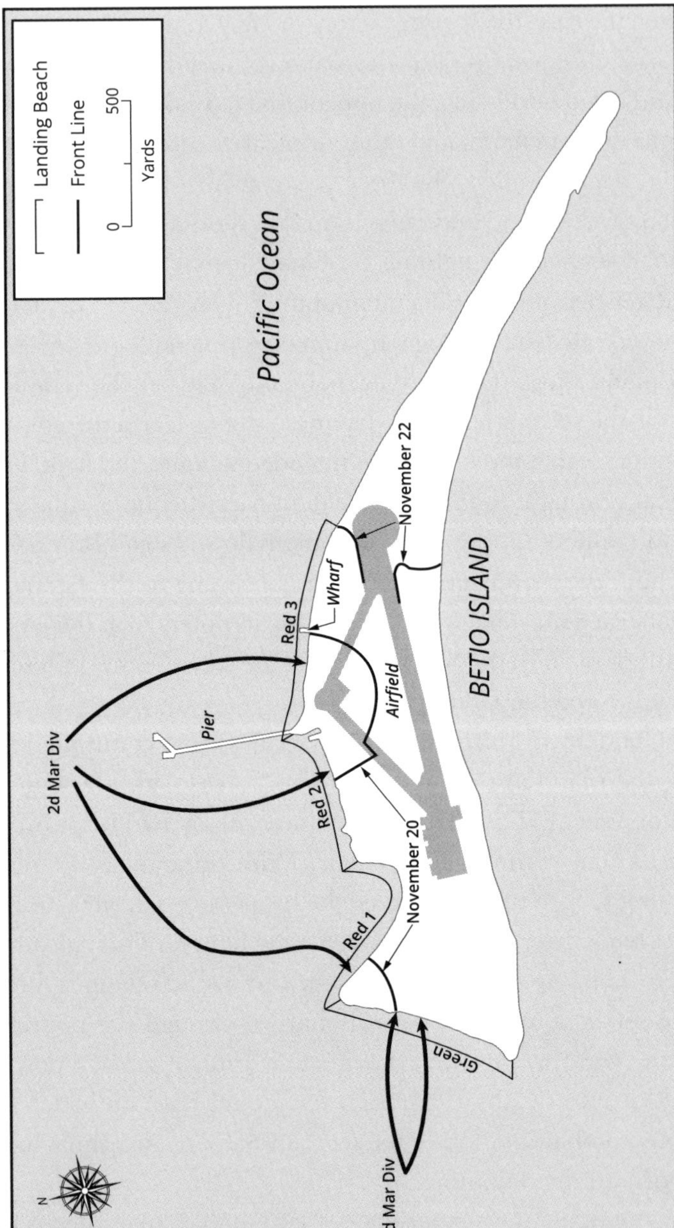

Prepared by Chris Robinson

Marines had virtually walked ashore on August 7, 1942. As the general himself remarked the day following the landing, "I'm beginning to doubt whether there's a Jap on the whole damned island."[34] Successive jungle battles on Guadalcanal also did little to test and refine the Americans' amphibious assault doctrine and capabilities. In that task, the Marines remained inexperienced and untested. It was true that "teamwork took and kept Guadalcanal," as two historians later determined.[35] But while complementary combined arms warfare protected the airfield and secured success, the Americans were not forced to apply those principles in the sand and surf of an opposed landing. Furthermore, once the 1st Marine Division secured Henderson Field, the campaign became primarily a defensive battle of attrition. Front lines remained generally static. The need for detailed coordination faded. Teamwork certainly helped to deliver success, but that teamwork was not challenged in a dynamic or kinetic fashion. In the months and years ahead, success would require far closer coordination and cooperation. The Navy and Marine Corps would need complementary triphibious warfare. And they would need it on the beach.

EVALUATION DAY: THE AMERICAN ATTACK ON TARAWA

As the Allies continued their southwest Pacific advance toward the Japanese stronghold at Rabaul under the resurgent General Douglas MacArthur, Admiral Chester Nimitz evolved his plan for a parallel drive across the Central Pacific. Indeed, Admiral Ernest King, Chief of Naval Operations and Commander in Chief, United States Fleet, had encouraged such an advance throughout 1943.[36] Nimitz's enterprise intended to attack and seize the Gilberts, Marshalls, and Marianas on its way across the ocean, all the while avoiding unnecessary bloodletting and gradually reversing the Japanese perimeter. First and foremost, King and Nimitz embraced the idea because of its inherent dependence on their cherished Navy. While MacArthur's advance through the Southwest Pacific promised an intractable commander and the inherent friction of Army-Navy cooperation, an advance through the Central Pacific would remain neatly in the lane of the U.S. Navy. At the same time, the route was at least theoretically familiar to the Marine Corps. War Plan Orange and strategists such as Pete Ellis had predicted and theorized such an advance for more than two decades. To open such an avenue, Nimitz set his sights on the Tarawa and Makin atolls in the Gilbert Island chain, more than two thousand miles southwest of Hawaii.[37]

As Nimitz's staff refined the plan, subordinate commanders turned to their tasks. The most formidable fell to Major General Holland M. "Howlin' Mad" Smith and the recently christened V Corps, composed of the 2d Marine Division and the Army's 27th Infantry Division. A former lawyer from Alabama, Smith's service in World War I spanned the Americans' most notable battles, including Belleau Wood as well as the St. Mihiel and Meuse-Argonne offensives. Following the war, Smith played a pivotal role in the Corps' preparation for amphibious war. He was an indomitable and spirited Marine who consistently secured the admiration of his men. On the other hand, Smith made equally passionate enemies who bemoaned his stubborn nature and his parochial attachment to the Marines (ironically, Smith had first lobbied the U.S. Army for a commission, only to find their appointments filled). Personality aside, the hard-charging Smith seemed the ideal commander for the tall task of seizing the hostile Tarawa atoll.[38]

Tarawa's key island of Betio, with its existing airfield, became Smith's primary objective, which he allocated to Major General Julian Smith (no relation) and the 2d Marine Division. After a hasty intelligence assessment, the subordinate Smith acknowledged the challenge of his task. Composed of level terrain, Betio Island promised its Japanese defenders extended fields of fire from which to contest an Allied landing. Furthermore, a natural coral reef encircled and protected most of the island. At low tide, the reef inhibited if not precluded any approach toward the beach. Though modest in size, Betio's geography presented the Marines with a significant problem.

Complicating the natural barriers were the sustained efforts of the Japanese garrison. After capturing the former British territory in the days following Pearl Harbor, the Japanese commander Rear Admiral Meichi Shibasaki quickly set about fortifying the atoll. Throughout 1943, as an American assault seemed more and more likely, Japanese defenders strengthened their fortress. By autumn—with more than five hundred concrete bunkers, 8-inch naval guns, and a frightening web of mines, barbed wire, and machine gun positions—Shibasaki had reason to boast that "a million Americans couldn't take Tarawa in 100 years."[39] Included in Shibasaki's 5,000-man garrison was an elite 2,600-man detachment that guarded Betio Island's meager six-tenths of one square mile. The island's determined Japanese commander had no intention of surrendering the beach as construction troops on Guadalcanal had done. Instead, Shibasaki's troops would fight over every foot of sand.[40]

Both the senior and junior Smiths desired a lengthy naval and aerial bombardment of the hardened island before their Marines went ashore. As the reconnaissance efforts of the American submarine *Nautilus* and captured Japanese radio traffic had revealed, Betio would prove a daunting target. Why not ease the task of the landing force, they reasoned? Yet senior Navy leadership, out of lucid strategic concern, could not abide an extended prelanding bombing. From their vantage point, surprise was essential; an extended preliminary attack would betray that very principle and put U.S. warships in danger. By the end of the planning phase, the principle of surprise prevailed over suppression. The Americans would hold their cards close and limit preparatory destruction. The decision boded ominously for the landing force. By safeguarding friendly ships and aircraft, the Marines of the 2d Division assumed an even more dangerous mission on the beaches of Tarawa.[41]

At 5:00 on the morning of November 20, 1943, after several days of innocuous aerial attacks, the American task force commenced its naval barrage against Betio. The shelling that began just a few hours before the landing force struck the beach was a stunning display of firepower. Three battleships, four heavy cruisers, and nearly two dozen destroyers composed Rear Admiral Harry W. Hill's naval attack force, which brought naval ordnance ranging in diameter from 3-inch to 14-inch shells. Together, the warships delivered more than 2,500 tons of shells on Betio's formidable positions and forced the Japanese defenders into their bunkers. The Marines expected fierce resistance on the beach, but Admiral Hill's spectacular display of naval might buoyed their spirits. Accompanying the landing force as it made its way ashore, American war correspondent

Robert Sherrod described the aura succinctly: "Surely, we all thought, no mortal men could live through such destroying power."[42] Marine Arvin Bowden, also observing from his landing craft, found comfort and relief in the American salvos: "We didn't think that they [the Japanese] would be able to do much. In fact, we kind of thought that the Navy was going to ship us in some ice cream."[43]

Yet the American plan soon splintered into chaos and confusion. U.S. Navy transport vessels dropped anchor in the wrong locations, and individual landing craft struggled to find their assigned wave positions once loaded with Marines. The predawn air strike came almost thirty minutes late, and several critical ships (including the battleship *Maryland*) lost radio communications early in the struggle. If this was not enough, a headwind slowed the landing craft as they churned ashore, further delaying the Marines' assault. As a few prophetic staff officers had worried, there was not enough water covering Betio's coral reef for the Landing Craft, Vehicle, Personnel (LCVPs, also known as Higgins boats) to cross. The Americans' plan of attack was rapidly deteriorating.[44]

To make the most of his crumbling timeline, Admiral Hill ordered the landing waves to delay their advance in order to properly synchronize the disparate elements of his task force. Operating from an initial "H-hour"[45] of 8:30 a.m., Hill delayed the landing first to 8:45 and then to 9:00. Yet even this adjustment failed to harmonize the American team; the landing craft soon fell behind their new timeline. Beset by Tarawa's menacing coral reef and still plagued by an unfavorable headwind, the landing craft coxswains labored in vain to make up lost time.[46]

At this crucial moment—and lasting for the final twenty minutes of their voyage ashore—Julian Smith and his 2d Marine Division lacked their most advantageous weapon: the naval guns of Admiral Hill's thirty battleships, cruisers, and destroyers assembled offshore. In strict accordance with their preestablished (if modified) timeline, the sea-based guns went cold at 8:55. Plagued by both faulty communications (further aggravated by the shock of the large guns) and a dense cloud of smoke that obscured their view, Hill's warships sat idle and unaware as the Marines' landing craft churned through the surf, still thousands of yards from shore.[47] For Smith's men, the lapse came at the most inopportune moment, when the landing force was in the most vulnerable phase of its attack. Corps naval gunfire officer E. G. Van Orman reported, "The fire stopped on schedule, although the boats and troops were yet far from the beach and subjected to murderous fire of unneutralized batteries."[48]

Tragically for the Marines of the 2d Division, Hill's warships were not the only silent weapons in the American arsenal as the landing craft hit the beach. In the opening hours of the assault, the Marines' field artillery remained offshore (not slated to land until that afternoon) while their medium Sherman tanks—moving ashore in untracked Higgins boats and mechanized landing craft—failed to clear Betio's coral reef. Having to unload and press ashore under their own power, the tanks did not join the initial assault troops for nearly two hours.[49]

American carrier aircraft suffered from debilitating coordination problems at the same time. On several occasions during the preliminary bombardment, American battleships paused their sequence to allow aircraft to strafe the beaches. Yet the pilots never appeared.[50] Unaware of Hill's ordered delay, and suffering from their own faulty communications procedures, carrier squadrons failed to adjust their attack window. Along with the gunfire ships, they ended their supporting fires while the landing force was still thousands of yards offshore. Even when the American pilots did appear overhead, they struggled to maintain a continuous flow of air support, which left the landing force vulnerable to the presighted fires of the Japanese defenders.[51] Accordingly, in the opening hours of the attack, the infantrymen relied principally upon their organic weapons: M-1 rifles, Browning automatic weapons, and eventually the medium Sherman tanks that trickled ashore.[52] Put simply, the disparate units of the American task force failed to harmonize their actions and failed to achieve their collective potential. Without adequate fire support, the Marines found themselves perilously exposed at the decisive moment.

At 9:13 the vanguard elements of the 2d Marine Division finally reached the seawalls of Betio. Yet even as the landing force made its way across the beach, the American task force continued to suffer from paralyzing coordination problems. Even though the Marine landing force included a distinct air coordination team (labeled an air liaison party), the ground and aviation components failed to harmonize their assault. Pilots miscommunicated their intentions over the radio, infantry commanders struggled to pinpoint ground targets for the aviators, and ground spotters wrestled to find common reference points or grid locations to coordinate action with the pilots. Inexplicably, the pilots and ground-based spotters were operating from different maps and target diagrams. Most pilots chose to fire on broad enemy positions, thereby degrading the effectiveness of their munitions.[53] In the absence of effective fire coordination, the Marines struggled to advance.

On top of this disturbing deficiency in air-ground cooperation, communications challenges plagued the 2d Marine Division as it struggled to advance against the preplanned gun lines, frustrating obstacles, and tenacious enemy resistance of the Japanese detachment. Just as the Marines needed a crescendo of fire support against inland targets, dysfunction resurfaced. Turning to their primary tool for shore-ship communications, the Marines found many of their Jeep-mounted radios lost, damaged, or destroyed during the trek ashore. Trying to patch together at least a few working sets, U.S. troops cannibalized various radio components and established a few contact frequencies with nearby ships and pilots. Without the full firepower of the American task force, the Marines' impromptu solutions had to suffice.[54]

Communications difficulties were not unique to the supporting firepower offshore and overhead. Indeed, many of the Marine ground units fought to maintain radio contact even among themselves. Battalion and regimental commanders were unable to combine, compare, and prioritize enemy targets for attack. Units unnecessarily repeated requests for fire support and, in too many cases, reiterated the same target request that an adjacent unit had already coordinated. Poor radio discipline presented its own problems, as radiomen consistently crowded the tactical frequencies to pass extraneous and even irrelevant information. Each individual complication—whether damaged equipment, congested radio nets, or redundant fire support requests—fueled an unforgiving cycle of confusion and disorder within the American task force.[55]

Shibasaki's well-trained defenders compounded the Marines' dilemma in the first few hours of combat. From a prepared firing grid that accounted for each square yard of Betio, Japanese mortarmen and machine gunners surged their fires as the attackers struggled ashore. The Americans' coordination lapse provided even further opportunity for the defenders to recover from the preliminary bombardment and organize as the Marines made their way ashore. With prearranged aiming stakes, interlocking machine gun coverage, and webs of barbed wire and tetrahedra scattered across the beaches, Shibasaki's men offered deliberate, well-planned resistance at each step. They took advantage of the breakdowns in U.S. coordination by synchronizing their own efforts and filling the American gaps in naval and aerial support with their own threatening barrage.[56]

Thrown from their timeline and facing steadfast Japanese resistance, Julian Smith and the 2d Marine Division struggled to build the momentum so necessary for success in an amphibious assault. Hours into the attack, the American offensive showed little promise. By late afternoon on November 20, Smith ordered the 6th Marine Regiment to board their landing craft and head ashore. This order committed his entire reserve element. By nightfall—and in spite of the costly errors in communications and battlefield coordination—the Marines had secured a tenuous foothold on the beaches of Betio (in some cases just one hundred yards inland). They hastily dug defensive positions, mounted lookout posts, and prepared for the Japanese counterattack that was sure to come. As the sun set low over the water, Smith transmitted one of the war's historic messages to his senior commander afloat: "situation in doubt."[57]

Fortuitously, no synchronized Japanese counterattack ever came. Though the initial American barrage had proven uncoordinated and—by most definitions—ineffective, it had knocked out Japanese communication lines and towers. Without effective control of his troops, Shibasaki failed to mount a forceful response throughout the day. As American luck had it, the Japanese admiral lost his own life in a shore blockhouse that very afternoon.[58] Stripped of their boisterous and determined commander, the Japanese defenders mounted only local, uncoordinated strikes. Though ferocious, their efforts failed to produce results. As the Marines clung to their modest foothold that first night ashore, the balance of firepower began to shift in their favor. Overnight, several howitzers landed on the nearby island of Bairiki to support the ongoing assault. Lighter 75-mm pack howitzers made their way onto the beaches of Betio. The Marines' medium tanks provided equally decisive firepower as they too found their way ashore.[59]

The following day, in spite of the Americans' early mistakes, the battle began to shift in their favor. Reinforced by the reserve regiment as well as the landed artillery and light tanks that trickled ashore, the Americans pressed ahead yard by yard and slowly made their way across Betio Island. Early in the afternoon, and in sharp contrast with General Smith's ambivalent message the preceding day, Colonel David Shoup, in command of the 2d Division's Combat Team Two, transmitted an equally famous dispatch, this time full of resolve: "Casualties many. Percentage dead not known. Combat efficiency—we are winning."[60] Eventually disrupted by the relentless flow of Marines over the beach, Japanese commanders struggled to coordinate a focused defense. Bottled into withering pockets of resistance on the island's southern coast, the defenders fought on despite the shifting momentum. Though they had lost many of their large 8-inch naval guns, they sustained machine gun and mortar fire from secondary and even tertiary defensive positions. For its part, the 2d Marine Division ground forward under the cover of its 75-mm howitzers and 37-mm light tank guns.[61]

By the morning of November 22, the Marines had seven thousand men ashore. Conversely, Japanese numbers had dwindled to just one thousand troops. In a last-ditch effort later that evening and into the night, Japanese officers ordered a final series of counterattacks. The American lines held firm, and when day broke the next morning, the Marines initiated their final advance. At 1 p.m. on November 23, the Americans declared Betio secure. Shockingly, only 146 of Shibasaki's original 5,000-man detachment survived to surrender. The remainder of the Japanese troops and Korean laborers died or went missing in the sand and surf of the ravaged island. Despite a costly series of early mistakes in the contest, the Americans gradually overcame their self-inflicted challenges and their determined enemy through firepower ashore and several instances of bold leadership. Some Japanese prisoners mentioned the Americans' firepower advantage, but they reported to their captors that the continual, dogged flow of Marines over the beachhead truly broke their morale. General Julian Smith—perhaps tempered by the experience—summarized the battle more bluntly: "We made fewer mistakes than the Japs did."[62]

ASSESSING TARAWA: LESSONS AT HOME AND ON THE FRONT LINES

As U.S. Marine and Navy forces recovered from the bloody contest, the American public at home struggled with the newfound realities of war in the Pacific. Determined to build resolve on the home front, President Franklin Roosevelt approved the release of gory combat footage in the 1944 film *With the Marines at Tarawa*.[63] Most war correspondents struggled to translate their experiences in the battle, with reporter Robert Sherrod concluding that "words are inadequate to describe what I saw on this island."[64] As the pictures, film reels, and first-hand accounts attested, the Pacific theater promised ferocious violence and utter destruction.

The disturbing reports and camera footage from Betio Island led some to question the strategic value of the tiny island. At least a subset of the citizenry, including politicians, demanded justification for the staggering price paid in American blood.[65] *Life* magazine put the challenge bluntly: "Was such a fight not too costly for a patch of sand two and a half miles long and 800 yards wide? What could be worth suffering such anguish for?" Nonetheless, *Life* answered with an impassioned defense: Tarawa displayed the courage and resolve of the U.S. Marines and "brought home, as it needs to be brought home again and again, the fact that there is no cheap short cut to win wars."[66]

While the American public reeled and debated in the aftermath of the Gilberts offensive, U.S. military forces organized their own professional evaluations. In the weeks following the fight for Tarawa, officers up to and including Major General Holland Smith (commander of V Corps) directed their individual units and staffs to execute a thorough postbattle study of the assault.[67] The internal investigation spanned the entire task force. Each platoon, ship, squadron, and section faced scrutiny. Indeed, even as the men of the V Corps sailed back from the Gilbert Islands, the process advanced.

Comments, judgments, and recommendations passed up the chain of command. The report culminated onboard the flagship of the Task Force 54 commander, Admiral Richmond "Kelly" Turner. Compiled, revised, and formatted, the final product totaled more than seven hundred pages. With a want of creativity, the title read *Headquarters Fifth Amphibious Corps Report on Gilbert Islands' Operation*.[68]

From the outset, the officers of the V Corps expected their careful staff work to produce tangible lessons for future operations. Consequently, Smith and Turner's voluminous report produced a litany of specific recommendations for everything from communications to logistics to naval fire support. In many cases, the Tarawa failures generated immediate corrections. The rather ineffective prelanding naval barrage significantly influenced subsequent bombardments, especially in length and volume. American preliminary naval barrages of 1944 and 1945 were to be measured in days, not hours, as had been the case in the Gilberts. Shipboard gunnery officers also acknowledged that proximity chiefly determined the effect of naval fires ashore. In future bouts, U.S. Navy ships would creep closer and closer to the shoreline to achieve maximum destruction against hardened enemy positions. Hoping to refine naval targeting procedures, commander in chief of the Pacific Fleet Admiral Chester Nimitz directed an extensive battlefield analysis of Japanese blockhouses and bunkers on Tarawa.[69] From top to bottom, the Americans labored to improve their naval gunfire support of future amphibious landings.

The report saved its more passionate critique for the general integration and coordination of fire support during the fight for Tarawa. Particularly during the struggle for Betio Island, American officers learned that unity of effort did not come easily in a triphibious attack. In blind adherence to their predetermined timeline, and in futile attempts to accommodate various air and naval fires, the V Corps had failed to synchronize its land, sea, and air forces. Holland Smith's own postbattle summary stated that "every effort is being made to correct the obvious lack of coordination."[70] As the authors acknowledged, no single weapon or tactic—be it a naval cannon, an aviation bombardment, or a ground assault from an infantry platoon—could carry the day alone. The strength of combined arms lay in their coordination.

Navy and Marine officers drew from Tarawa the lesson that in future Pacific operations, fire support had to remain constant and flexible throughout the attack. In particular, naval guns and supporting aircraft had to provide robust firepower as landing waves approached and arrived on the shore. Aviation liaison officers—those responsible for directing aerial attacks ashore—criticized the extended gaps in coverage at Tarawa and petitioned pilots to minimize any breaks between strafing runs. As Colonel Peter Schrider, the V Amphibious Corps air officer, concluded: "Greater coordination in timing of air attacks is imperative."[71] In almost lockstep agreement, Marine Major E. G. Van Orman, the Corps naval gunfire officer, shared his disdain for Tarawa's scripted timeline. He proposed that naval fires "be lifted with reference to the progress of the landing craft rather than on a time schedule." He further recommended that naval gunnery officers incorporate recent lessons from land-based artillery experience: "It is my belief that it [naval gunfire] can be fired as an artillery rolling barrage to a certain degree."[72] Across the board, American officers appealed for integrated fire support as the landing force closed upon and attacked across the formidable beach.

Yet effective coordination on the battlefield required reliable means of communication amid adverse conditions. Here again, American units had struggled at Tarawa. Even as the V Corps turned the bows of its landing craft toward Betio, communications failed to hold the American task force together. Marines riding amphibian tractors ashore found no radio sets with which to request fire support and direct air or naval strikes. Clearly, these craft needed such capabilities in future battles. The corps signal officer insisted that future landing forces "must be prepared to request and control fire support *while* still embarked in landing craft."[73]

Even the Marines with functioning radios found their gear did not meet the task. Tactical receivers were ill-suited for littoral combat and proved dangerously bulky as the landing force waded ashore. When Japanese resistance mounted on the shoreline, the Marines lost many of their radios in the harrowing journey. To compound their communications challenges, several units—perhaps in the panic of combat—used the air support frequency channel as a general information net. This cluttered the radio channel with friendly position updates, extraneous requests, and ancillary information that impeded the efforts of pilots and ground liaisons to communicate clearly and directly.[74] Both equipment failures and procedural errors deprived the landing force of essential fire support from nearby ships and aircraft.

In their comprehensive postbattle investigation, American naval officers also turned attention to battlefield awareness (or lack thereof) among U.S. troops, and specifically their inability to recognize and adapt to the changing combat conditions on Tarawa. Units embarked at sea and in the air suffered from an inaccurate—and often delayed—picture of the battlefield. Inherently detached from the front lines in both latitude and altitude, American ships and aircraft depended upon the infantry and supporting entities ashore to act as the eyes and ears of the triphibious task force. But the landing force—preoccupied with its own tasks—failed to transmit regular updates on friendly unit positions, enemy strongholds, and the progress of the attack. The Marines ashore thus reduced the effectiveness of their supporting arms. Without timely and precise updates, U.S. ships and aircraft could not provide immediate support when ground units needed it most. This want of common information contributed to the threat of friendly fire.[75] As the report highlighted, the Americans' faulty battlefield awareness at Tarawa negated a principal advantage of the U.S. force: complete command of the air and sea.

Taken in sum, U.S. fire support coordination at Tarawa displayed three evident failures. First, as the landing force floated ashore, American allegiance to the prearranged timeline inflicted a deadly hiatus of fire support just as the Marines approached the point of greatest vulnerability. Second, and compounding their situation, the V Corps found its communications gear entirely unsuited for the conditions of an amphibious assault. Third, even when radio sets were available and functioning, American units found themselves plagued by dissimilar maps, unrehearsed techniques, and unfamiliar lexicon. The task force failed to fight as one cohesive team. Even in spite of deliberate interwar training and decades of conceptual war planning, several significant problems went unacknowledged and unresolved. As the naval historian Samuel Eliot Morison concluded, "Ignorance of how to tackle a strongly defended coral atoll surrounded by a fringing reef was responsible for most of the errors in this attack."[76] From the integration of supporting arms to communications procedures and battlefield awareness, American units at Tarawa failed to achieve their combined arms potential. In future campaigns, the three arms of the triphibious force would have to learn to fight as one synchronized team.

Yet all was not lost. The Americans had—even if at shocking cost—taken the Tarawa atoll. As certain observers reasoned, the Marines had to cut their teeth somewhere. Holland Smith, in bureaucratically passive language, resolved that "the lessons learned from this operation point to modification of certain techniques to be employed in operations continuing across the Pacific."[77] And the lessons were many. Combat experience on Betio taught American forces the utility of the flamethrower in clearing Japanese bunkers and the need for many more armored amphibian tractors.[78] Amid these concerns, Navy and Marine officers resolved to improve the coordination of triphibious fire support. Indeed, the American response to the trauma of Tarawa proved crucial in the succeeding campaigns of the Pacific War.

CHAPTER 3

BUILDING A "SPIRIT OF COOPERATION"

COORDINATING TRIPHIBIOUS FIREPOWER IN THEORY

In a 1973 lecture at the Royal United Service Institution, military historian Michael Howard compared peacetime military forces to ancient mariners on the high seas. Beset by heavy fog and poor visibility—and without the aid of modern instruments—the Sailors were forced to rely on assumptions and inclinations rather than science and certainty. With more hope than assurance, Sailors trusted their dead reckoning and nautical instincts to guide them through the storm. In a similar manner, Howard argued, modern armies and navies navigated periods of peace with uncertainty and speculation. Unsure of what the next conflict might bring, such military forces prepared for war with no manner of confirming their assumptions, doctrine, tactics, or weapons. In late November 1943 the Marines' assault on Tarawa embodied Howard's analogy. Having broken through the fog of the interwar peace, the U.S. Navy and Marine Corps finally had a reliable gauge by which to mark and adjust their methods.[1]

In the weeks and months following the fight for Tarawa, American officers turned diligently to their failures in coordination. Specifically, their postbattle recommendations fell into three general categories: the agencies responsible for integrating American fires, the equipment provided for such teams, and the incorporation of those specialized teams within the broader organization of U.S. forces in the Pacific.[2] Seen clearly in the Americans' coordination challenges at Betio Island, each of these categories demanded swift and industrious improvement if the Navy and Marine Corps were to mature their amphibious approach, ensure the success of future landings, and reduce the butcher's bill of imminent assaults.

Though the American aerial and naval gunfire coordination teams at Tarawa had evidenced a want of synchronization, they were no novel construct in 1943. Even during the interwar period, coordination units were a steady—if underemphasized—piece of the organizational structure in amphibious operations. Shore fire control parties and air liaison parties each had their task: to direct and integrate the cacophony of fires during a contested landing. Fire support was critical in putting troops ashore; even in the interwar period, these agencies were expected to deliver the necessary support.

As the Marines' 1934 *Tentative Manual for Landing Operations* dictated, naval gunfire teams would accompany the landing force ashore and supervise gunfire from supporting vessels. Under the charge of the senior U.S. Navy officer ashore (or "Navy officer in tactical command"), these control teams would pass fire requests from troop commanders to the individual ships or fire support groups. Ostensibly versed in the nuances of naval gunfire, these Sailors would introduce a "common language" between American forces ashore and afloat.[3] In theory, the intermediaries could advise, translate, and modify requests in accordance with the naval gunfire assets available. Fire control teams would reflect an intimate knowledge of the "power and limitation of each firing ship . . . in order that the tactical plan may be based upon definite ships' gunfire."[4]

The intricacies of controlling and coordinating air support ashore were less developed, but they were present in theory before Japanese planes struck at Pearl Harbor. Marine aviators had in fact developed dive-bombing techniques and matured their use of tactical air power during their early twentieth-century interventions in places such as Haiti, Nicaragua, and the Dominican Republic.[5] The experience led one young officer, Marine Captain Harold D. Campbell, to recognize that "aviation will produce its greatest efficiency when used in liaison with the other arms and in working for their success, because, in any war, tactics consist in assuring the coordination of all forces."[6] But recognition by young officers such as Campbell did not immediately equate to doctrinal development within the Corps. Controlling techniques stagnated, and there was no general reform of the coordination of firepower. Voices like Campbell's were isolated and did not attract an institutional response. Although the Marines' *Tentative Manual* championed the significance of air support, it did not organize dedicated control teams or establish deliberate techniques for applying aviation fires ashore. Instead, the manual noted rather vaguely that aircraft "should be able to communicate directly with radio stations of ground units."[7] At this early juncture, most Marines appeared content to emphasize close air support without developing its means.

In short, although naval officers—Navy and Marine—recognized the essential functions of air support and naval gunfire long before the amphibious assault on Tarawa, the tasks failed to garner significant attention or resources from the peacetime naval service. With no experience synchronizing fires in combat, and little prioritization from interwar leadership, the coordination teams were destined for a disappointing debut on the beaches of Betio Island. American progress in controlling triphibious firepower had waited for the cold and unforgiving lessons of combat. And Betio had provided lessons in abundance.

ADDRESSING THE LESSONS FROM BETIO

One glaring weakness of the war's early fire control teams was a fundamental, perhaps inexcusable, error: they lacked adequate training. Although fire control and coordination were present conceptually, training rarely made it to the top of a commander's priority list. Sailors and Marines, even those serving on coordination teams, were generally unfamiliar with the capabilities and limitations of naval gunfire. Their inexperience and resultant lack of confidence bred skepticism in the men they supported and the units they served.[8] The teams' inexperience further explained the combat troops' mistrust of air support. One bulletin reported an unsettling reality after a 1943 amphibious exercise off the coast of California: "No air-ground liaison was attempted because there were no air or ground units [available] trained in this phase of amphibious operations. This training is now underway."[9] The bulletin offered a blistering critique of the inadequacy of naval support: "Ships must realize that for *call* fires they must take orders from the Shore Fire Control Party assigned." Citing the need for swift fire support, the memo determined that "naval gunfire during this type of operation is effective only when it can be placed *rapidly* on the enemy. Seconds delay in naval gunfire may cause untold casualties on our infantry."[10]

Other critics charged that the infantry, gunfire ships, and aircraft squadrons were in fact well-trained but that their experience and proficiency lay in their own singular brand of combat. Prewar and even early war training disproportionately focused on the distinct tasks of each arm rather than a comprehensive application of triphibious warfare. In 1942 Navy lieutenant R. D. Hunt Jr. admitted that "[our] modern fire control system is designed for naval combat involving battle at sea" rather than in support of an infantry landing.[11] He complained that aerial "spotters"—those assigned to observe, record, and adjust naval gunfire—were only skilled in tracking waterborne targets, not enemy positions ashore. Compounding the problem, aerial spotters were accustomed to nautical charts and methods, not land-based grids and targeting procedures.[12] Hunt was not alone in his critique. Marine Lieutenant Colonel William Oldfield reported a glaring example of imprecision (and improvisation) on Guadalcanal, where a naval gunfire spotter directed a ship to fire on an enemy position. The observer—without any common reference points by which to guide the offshore gunners—vaguely directed the ships to engage Japanese troops "north of the Poha River on the third hill covered by coconut trees."[13] With no uniform maps, American coordination teams struggled to improvise on the triphibious battlefield.

Compounding the inadequate prewar training in fire control and coordination was a cultural (and quite parochial) rift between the distinct entities of the American naval service. That cultural chasm, aggravated during the heightened independence of the interwar peace, endured into the opening campaigns of World War II. Donald M. Weller, who went on to become a central architect of naval gunfire planning in the Pacific campaigns and a major general in the Marine Corps, testified that even into the early years of the conflict, service parochialism hampered the integration of American firepower. Weller claimed that Navy officers "were not in sympathy with the mission of supporting troops—after all, ships were built for combat at sea against other ships."[14] With a predilection for decisive battleship engagements on the high seas, these Sailors had little appetite for supporting landing operations. But the Marines were equally guilty of an insular, skeptical, and uncooperative attitude. Even in 1942 infantrymen placed marginal faith in shells launched from Navy vessels miles from shore. Instead, most Marines believed that ships' capacity for inflicting friendly fire casualties outweighed their tactical utility in an amphibious assault.[15] As Oldfield summarized it, Marine officers of 1941 and 1942 viewed naval gunfire support "with a jaundiced eye."[16]

In both the Solomon and Gilbert islands, then, inexperience and inter-community rifts presented a dangerous obstacle to performance. Shore fire control parties at Tarawa—having spent the majority of their training time at sea—were unversed in the organization, characteristics, and techniques of the Marine infantry.[17] In some cases, naval personnel dismissed and even resented their assigned task. And the Navy's disinterest in naval gunfire support promised that the task of naval fire control would fall to the most expendable Sailors. Weller noted that "in those naïve days [fire control] parties were made up of young and 'available' naval officers whose knowledge of the landing force problems was limited . . . [the teams] were reinforced by members of the 'radio gang,' usually led by a salty chief, whose demeanor indicated extreme displeasure with the whole affair."[18] Alienated by their divergent experiences, American land and sea forces struggled to communicate clearly, appreciate the utility of their counterpart, and combine their capabilities into a harmonized assault.

If inadequate training and cultural divisions were not enough to stymie American firepower integration in the Pacific, a want of adequate equipment also hindered their efforts. Even into the first year of World War II, shore fire control and air liaison parties trained and fought without the necessary equipment for their specialized task. As Lieutenant Hunt described, these communications shortfalls made the difficult task of coordination even more laborious.[19] When the teams deployed for a particular training maneuver or combat operation, they borrowed radios and supplementary communications gear from the infantry divisions and artillery battalions that they joined.[20] But naturally, the equipment they borrowed—and in many cases scavenged for—was not suited for ground-to-air or shore-to-ship communications. The radios and auxiliary gear such as telephone wire and handsets were susceptible to water damage, and troops lacked the proper storage cases to protect against the surf and spray during their harrowing voyage between ship and shore.[21]

The oversights were difficult to justify. Officers with even the most elementary experience in coordinating naval gunfire or air support ashore understood the necessity of communications. As Hunt made clear, gunfire control teams could only meet their task if communications between ship and shore were "rapid, reliable, and efficient."[22] A 1943 general order from Holland Smith reflected similar emphasis: "It must be noted that the effectiveness of a Shore Fire Control Party is entirely dependent upon COMMUNICATIONS!"[23] Yet without organic and suitable radio sets, the challenge of synchronizing and adjusting firepower from offshore and overhead was nearly insurmountable.

In the first two years of the war, and largely as a consequence of the cultural barriers between Navy and Marine entities, fire control and coordination teams had low priority in training and resources and failed to realize their battlefield potential. Their impoverished status hindered their effective incorporation and destined them to a transitory existence within the American naval service. Rather than remain a standing component of the Marine landing forces that they supported, the shore fire control parties and air liaison parties were mobilized only as necessity dictated. When an approaching operation called for integrated air and naval fires, the units were dispatched. At the action's conclusion, the teams were recalled to higher headquarters to await their next marching orders.[24] Unsurprisingly, these early fire control teams struggled to develop solidarity and credibility with the infantrymen they fought alongside. The parties endured a reactive and nomadic life cycle that kept them in constant rotation between various Marine divisions. The rhythm compounded their existing training deficiencies. Though these limitations were most certainly driven by reasonable managerial concerns over manpower, efficiency, and budget constraints, they nonetheless degraded the working relationships and general effectiveness of coordination units through 1943.

BUILDING A "SPIRIT OF COOPERATION"

The officers who assessed American firepower following the battle for Tarawa agreed that their specialized fire control teams required hasty remediation. For U.S. combat power to achieve its full potential in the Pacific, the

Navy and Marine Corps needed to recraft the organization, training, and equipping of both shore fire control and air liaison parties. Tactical commanders and staff officers—both at sea and ashore—needed to familiarize themselves with the intricacies, capabilities, and limitations of naval and aerial fire support.[25] In short, a harmonized performance on the battlefield required a foundation of shared understanding and appreciation.

Navy Lieutenant Hunt and Marine Lieutenant Colonel Weller both argued that common trust and credibility would deliver success, but only if the distinct entities acknowledged a higher shared mission. Hunt counseled shipboard gunners and support personnel to embrace the task of naval gunfire support and adjust their methods to provide responsive, effective fire. He similarly challenged the infantry units to accommodate fire control teams, imploring them to build a "spirit of cooperation," a dynamic "without which no landing operation can succeed."[26] Reflecting on the transformation of fire control and coordination in 1942 and 1943, Weller described a similar need for cultural change: "The [liaison] officer had to know more than the rudiments of the organization, tactics, and techniques of this battalion of riflemen, if he was to fill his supporting role in full measure. In short, these officers had to be grounded in both camps."[27] To excel on the modern battlefield, the troops needed cultural integration and common trust.

As frustrated as Hunt and Weller might have been, the combat operations of 1942 and 1943 gave American troops both the opportunity to observe and the stimulus to refine their approach to triphibious war. In both naval gunfire and aerial support, the Navy and Marine Corps' failures stirred creativity and bred novel solutions. If the services had indeed broken through the interwar "fog" of historian Michael Howard's seafaring analogy, the Americans were determined to incorporate recent lessons, chart a new course, and set sail in the clear skies beyond the storm.

In the closing months of 1943 the U.S. Navy and Marine Corps responded to the underacknowledged and underresourced coordination teams of the prewar construct and unveiled a nascent unit charged with the task of comprehensive firepower integration: the joint assault signal company (JASCO). The idea to consolidate and integrate fire support efforts under one common umbrella actually originated with Major General Alexander A. Vandegrift and the 1st Marine Division on Guadalcanal. But it took the jarring American experience in the Tarawa atoll to give the concept institutional traction. At Vandegrift's behest, the joint chiefs of staff agreed to reorganize the various fire support teams into the creative JASCO construct.[28] The companies would serve as administrative headquarters for the subordinate shore fire control parties, air liaison parties, and shore party communications sections.[29] While each entity remained responsible for its own specialized task, the JASCO construct brought the disparate sections together for the first time under a single, unified heading. Under the new arrangement, fire support teams would train, organize, deploy, and fight as a comprehensive unit.[30]

Wholly adaptive in nature, the JASCO initiative was mounted to address early war deficiencies in fire support coordination. In streamlining and centralizing the task, the Navy and Marine Corps hoped to improve the efficiency, responsiveness, and integration of naval and aerial fires in support of an amphibious landing. Despite its label, the 1943 JASCO was significantly larger than a typical line company—what one veteran labeled a "heavy company in the sense of numbers."[31] In effect, the various naval, air, and communications sections each equated to their own virtual company of roughly 100 men, plus headquarters personnel, for a total JASCO strength of 412 troops in its original table of organization and equipment.[32] At such a manning, the JASCOs reflected the growing prioritization of fire control and coordination within the American armed forces. Together, the heavily manned teams were meant to serve as the "essential links between the land, sea, and air elements in operations against the enemy."[33]

While introduced as an administrative adaptation, the JASCO endeavor quickly spurred developments in more practical considerations, namely in the training and equipping of U.S. coordination teams. Although the basic functions of the naval fire and air liaison teams remained constant, they encountered newfound prioritization from senior commanders and staff officers alike. Given the Marine Corps' growing claim to amphibious operations, the service incurred primary responsibility for training and developing the novel units.[34] Now with a reinforced communications section to support their efforts, the teams attached to a standing Marine division and merged into the structure of the landing force as each amphibious operation approached. After assignment to a particular division, the JASCOs broke themselves into thirteen subordinate teams: one liaison section for division headquarters, one for each of the three regiments of the division, and one for each of the nine battalions of the division.[35] Thus, every ground maneuver element above the company level had familiar and consistent access to both air and naval fire support.

Once ashore with the landing force, the JASCO shore fire control parties—at the direction of their respective battalion or regimental commander—recommended, requested, observed, and adjusted naval gunfire from supporting ships. Using handheld tactical radio sets, control parties at the battalion level passed fire missions to their regimental and then division counterparts. At each additional tier, the senior control parties could supervise and, as necessary, triage the incoming requests. In the chaotic and compressed circumstances of an amphibious assault, calls for fire support were often balanced against myriad competing demands. The senior naval gunfire liaison officer ashore (usually operating with the division commander) had ultimate authority for the outgoing requests. The procedure was nearly identical for air liaison parties. Requests traveled vertically within the structure of the landing force and then jumped from the senior air liaison officer ashore to the supporting aircraft squadrons.[36]

American fire control teams quickly benefitted from several structural consequences of the JASCO reorganization. The companies now had the ability to train cohesively as one team prior to an amphibious landing and then reflect collectively on their performance in the aftermath of the battle. Rather than the ad hoc and fleeting arrangements of the pre-JASCO years, shore fire control parties and air liaison parties could build on common experiences and trends. The more stable organization also allowed JASCOs to develop unit camaraderie, which had been missing in many early coordination teams. As in any human enterprise, relationships mattered, and the JASCOs now had a foundation from which to build rapport. But arguably the most significant effect of the restructuring was the longest overdue—JASCOs now had their own dedicated equipment, both for training and for combat. Finally, their kit was specifically suited for both the daunting conditions of the amphibious assault mission and their unique technological demands in communicating across the three domains of land, sea, and air operations.[37]

Administrative change was crucial, and the JASCOs delivered several important developments in that regard. But practical training was arguably more germane, especially within the throes of an ongoing global conflict. As one postwar doctrinal publication argued, rigorous, realistic, and integrated training was the only antidote to battlefield disorder. Static and unimaginative training—often the type associated with interwar periods—"tends to break down integration of firepower with the [ground unit's] scheme of maneuver due to: safety regulations, shortage of training ammunition, and lack of suitable firing areas. The natural result of this condition is an uncertainty as to what fire support can do, and a failure to take advantage of available firepower in initial operations."[38] To truly adjust their course in amphibious fire support, Navy and Marine leaders turned their attention to practical, intrawar training.

Luckily for the JASCOs, naval gunfire training had already received energetic support from Admiral Chester Nimitz himself in September 1943. Intent on evolving the infrastructure of naval gunfire training, Nimitz directed the V Corps to select and establish a dedicated firing range in the Pacific theater. The commander in chief of the Pacific Fleet undoubtedly envisioned a replica of the site at Bloodsworth Island, lying just off Maryland's Eastern Shore in the Chesapeake Bay. Relatively isolated and completely uninhabited, Navy ships assigned to the Atlantic Fleet had battered the ranges at Bloodsworth since the attack on Pearl Harbor. But as American ships, men, and munitions all poured into the Pacific, Nimitz acknowledged the need for a new, more intricate, and more proximate range where American forces could train on their way to war with Japan.[39]

Whether in anticipation of Nimitz's directive or having launched their own proactive reconnoitering, the staff officers of Holland Smith's V Corps gave Nimitz a swift solution. Less than three weeks after the order, Smith's lieutenants researched and settled upon Hawaii's remote Kahoolawe Island, just south of Maui and east of Lanai.[40] The rugged, dry, and necessarily unpopulated island of approximately forty square miles provided ideal features for the work about to begin. And begin it did. Just six weeks after Nimitz's instruction, at 8:18 on the morning of October 21, 1943, the 14-inch guns of battleship *Pennsylvania* christened the Kahoolawe range. By the end of the month, the training center and its newly formed cadre of instructors (the naval gunfire training section) graduated five more American ships, initiating a steady stream of curricula that would become an instrumental primer for American warships passing through Hawaii. As Marine veteran and postwar historian Robert D. Heinl put it, "Kahoolawe's throbbing tempo of wartime activity had commenced in dead earnest."[41] In short time, the island became not only the center of naval gunfire training in the region, but also a major hub for emerging JASCO units to form, train, and deploy. Under the direction of naval gunfire liaison officers freshly rotated out of combat billets, Kahoolawe expanded to include joint training exercises, communications drills, and extensive live-fire maneuvers.[42] Its rapid growth led Heinl to proudly label the American outpost "the most shot-at island of the Pacific."[43]

Kahoolawe's charter and initial salvoes preceded the battle of Tarawa, but the school's development quickly mirrored the lessons that American troops extracted from their assault in the Gilberts. By December 1943 the naval gunfire training section had crafted a comprehensive curriculum meant to prepare JASCO personnel for the rigors of combat in the Central Pacific. The school stressed water survival, the ability to perform under fire, communications skills, landing craft familiarity, and a rudimentary introduction to naval gunnery.[44] Kahoolawe instruction was broad but elementary, reflecting a desire for the general tenets of amphibious warfare and modern firepower coordination. Though it would take time to mature—and lessons would continue to flow from operational units back to the Hawaiian outpost—the naval gunfire training section provided the institutional scaffolding and increased resources that might allow U.S. Navy and Marine forces to master the art of triphibious fire support.

PAIRING THE TOOLS: AMERICAN TECHNOLOGICAL DEVELOPMENTS IN TRIPHIBIOUS WAR

While American officers improved their training facilities in the Pacific and pursued a more coordinated tactical effort within their naval task force, they also turned attention to the tools that made triphibious warfare possible. Though many ship and aircraft development programs had begun in the peaceful but anxious years of 1938 and 1939, American factories could not produce advanced planes or massive warships overnight. Thus, 1943 became a year of industrial realization for the Americans. For the infantrymen focused on seizing the next assigned beach in the Central Pacific, few programs could have been as welcome as the *Iowa*-class battleships.

Directed in the summer of 1939 and expanded under President Franklin D. Roosevelt's Two-Ocean Navy Act of 1940, the *Iowa* line delivered the most advanced capabilities in offshore fire support. The first out of the dry dock, class namesake USS *Iowa*, was commissioned in February 1943 and transported Roosevelt both to and from the Casablanca Conference before sailing for combat in the Pacific. Nearly nine hundred feet long, *Iowa* totaled 45,000 tons displacement, a 10,000-ton increase over the most recent generation of U.S. battleships, the *North Carolina* class of 1937. And the ship's armament matched its nautical footprint. *Iowa* carried nine 16-inch guns in the main battery and another twenty 5-inch guns in the secondary compartment. Most impressive of all, under the power of four steam turbines, the floating armories of the *Iowa* class could make more than thirty knots through the water.[45] Ultimately, the class put three of its four battleships (*Iowa*, *Missouri*, and *Wisconsin*) into service behind the V Corps in the Central and Western Pacific.

In the air, too, American engineers allowed the Navy and Marine Corps to prosecute amphibious assaults with more speed, firepower, and precision. For the first two years of the war, naval fighter pilots relied upon the Grumman F4F-4 Wildcat as their primary fighter. With folding wings that complemented carrier operations and a rugged construction, the Wildcat earned a reputation as a dependable and versatile machine. But as war advanced across the Central Pacific, the plane's weaknesses attracted increasing attention and frustration. Under the best of conditions, the F4F-4 could reach a peak combat speed of just over three hundred miles per hour and took more than twelve minutes to climb to 20,000 feet. Though it carried six .50 caliber fixed guns, it could only deliver a pair of 100-pound external bombs to the beach.[46]

In the autumn of 1943 American carrier pilots welcomed an upgrade: the Grumman F6F Hellcat. Boasting a two thousand–horsepower Pratt and Whitney engine, the Hellcat promised increased performance and protection. With a slick weight of nine thousand pounds, the F6F carried over the Wildcat's six machine guns but upgraded the external bomb capacity from 200 pounds to 2,000 pounds and added six 5-inch rockets for additional demolition. The Hellcat could reach 20,000 feet more than ninety seconds faster than its predecessor and was capable of four hundred miles per hour through the air. Most importantly, it could outfly its Japanese nemesis—the Mitsubishi Zero—at altitudes over 14,000 feet.[47] Though designed as a fighter, its remarkable payload allowed the Hellcat to spend its initial flight as a trusty ground attack air support platform and then transition to a nimble fighter. As the accomplished naval pilot John Thach recalled, "You drop your bomb, [and] then you've got the world's best fighter."[48]

If 1942 had been dark and dispiriting, 1943 delivered hope. After a hard-fought and long-awaited victory on Guadalcanal, U.S. forces triumphed in their Central Pacific debut at Tarawa in the Gilbert Islands. Though the operation carried a heavy butcher's bill and revealed several areas for concern, the assault opened a second axis of advance in the Pacific Theater and validated the Marine Corps' ability to seize a heavily defended shore. And the surging stream of American production buoyed Allied confidence all the more. In 1943 alone the Navy received 18,434 ships and submarines and more than 16,000 landing craft from American industry. In the same twelve-month span, U.S. factories doubled the combined output of their German and Japanese counterparts.[49] The war was far from over, but 1943 convinced Allied leaders that both time and surging wartime production were on their side.

CHAPTER 4

ON TO THE MARSHALLS

COORDINATING TRIPHIBIOUS FIREPOWER IN PRACTICE

As American industry hit its stride, new units paralleled the new gear that flowed to the Pacific. In early 1944 the recently christened joint assault signal companies prepared for their first combat test. Their crucible would come in the Marshall Islands, a sprawling but strategically placed chain in the Central Pacific. Allied war planners knew that a successful assault on the Marshalls promised two enviable advantages. First, the effort would reduce the enemy perimeter in the region by denying the Japanese strategic anchorages and air bases across the island chain. The second benefit followed the first in consequent logic: American forces could occupy and strengthen existing surface and aerial hubs in the Marshalls to expand their own strategic air and naval campaigns against Japan.

The Kwajalein Atoll comprised the nucleus of Japanese strength in the Marshalls; it quickly became the Americans' primary objective. A triangular-shaped string of islands roughly seventy miles in length and twelve miles in width, the atoll boasted five principal air bases (one under construction) and a robust naval base. The American assault would rest on simultaneous attacks against Roi-Namur and Kwajalein islands as well as the atolls of Enewetak and Majuro. Though it had received fresh divisions since the battle for Tarawa (one, the 4th Marine Division, was just six months old and without combat experience of any kind), Major General Holland M. Smith's V Corps remained the principal landing force. By this point in the war, the corps was an amalgam of Army and Marine forces; Smith assigned Kwajalein Island to his 7th Infantry Division (U.S. Army) and gave responsibility for the Majuro Atoll to the 2nd Battalion of the 27th Infantry Division. That left Roi-Namur for Smith's 4th Marine Division, with Major General Harry Schmidt commanding.[1]

From the earliest stages of planning, the 4th Marine Division's assault on Roi-Namur benefitted from the lessons of "Bloody Tarawa." Having petitioned for a deliberate and protracted preliminary bombardment, Marine officers watched approvingly as U.S. aircraft pounded Roi-Namur for thirty days prior to the assault. Instead of the "modest" three-hour naval shelling that preceded the Marines' landing at Tarawa, American ships and planes blasted Roi-Namur with six thousand tons of ordnance before the Marines set foot ashore. The expenditure was nearly a threefold increase over the Tarawa barrage some nine weeks earlier.[2]

The Americans scheduled D-day for January 31, 1944. However, Operation Flintlock would commence not with the main landings at Kwajalein and Roi-Namur, but with the seizure of preliminary positions meant to aid the principal attacks. To buttress their firepower, the V Corps' D-day operations focused on landing 105- and 155-mm howitzers on several undefended islands neighboring Kwajalein and Roi-Namur. By nightfall on January 31 the 14th Marine Artillery Regiment had established several firing positions within range of the primary landing beaches. Throughout the night, Marine artillerymen peppered Roi-Namur with "harassing fires" meant to distract and badger Japanese troops. Most importantly, and unlike the American attack on Tarawa, the howitzers stood registered to support the morning assault.[3]

As dawn broke the following morning, the Marines queued up to load their landing craft while American fire support approached its prelanding crescendo. This time, however, U.S. ships and aircraft benefited from the practical, hard-earned lessons of the attack on Tarawa. Rather than repeating the "area bombing"[4] tactics used in the Gilbert Islands, carrier aircraft launching from Rear Admiral Marc A. Mitscher's Task Force 58 identified specific enemy targets and focused on precision bombing techniques. Such deliberate efforts led to more efficient and effective fire support from above.[5] In one instance at Roi-Namur, carrier pilots learned that a steep aerial dive executed from two thousand feet down to fifty feet across an enemy position made for "highly successful" strafing fire.[6] Positioning and precision, it seemed, made all the difference.

Also reflecting on the experience at Tarawa, Rear Admiral Richard L. Conolly, commanding Task Force 53, the Northern Attack Force, determined to provide effective and continual naval gunfire support as the Marines went ashore. He directed his fire support groups to sail in close to the enemy shoreline in order to accurately identify Japanese positions and increase the destructive power of each salvo. Firing from "point blank" ranges of less than two thousand yards, Conolly's Sailors assumed far greater risk to themselves and their ships to improve their effects ashore.[7] Despite the added danger, the admiral's subordinates applauded his audacity. Commanding the battleship USS *Tennessee*, Captain R. S. Haggart wrote that from "personal observation of the targets" he could not believe that the ship's objectives "could have been more thoroughly destroyed."[8] The commander of Destroyer Squadron One called the close-in firing positions "ideal" and argued that the effect was far more than physical: "Not only is such fire destructive to the enemy but it is bound to give a boost to the morale of the landing troops as they pass by on their way in."[9] The captain's impression was correct. The impressed and thankful Marines at Roi-Namur approvingly nicknamed the bold admiral "Close-In Conolly," a title he would hold for the remainder of the war.[10]

In addition to his standard complement of battleships, destroyers, and cruisers, Conolly also unveiled a creative, modified naval vessel meant to provide critical fires within the final one thousand yards of the Roi-Namur shoreline. As the Marines' landing craft made their final approach and the heavy 16- and 14-inch guns of Conolly's armada were forced to lift their fire from the landing beaches, recently adapted landing craft, infantry (LCIs) under the direction of Captain E. R. McLean and Commander J. C. Woelfel, filled the void in firepower. Though the craft were intended to ferry troops ashore in an amphibious landing, McLean and Woelfel's nine LCIs boasted twenty-four 4.5-inch rocket tubes, two 40-mm guns, and several .50-caliber machine guns each. Aided by a shallow draft of less than six feet that allowed them to navigate just offshore, the LCIs blasted Japanese positions with rockets as the Marine landing waves closed between 1,100 and 600 yards from the beach. As the Marines entered the final five hundred yards of their approach, the gunboats "swung off to the flanks, and continued firing," raking the landing beaches with their 40-mm cannons and .50-caliber machine guns.[11] Captain McLean commented after the battle, "In our LCI gunboats we have developed a very fine close-in weapon as they can deliver effective support until the waves *actually* hit the beaches."[12]

The Japanese detachment on Roi-Namur presented a similar defense—in both size and style—to what the Marines faced in their earlier attack on the Tarawa atoll. Some three thousand Japanese soldiers and laborers had constructed an intricate web of mutually supporting positions designed to maximize firepower at the beachhead. The decision was, as historian Theodore Gatchel has pointed out, a conceptually "stagnant" one. The Japanese remained focused on the waterline instead of pursuing a more comprehensive defensive approach.[13] Fighting from trenches that paralleled the length of the beaches, the defenders were both well camouflaged and well protected. Pillboxes, concrete walls, and reinforced fighting holes threatened to complicate the Marines' advance. As in the Gilberts, the Japanese would make the shoreline their bid for success, hoping to stall the American operation before it could gather momentum.[14]

At precisely 11:57, after a full morning of air and naval bombardment, the first Marines advanced onto the beaches of Roi-Namur, and control of air and naval fire support shifted to the newly minted 1st Joint Assault Signal Company. As envisioned in their original charter, the JASCO teams dispersed themselves among the landing force according to practicality and priority: shore fire control parties (SFCPs) consisting of one naval gunfire liaison officer and five to seven enlisted personnel trekked ashore alongside each infantry regiment and battalion. Each SFCP debarked their landing craft with one TBX radio and one SCR-536 radio, both configured to match the radio nets of the infantry units they supported as well as the naval gunfire common channel that connected them with offshore vessels.[15] With both frequencies operational, the fire control parties could monitor the general radio chatter of the gunfire ships and adjacent SFCPs as they exchanged updates and requested support. Though ad hoc support developed as needed, each ship was preassigned a particular sector of the objective. When a liaison officer and supporting ship commenced a particular fire mission, they switched to an alternate channel to minimize interference and confirm the details of the request.[16]

At first, little air or naval support was required. Thanks to the intense prelanding barrage, the Marines encountered virtually no resistance in the first three hundred yards across the beach. For a moment, at least, the attack mimicked the precision of a martial parade, and the "main landing was accomplished unopposed."[17] Yet as the operation on Roi-Namur progressed and the Americans encountered Japanese positions not targeted in the initial bombardment, the 4th Marine Division increasingly turned to its air and naval fire support. Shore fire control parties quickly established communications with their offshore counterparts and began coordinating naval strikes ashore. In the short twenty-six hours of combat on Roi-Namur, the control parties directed "call fires"[18] that totaled 7,000 rounds of 5-inch shells, 350 rounds of 8-inch shells, and 350 rounds of 14-inch shells onto the single square mile of the island.[19]

The Marines' assault ashore soon became a complementary, combined arms affair. The 23rd Marine Regiment, assigned to seize Roi's principal airfield, advanced behind careful tank-infantry coordination. When the 23rd Marines' progress stalled in the face of three determined Japanese naval air groups on the northeast corner of the island, the Marines turned to their JASCO attachment. Within moments, the shore fire control party directed a string of 5-inch salvos from the light cruiser *Santa Fe* onto the stubborn Japanese airmen. Watching the harmonious assault from above, one American air observer reported, "ONLY TWO REMAIN WHO HAVE NOT AS YET MET HONORABLE ANCESTORS."[20]

American carrier air support added its own effects to the cacophony of fires on Roi-Namur. On February 1 U.S. pilots operating from Rear Admiral Mitscher's Task Force 58 flew 238 sorties over the Marshall Islands. The day's air operations included more than ninety missions in direct support of ground troops, delivering 119 tons of bombs and 176,600 rounds of .50 caliber ammunition onto the beaches.[21]

The commander support aircraft (CSA), embarked with Conolly and working from the joint operations room of USS *Appalachian*, managed and controlled aircraft in support of the Marines ashore.[22] Throughout the battle, airborne observers provided the CSA regular radio updates on friendly positions, enemy movements, and the progress of the landing force. As infantry units ashore encountered stubborn targets, they turned to their accompanying air liaison parties (ALPs) to contact the CSA and his staff offshore. Once the CSA granted approval, his staff assigned an aircraft (or flight of aircraft) in support, and the mission commenced. Though the process allowed for meticulous management from the experienced CSA and an orderly "air space" above the battlefield, it also proved cumbersome and fragile. At any one of the relays between the front-line infantry forces and the CSA offshore in *Appalachian*, delays and miscommunication threatened the effectiveness of American close air support in the Marshalls.[23]

Once assigned to a specific mission, pilots established radio communications with the on-scene airborne coordinator, a senior naval aviator circling the battlefield and responsible for providing order to friendly aircraft. He shared relevant safety information to the incoming pilot and served as a localized air traffic controller, directing friendly flights around the battlefield. When in support of ground troops, pilots raised and monitored a second frequency that allowed them to speak directly with the appropriate ALP. In this final conversation, the air liaison officer identified friendly ground units for the pilot and confirmed target coordinates before the air strike commenced. Unlike at Tarawa—where American pilots and ground units struggled to speak a common language—air liaison officers and pilots in the Marshalls confirmed their targets through both ground coordinates and a pre-established target identification number, developed from reconnaissance imagery before the battle.[24]

The effects of the Americans' increased coordination in the Marshalls were tangible. Throughout the assault on Roi-Namur, pilots synchronized their strikes with both ground and naval fires. The 1st JASCO—through its subordinate SFCPs and ALPs—provided critical support in coordinating the various components. Unlike at Tarawa, and even in spite of several delayed carrier strikes, the Marines judged their air support dependable and continuous, their naval gunfire responsive and accurate. In several instances, Marine infantrymen reported the JASCO's ability to deliver near-immediate naval gunfire.[25] Air support was usually soon to follow, and with comparable effects. The CSA overseeing aviation support on Kwajalein and Roi-Namur recalled, "Aircraft movements were controlled with a view to minimizing mutual interference. Artillery and naval gunfire were lifted only when heavy air bombardment was required on targets which had not proven vulnerable to naval gunfire or artillery."[26]

In large part due to effective fire support from Conolly's Northern Attack Force, the 4th Marine Division declared their objective secure at 2:18 p.m. on February 2, 1944. By any account, the victory on Roi-Namur was rapid; the first landing wave had stepped ashore less than twenty-seven hours earlier. In several cases, the Marines' aggressive pace compromised safety as American ships and aircraft struggled to keep their fires safely in front of their fellow troops.[27] In welcome contrast to the shocking casualty counts at Tarawa, the landing force suffered just 129 killed and 436 wounded. In a now-discernible trend that connected Guadalcanal, Tarawa, and the Marshalls, the Marines killed 3,472 enemy troops and took just 99 Japanese prisoners on Roi-Namur.[28] As brutal as armed conflict inherently is, war in the Pacific was approaching a new and entirely awful tier.

Tank-infantry tactics and field artillery both contributed to the triumph, but most troops fighting ashore credited the victory to U.S. naval fire support. Various American officers claimed that the "overwhelming" amount of naval gunfire—both before and during the assault—secured the Marshalls. The commanding general of the 4th Marine Division estimated that between fifty and seventy-five percent of enemy troops on Roi-Namur were killed by air and naval fires.[29] Several Japanese prisoners of war "testified that the terrific blasting effect of the heavy and continuous bombardment terrorized the defending forces and reduced their [defensive] effectiveness."[30]

Yet even alongside such sincere recognition, postbattle reflections in the aftermath of the Marshalls offensive brought careful critique to the Americans' evolving system of fire support in the Pacific. Though naval and aerial fires achieved obvious effects on Roi-Namur, U.S. Navy officers in particular identified several shortcomings in the coordination and execution of those fire missions. As Japanese troops learned to counter American bombardments with more defensive cover and to wait out the preliminary shelling, they would counteract the impressive effects observed in the Marshalls.[31]

Navy and Marine units needed closer coordination if they were to succeed in a larger offensive against a better equipped and more established defensive force.

Principally, Navy and Marine officers acknowledged a need for closer integration between the various components of the American triphibious force. At Roi-Namur, land, sea, and air units failed to appreciate both the capabilities and limitations of their peers. In command of Carrier Air Group 9 at Roi-Namur—a unit composed of F6F-3 Hellcat fighters, SBD-5 Dauntless dive bombers, and TBF-1 Avenger torpedo bombers—Lieutenant Commander P. H. Torrey described the dynamic carefully:

> The capabilities of a carrier's deck do not seem to be fully appreciated by those making out the air plan. The same might be said for those directing the operations of aircraft from the ground in support of a landing. The entire air plan on the day of landing is constructed around the time of landing, the crucial point of the entire operation. Flights are arranged in order that H-hour occurs about midway of the period of the flight to allow for maximum leeway on either side. However, H-hour both at Tarawa and Roi was changed [in mid-operation] so that the flight was required to remain even beyond that allowed extra time and was very nearly forced to return. If such was the case and had incoming flights been detained for even a short time by unfavorable weather, no air support would have been available at all. . . . The restrictions carrier operations should impose on any change of time of landings should be thoroughly appreciated by those directing these operations if the proper support is to be obtained.[32]

The commander of Carrier Air Group 6, Lieutenant Commander D. B. Ingerslew, echoed Torrey's concern, recommending that "greater effort be made by ground forces to maintain prearranged schedules."[33]

The aviators were hardly the sole critics. Other components of the triphibious force voiced their own concerns that often returned the blame to the pilots. While aviation officers such as Torrey and Ingerslew called for rigid adherence to an attack timeline, naval gunfire personnel clamored for more flexibility across the composite unit and a deeper knowledge of naval gunfire capabilities, specifically within the landing force. To achieve an effective, coordinated assault, land, sea, and air forces needed to tune their support to the progress of the landing force—whether afloat or ashore—rather than adhere to a prescriptive timeline.[34] The rub, of course, was in the balancing of both points of view.

Both practical and cultural issues contributed to the rift between American aviators and their counterparts in the infantry. From their earliest days in flight school, naval pilots learned to rely on prescribed checklists and exact specifications. Timelines were not only convenient; they were critical. When a pilot launched from his carrier, his fuel gauge became a supreme authority. It determined—in direct fashion—how long he would remain aloft and, accordingly, how much support he could provide. Fuel levels were neither flexible nor negotiable. Specific feet of altitude and precise fuel readings drove the aviators' decision-making. The infantryman, on the other hand, was taught to embrace chaos and friction. On a dynamic battlefield, rigidity was both foolish and detrimental. Such recognition did not preclude planning within the infantry, but it did elevate a spirit of flexibility and adaptation.[35]

Aviation and naval gunfire officers did find agreement in certain matters, most notably in their disappointment with the Marines' inadequate knowledge of supporting arms coordination. While naval gunnery crews complained that landing force personnel lacked the training and experience to properly apply sea-based fires, aviators argued that the same infantry units often dismissed aviation support out of hand.[36] The CSA at Roi-Namur charged that landing force commanders failed to clearly express their expectations. As a result, "many [air] attacks were made with the hope, rather than the assurance, that they would be of benefit to the troops. . . . Battalion Commanders may not have been sufficiently familiar with, or confident in, the use of this relatively new weapon." Because of such limitations, he wrote, the full potential of naval air support "is yet to be realized."[37]

On occasion, breakdowns in "shared understanding" led American forces to the precipice of disaster at Roi-Namur. On the second day of battle, an unnamed destroyer flagrantly retreated from its firing position and left a Marine unit ashore devoid of naval gunfire support at a crucial moment in the operation. Rear Admiral Conolly called the move "a serious error in judgement on the part of the Commanding Officer." Though he chose to keep his condemnation anonymous—likely to protect the reputation of the captain and crew—Conolly levied a scathing critique all the same:

> The fact remains that (USS _ _ _ _ _) with her 5-inch guns and close range machine guns, was not at hand, and the assault waves moved forward covered only by LCIs. It is absolutely vital that fire support units remember that they are supporting the landing of foot troops. Everything must be coordinated to get them ashore safely. If a ship is assigned to render close support until 5 minutes before the troops land, the commanding officer of the ship concerned must remain and provide that support, even if the landing time is delayed for hours at a time, unless specifically ordered otherwise by superior authority.[38]

Even if the guilty destroyer itself escaped recognition, "Close-In" Conolly extracted the lesson for his Sailors to absorb.

To address such lapses in coordination, Navy and Marine officers of Conolly's attack force prescribed an overhaul in pre-operation training. Under the haste of American preparation for the Marshalls offensive—by now a seemingly unavoidable dynamic in the war—the landing force received only "elementary and basic amphibious training" while the vast majority of supporting aircraft did not take part at all in preparatory rehearsals, primarily because the carriers' robust operational calendar precluded participation in the Hawaiian-based exercises.[39] The JASCOs, hastily organizing according to their post-Tarawa charter, arrived just in time for the final preparatory maneuvers.[40] Although most naval gunfire ships did execute a training curriculum before sailing for the Marshalls, they did not integrate their training with the Marine landing force.[41] Separate drills might have promised safety for the men, but they also meant that complex problems over command, control, and coordination went unacknowledged and unaddressed within the task force.

In response, American officers called for an integrated and lengthened training period for each entity of the triphibious team. If disparate units were to build credibility and shared understanding and avoid dangerous lapses in combat, they needed to train as one unified team before the first naval salvo, aerial attack, or wave of Marine infantrymen.[42] Isolated training—with ships, planes, and landing craft at separate locations and focused on individual capabilities—was incomplete and made American troops complacent, giving them an elevated and at times false sense of confidence. Most importantly, just as they had during the interwar period, isolated exercises ignored the messy and acute challenge of coordination for the actual battlefield, where lesson-learning exacted far more blood.

Insufficient training not only left tactical problems unresolved prior to the Marshalls; it also contributed to deeper relational weaknesses within the V Corps and its supporting factions. By failing to expose the ships, carrier squadrons, and Marines to one another adequately in training, the American attack demanded "personal cooperation between strangers."[43] Infantry, aviation, and naval gunnery personnel struggled to appreciate the perspective, requirements, capabilities, and limitations of other specialties. The triphibious team needed comprehensive association and common rapport if it was to achieve its fullest potential.

Because of their unique position at the nexus of triphibious operations, Navy and Marine observers alike identified the novel JASCO as a fitting vehicle to foster closer integration and understanding among American forces in the Pacific. The specialized companies had performed capably, though not exceptionally, in their first Central Pacific test and received many of the same criticisms levied at the naval crews, aviators, and infantrymen: JASCO units were inexperienced in the art of applying air and naval fires, their introductory training was hurried and insufficient, and they lacked a certain rapport with the pilots and naval gunners with whom they interacted.[44] Criticisms notwithstanding, the JASCOs remained the most suitable medium of change, and both their responsibilities and their expectations grew in the coming months of war. As the emerging bridge between American land, sea, and air forces, the units were well positioned to light the path forward in triphibious integration.

Although tactical commanders and staff officers at the individual battalion, ship, and squadron levels were the first to diagnose and address concerns in battlefield coordination, senior commanders quickly threw their institutional weight behind the reform effort. General Holland Smith advised after the assault on Roi-Namur that "the closest possible cooperation with corresponding naval echelons is essential."[45] Admiral Conolly, himself becoming a tireless advocate of naval fire support, wrote: "It cannot be too strongly emphasized that the effects of [aerial] bombing and [naval] gunfire are complementary. Each can contribute destruction of certain elements of defense, personnel, and structures. Properly timed and coordinated the power of the combination . . . is multiplied several fold."[46] At the highest and lowest tiers of battlefield command, the offensive in the Marshalls convinced American commanders of the need for closely choreographed triphibious operations.

VICTORY IN THE MARSHALLS: PLATEAU OR PRELUDE?

American success in the Marshall Islands gave grounds for optimism at the highest levels of U.S. wartime leadership and reinforced confidence in the Navy and Marine Corps' ability to carry out amphibious war. In particular, the victory evidenced the progression of U.S. amphibious forces in the months since the attack on Tarawa. As Admiral Ernest King's staff summarized in a comprehensive after-action report: "The various factors and steps in our success did not just happen; they were brought about." For King's staff, the most valuable adjustment "brought about" was the Americans' deliberate emphasis on massing firepower against the enemy. The report's introduction concluded: "The rapid advances on shore with but moderate losses were possible only because of the intensity and thoroughness of the preliminary bombings and bombardments and the effective support of artillery and naval vessels in providing barrage and call fires as needed."[47]

American use of air and naval fires in the Marshall Islands surpassed any precedent to date in the Pacific War. Slowly but surely in the amphibious contests of the Pacific War, firepower was becoming king. In December 1943, a full month before Army and Marine troops touched down on the beaches, Army Liberator bombers worked the Marshall Islands over with

601 tons of ordnance. As the naval task force steamed for its objectives, Rear Admiral Mitscher's fast carriers of Task Force 58 dropped another 1,156 tons of bombs.[48] And yet only then did the naval cannons begin adding to the deluge. On Roi-Namur alone, U.S. Navy gunners delivered 18,559 5-inch, 3,337 6-inch, 783 14-inch, and 882 16-inch high-explosive shells for a total naval tonnage of 2,251 tons.[49] Associated Press correspondent and eyewitness Alva Dopking understandably labeled it the "heaviest naval bombardment in history."[50] All told, American naval guns drowned Roi-Namur with more than three pounds of ordnance per square yard, a higher ratio than any previous amphibious assault of the war. And having corrected their prewar doctrine, U.S. fire support ships now targeted precise, specific fortifications rather than laying down general "area fire."

In large part because of overwhelming American sea and air power, the nation's position in the Pacific appeared promising in the early spring of 1944. In a formal report to the Secretary of the Navy that April, just weeks removed from the overwhelming American victory in the Marshalls, Admiral King expressed unqualified confidence in American military power and the now-visible road to victory. Amid an increasingly successful submarine campaign that was denying Japan desperately needed fuel reserves and ongoing amphibious landings that overwhelmed Japanese positions through aerial and naval firepower, King concluded,

> The war against Japan has gone increasingly well of late. From their posts of maximum advance in the Pacific, the Japanese have been driven back progressively by a series of offensive operations. Important as our own advances toward Japan are, they do not fully represent the improvements in our position. Japanese capacity to maintain the war at sea and in her advanced areas has suffered increasingly, due to the loss of vital shipping, while the growth of our power in the Pacific enables us to threaten attack on the Marianas and Carolines and Kuriles, which may be called the intermediate zone of defense of the Empire. . . . the current and prospective circumstances in the Pacific Theater present a situation which must be as dark and threatening to Japan as it is full of promise to us.[51]

Reporters, too, seemed to acknowledge the optimism of the moment. After landing alongside Marines at Roi-Namur, Alva Dopking reported that "the cockiness of the Japanese was gone. They looked frightened. One trembling prisoner told an American officer, Lieutenant William Brown of Scarsdale, N.Y., that he and others on the island knew that the Japanese no longer had a chance to win the war."[52]

The Marshalls had been something of a relief for American forces. The rapid victory hastened the Allies' timeline in the Pacific and convinced Admiral Chester Nimitz and the joint chiefs to bypass the Japanese fortress at Truk altogether. That decision freed up several Marine and Army divisions, expedited the looming assault on the Marianas, and contributed to growing American confidence in the war effort.[53]

But if many equated triumph in the Marshalls with sure and certain victory in the broader conflagration, others tempered their enthusiasm with the grave realization that the road to Tokyo still spanned some 2,800 miles. Along that path stood fortified Japanese citadels manned by resolute defenders. How would future assaults compare? Holland Smith, himself prone to elevated confidence when discussing his own Marine forces, seemed to temper the fervor after the American campaign in the Marshalls: "There is still much to be desired to improve planning, improve the coordination of efforts and prepare for the attack of more difficult objectives."[54] In fact, it was the very seizure of "more difficult objectives" that would define the final year of war in the Pacific.

CHAPTER 5

MORE SHELLS, MORE PLANES, MORE HARMONY

TAKING THE MARIANAS

In his 2016 study *The Soul of Armies*, political scientist Austin Long investigated how organizational culture directly fuels—or foils—battlefield success. In its prosecution of counterinsurgency warfare throughout the nineteenth and twentieth centuries, Long argues, the U.S. Marine Corps embraced a "managerial culture" that focused on internal operations, identity, and purpose. Along the way, the service intensified its infantry-centric approach to combat. When applied effectively, this cultural posture granted the Corps a high degree of initiative "at each level of command, giving officers wide latitude for decision and, correspondingly, high levels of responsibility for those decisions."[1] Along the way, combat experience in the Pacific, Central America, and the Caribbean helped the Marines coalesce "around a managerial culture emphasizing small-unit leadership with an infantry ethos."[2]

Though Long's investigation centers on military performance in a counterinsurgency context, the cultural traits that he identifies within the service help to explain the Marines' approach to amphibious warfare in the Pacific. The same autonomy, introspection, and flexibility that provided latitude in a counterinsurgency allowed local Marine commanders to integrate naval and aerial support in more effective and creative ways in the Central Pacific.

APPROACHING THE MARIANAS

American forces emerged from their assault on the Marshalls with newfound confidence in their ability to wage triphibious war. Aided by surging wartime production in the United States, Allied forces fought from a growing foundation of material and technological superiority. In 1944 alone the U.S. Navy built more than 40,000 ships of all sizes, ranging from aircraft carriers to specialized landing craft. By December of that year, the service was adding over 50,000,000 horsepower per month to its already massive flotilla. As Fleet Admiral Ernest King put it, "Our guiding policy is to achieve not mere adequacy, but overwhelming superiority." The Chief of Naval Operations went on, rejoicing in the now-realized potential of American industry: "The magnificent productive capacity of the United States has given us the greatest navy in all history."[3] For King's Sailors and Marines, the dark and dispiriting defeats of 1942 were but a faint memory. Having secured the Marshall Islands with relatively minimal bloodshed, the Allies remained on the march to Tokyo.

As the United States widened its material advantage, so too did it mature its tactical approach to warfare in the Pacific. Throughout 1944 U.S. forces continued to develop a novel brand of the amphibious assault. This modern version, theorized during the interwar years and advanced during the conflict's early combat operations against Japan, centered on surprise, speed, and mass. To these classical features, the Americans introduced an unprecedented degree of supporting firepower from the sea and air. In the Central Pacific, American triphibious units learned that overwhelming, meticulous, and carefully coordinated firepower could solve their most pressing tactical problems. Especially when meeting increasingly effective Japanese defensive methods in their advance across the Pacific, U.S. landing forces came to rely upon naval and aerial fires to first put the infantry ashore and then propel its attack against an entrenched and determined enemy.

PUNCTURING THE MARIANAS PERIMETER: THE BATTLE FOR SAIPAN

After weighing their 1944 strategic options, the representatives of the British-American combined chiefs of staff declared the Marianas their next objective in the Central Pacific. The choice made sense on a number of levels. An attack through the Marianas would cut Japan's naval supply lines and provide a forward base for the American submarine fleet intent on tightening its noose around Japanese shipping. With a dash of luck,

MAP 3. SAIPAN

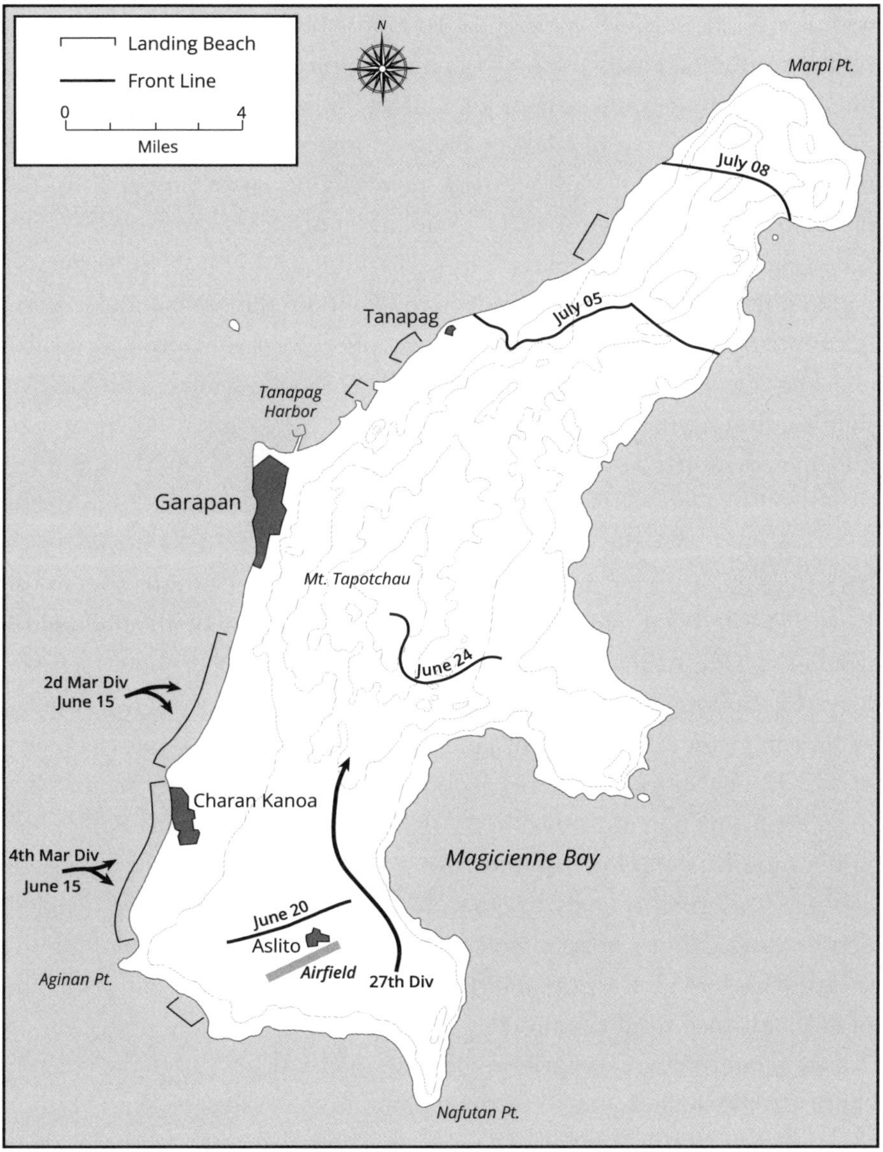

Prepared by Chris Robinson

the campaign might even draw the Japanese fleet into a climactic naval engagement on American terms.[4] The possibilities thrilled Admiral King and Admiral Nimitz. But American fever for the Marianas did not stop with the Navy; the U.S. Army Air Forces likewise welcomed the target. As the combined chiefs themselves had recognized during the Cairo and Tehran conferences, the seizure of Guam, Tinian, and Saipan islands in the Marianas chain would deliver a long-awaited dream: as the conference record itself labeled it, the "strategic bombing of Japan proper."[5] To the pleasure of General Hap Arnold, commander of all U.S. Army Air Forces, Allied control of the Marianas promised to put the novel B-29 Superfortress within range of the enemy's home islands. For both the Navy and the Army Air Forces, it was hard to envision a target offering greater strategic spoils.[6]

The chiefs' decision meant a sustained dual-axis advance, with MacArthur continuing the march toward Rabaul in preparation for his much-anticipated return to the Philippines, while Nimitz's Navy-Marine team continued its Central Pacific heading through the Marianas. MacArthur was disgusted with the decision, as it virtually extinguished his hopes of becoming the supreme and undisputed joint American commander in the Pacific Theater. Only a direct and unimpeded advance upon the Philippines would do, MacArthur believed, and Nimitz's Pacific Fleet should lend its powerful support. The Marianas were merely a distraction that would delay American victory in the war. In January 1944 MacArthur wrote Secretary of War Henry Stimson to share his displeasure and plead his solution: "Give me central direction of the war in the Pacific, and I will be in the Philippines in ten months. . . . Don't let the Navy's pride of position and ignorance continue this great tragedy to our country."[7] But the decision was made, despite MacArthur's noise. The combined chiefs of staff directed Nimitz to ready his team for action and strike the Marianas in mid-summer. The parallel advance would continue.

By geographical comparison, the Mariana Islands dwarfed the recently captured Marshalls. Lying some three thousand miles west of Pearl Harbor, the sprawling Marianas stretched nearly five hundred miles. For both Allied and Japanese war planners, the strength of the archipelago lay at the southern end. Only there could military forces find islands large enough to serve as proper naval and aerial bases. Among the suitable islands, American leaders turned their initial attention to two prospects: Saipan and Tinian. To Holland Smith and the V Corps fell the task of assaulting Saipan; to Major General Roy S. Geiger and the Third Amphibious Corps, the task of seizing Tinian.

Saipan presented the most daunting objective. The island stretched fourteen miles long and some five miles wide, but its chief obstacle was its interior terrain. Beginning with a stable plateau in the south—where the Japanese constructed their primary airfield—the island rose gradually and morphed into mountainous terrain in the center. Peaking at a height of more than 1,500 feet, the central highlands gave way to a hilly northern region. Ridges, peaks, caves, and ravines littered the central and northern sectors of the island. Unlike the relatively flat and predictable topography of former objectives such as Guadalcanal, Tarawa, and Kwajalein, Saipan presented a large and intimidating landscape.[8]

In the months before the assault, American intelligence officers assessed enemy strength on Saipan, categorized the island's landing beaches, and pored over aerial photography of the enemy outpost. Their prognosis was bleak, but time was of the essence. By May 1944 intelligence assessments revealed three airfields on Saipan and roughly 12,000 enemy troops. As American aircraft documented the arrival of Japanese reinforcements throughout the spring, intelligence officers pushed their estimate to 18,000 defenders. Even the modified appraisal was faulty, however, as aerial photography failed to capture the true inland strength of the Japanese detachment. In actuality, 30,000 enemy troops awaited the American landing. As a harbinger of the Pacific War's final year, Saipan promised both formidable geography and a reinforced defensive garrison.[9]

On June 11, 1944, U.S. forces commenced carrier air strikes against the Marianas—what had become the standard "softening up" operations that preceded American ground assaults in the Pacific. Admiral Mitscher's Task Force 58, composed of a staggering fifteen carriers and 1,200 planes, provided the sea-based air power, while Admiral Raymond Spruance retained overall command of the Fifth Fleet and its jaw-dropping six hundred warships. Paying particular attention to enemy aircraft, ships, antiaircraft batteries, and coastal defense guns on Saipan, Mitscher's pilots worked the island over during daylight hours. In their first strike alone, the now-experienced aviators destroyed 124 enemy planes and 13 ships. American fast battleships and destroyers joined the symphony on June 13, or "D-day minus two" in the operational vernacular (forty-eight hours before the infantry landing). The ships focused their efforts on mobile artillery targets and enemy fortifications on and near the landing beaches. The naval shelling proved complementary to the aerial bombing, at least from vantage points offshore. The destroyers sustained "harassing" fires throughout the night, intending to unsettle Japanese troops and remind them of the attackers' firepower advantage.[10] Aboard the cruiser *Montpelier*, seaman James Fahey reported his confidence: "We should have the Japs punch drunk by the time the Marines land Thursday morning."[11] The following day, U.S. ships and planes repeated the script for their audience. Fahey's reassurance only grew: "We did enough bombarding to last us a lifetime. . . . Thick smoke miles high was all over the island. I never saw anything like it before, it was like the great Chicago fire. Any large city would be in ruins if it took the shells and bombs Saipan took for almost a week."[12]

From his defensive position ashore, Japanese Private Yamauchi Takeo shared Fahey's awe. Being on the receiving end of the American volley, however, Takeo's emotions quickly moved from wonder to terror:

> I was eating a large rice ball when I heard a voice cry out, "The American battle fleet is here!" I looked up and saw the sea completely black with [ships]. What looked like a large city had suddenly appeared offshore. . . . The first salvos exploded along the beach. The extreme intensity of those flashes and boiling clouds of smoke still remain[s] in my mind today. They went sixty meters straight up! Huge guns! From battleships. A total bombardment from all the ships. The area I was in was pitted like the craters of the moon. We just clung to the earth in our shallow trenches. We were half buried. Soil filled my mouth many times. Blinded me. The fumes and flying dirt almost choked you. The next moment I might get it![13]

Stricken with fear yet well protected, Takeo and his fellow defenders weathered the prelanding barrage and awaited the Americans' vulnerable approach to the beach.

Spruance's battleships were threatening enough from their preparatory firing positions, but as the attack morphed from barrage to amphibious assault, the American warships brought even more destruction to Saipan's doorstep. As Navy and Marine officers had learned at Tarawa—and observed again in the Marshalls—effective supporting firepower had to mirror the movement of the landing force rather than adhere to a strict, predetermined timetable. In order to tether themselves to the progress of the landing force and to increase the effectiveness of their rounds, naval gunfire ships determined to "move in to extremely close ranges" while providing fire support ashore during the Marianas offensive.[14]

On June 15, 1944, D-day came to Saipan. With gunfire ships in immediate proximity and Mitscher's warplanes overhead, Holland Smith's joint Army-Marine landing force prepared for its entry in the battle. At 5:52 a.m., aboard USS *Rocky Mount* and in operational command of the joint force, Admiral Richmond Kelly Turner gave the ceremonial order: "Land the Landing Force." The scripted phrase set the attack in motion. Marines loaded their LVT (landing vehicle, tracked) assault craft, and coxswains made haste for the "line of departure," where each scheduled wave would rendezvous before churning ashore. The troops slated for the Saipan beaches, designated the "Northern Troops and Landing Force" and composed of the 2d and 4th Marine Divisions and the 27th Infantry Division (Army), totaled a staggering 71,034 men. The Marines were slated to land first; Smith intended to hold the 27th Division in reserve and, ideally, preserve it for follow-on actions.

From precisely 7:00 to 7:27, as the various landing craft staged, loaded, and circled their embarkation zones, Mitscher's carrier aircraft made a penultimate pass over the island. Sixty F6F Hellcats, 51 SBD Dauntlesses, and 54 TBF Avengers struck the landing beaches and proximate targets.[15] With the air strike complete, Turner's naval cannons resumed their barrage. As the Marine landing force closed the final eight hundred yards of its trek ashore, the naval guns went cold once again, and a flight of forty-eight Hellcats and twenty-four Avengers roared over the beaches in a final strafing and bombing attack. The planes sustained their support until the landing craft were one hundred yards from the shoreline, at which point the pilots shifted their aim one hundred yards inland.[16] Contrasted with the Americans' disarray at Tarawa, the Saipan attack unfolded with precision and harmony.

On account of the accurate and extended preparatory barrage that forced enemy defenders from the beaches, the initial landing proceeded smoothly for the Americans. From their landing point on the southwestern corner of the island, the Marines extended their foothold and made steady progress in the face of light Japanese resistance. But just as the 2d and 4th Divisions felt their momentum build, they encountered a wall of resistance behind the open beaches. Japanese troops "from prepared positions on commanding terrain" pummeled the landing force with preregistered artillery, mortar, and machine gun fire.[17]

As the attack began to stall, Marine lieutenant colonel Hollis Mustain was one of the first commanders ashore to augment his advance with "on call" air and naval fire support. With his First Battalion thrown on its heels, Mustain directed his air liaison and shore fire control parties to arrange offshore fire support. The JASCO teams soon had three destroyers, the battleship *Tennessee*, and a section of attack aircraft working with the First Battalion to turn back the Japanese counterattack. Mustain's outfit regained the initiative by early afternoon and destroyed two Japanese companies on Saipan's southern Agingan Point.[18]

Mustain's renewed attack was not the only reason for optimism that afternoon. By early evening, U.S. landing craft had ferried 20,000 troops, seven artillery battalions, and two tank companies ashore. Enemy resistance remained stiff, but the welcome firepower buttressed the Marines' front line on Saipan. As the artillery teams positioned, prepared, and registered their guns, American carrier pilots and naval gunners maintained their critical support. Having weathered a series of additional enemy counterattacks in the afternoon and evening hours, Mustain and his fellow Marines clung to a well-defended but promising beachhead as the sun dipped below the horizon on D-day.[19]

Challenged but holding, the battered Marines received welcome support the following day. Having taken more than 2,500 casualties and having realized that Saipan's enemy troop strength was much higher than the preliminary estimates, Holland Smith postponed the adjacent landing on Guam (slated for June 18) and instead sent the reserve 27th Infantry Division ashore to reinforce the Marines' position. The soldiers joined the American lines and rejuvenated the charge. Preceding their attacks with coordinated naval, air, and artillery support, the V Corps—now as a full-strength unit—fought its way across Saipan.

The coordinated fires were welcome, for the Japanese defenders under Lieutenant General Yoshitsugu Saito determined to play to their strengths. Although the detachment's construction efforts had fallen behind schedule in the early summer, leaving their material vision for the island incomplete, Saito and his troops leveraged their next best card: Saipan's rugged terrain. As the Americans advanced ashore, Japanese officers placed snipers in the dense sugarcane of the island's interior and sustained their web of interlocking machine gun and mortar fires that had begun at the water's edge. Some defenders died in place, while others retreated across successive ridges and coral cliffs to take up new fighting positions. Particularly as the assault wore on, Japanese commanders turned to their familiarity with the austere terrain and their preestablished defensive lines to combat the American advance.[20]

Against Saito's terrain-oriented scheme, the V Corps' progress was slow but reliable. American fire support sustained the attack. As naval guns helped to press the attack forward, one observer commended the destroyer *John Rodgers*' dependable fires, stating that "her firing left very little to be desired."[21] Another veteran of the battle recalled an unnamed Marine colonel who, while "tranquilly puffing a cigar," directed American naval gunfire against several Japanese tank companies threatening American lines on the night of June 16–17. Perhaps with a dash of embellishment, the Marine observer recorded the effects the following morning: "At dawn the colonel was still on the stump, still puffing, with thirty-one derelict Jap tank hulks around him."[22] That day, June 17, the 4th Marine Division and 27th Infantry Division reached Magicienne Bay, bisecting the island. The following day, the soldiers of the 27th secured Aslito Airfield, which the Americans renamed "Isely Airfield" after Navy commander and pilot Robert Isely, killed four days earlier while strafing the beaches of Saipan in a low-level bombing run.[23]

After four more days of gruesome fighting—marked by the Americans' increasing use of bazookas, flamethrowers, and tank-infantry assaults to clear Japanese bunkers—the landing force added another aspect of organic fire support ashore. Having cleared and repaired Isely Airfield on the southern peninsula, U.S. troops welcomed four Army P-47 squadrons to the airstrip on June 22–25. The effect—both psychological and material—was immediate. And again, as at Henderson Field on Guadalcanal in 1942, the aviators and infantrymen in the Marianas developed a mutual affinity and appreciation for one another. In complementary fashion, the grunts protected the airstrip, and the aircraft defended the ground units. By the final days of June, the Army P-47s had solidified their value, particularly in close air support strikes against hardened Japanese bunkers on Saipan.[24]

While benefiting from air power ashore, American units continued to rely upon naval gunfire and carrier aviation support throughout late June and early July. Naval gunfire regularly energized advances by the 2d and 4th Marine Divisions as well as the 27th Infantry Division, supplementing their now-reliable tank-infantry tactics.[25] Navy lieutenant Ben Bradlee, who would go on to serve as the executive editor of the *Washington Post*, recalled a particular radio exchange with a Marine lieutenant ashore on Saipan. Aboard the destroyer USS *Philip*, Bradlee was responsible for receiving and processing fire support missions off Saipan. His anecdote reflects just how far Navy-Marine cooperation had come by mid-1944:

> When the young Marine and I talked he was so close to the Japanese defenders that I could hear them yelling, whenever he transmitted his request for a barrage of 5-inch gunfire from us. I've lost his name, unfortunately, but this guy was one brave son of a bitch. He would ask for gunfire in such-and-such a place—often within a few yards of his foxhole—and would relay the coordinates he gave me to the gunnery officer. First "Fire," then deafening explosion. Then pause, while the 57-pound shells streaked toward their target, followed by comments from our unseen buddy. . . . "Bullseye" maybe. Often, even. And sometimes: "That was a little close, friends. Back off a blond one."[26]

Bradlee went on to describe the ships' feverish support of the Marines ashore. From just 1,500 yards off the coast—a dangerous distance for any warship, let alone a destroyer—the crew provided indispensable fire support. Bradlee recalled, "The *Philip* was firing so many rounds of 5-inch shells, wherever our forward area spotter wanted them, that we were concerned that the barrels were deteriorating."[27] *Philip* and its red-hot barrels were hardly alone in their duties. The gunnery officers from one task group estimated that during a six-day window in early July, they delivered a minimum of 25,495 rounds onto Japanese positions, an average of 4,249 shells per day.[28] Carrier planes also sustained their critical role on Saipan, conducting no less than 186 close support missions between June 28 and July 3.[29]

The firepower offshore and overhead, combined with Marine artillery and tanks, drove the American lines forward yard by yard. Captain Frederic A. Stott, fighting with the 1st Battalion of the 24th Marine Regiment, remembered a particular episode that reflected both the Americans' combined arms advantage and the eroding humanity of the Pacific War: "In the forenoon the company came upon large numbers of Japs pocketed in a ravine bed and practically defenseless. Air strikes, artillery, mortars, and small arms were employed with success and satisfaction. It is highly satisfying to pour out destructive fires with effect and without retaliation."[30] Six days later, at 4:15 p.m. on July 9, Lieutenant General Holland Smith declared the island secure. At 10:00 the following morning, troops formally raised the U.S. colors over Saipan.[31] Though threatening pockets of resistance remained—including thousands of spirited enemy troops—close and committed cooperation between American ground, air, and naval forces had delivered success in the Marianas.

The victory might have left U.S. troops with a stronger sense of achievement but for the harrowing acts they witnessed in the final stages of the battle. As soldiers and Marines closed the perimeter on the northern tip of the island, as many as one thousand civilians proved themselves unwilling to abide Allied capture. Zealous Japanese soldiers assisted those struggling with the decision. As his unit advanced, Captain Stott recorded one of the many grisly scenes. At the tip of Saipan's Marpi Point, one hundred civilians gathered in an ever-tightening bunch. The Marines sent forward interpreters to beg for the group's surrender. Their appeals were fruitless, and Stott struggled to comprehend what followed:

> Almost imperceptibly a psychological reaction seemed to emerge, and the people drew closer together into a compact mass. It was still predominantly civilian, but several in uniform could be distinguished circling about in the throng using the civilians for protection. As they huddled closer sounds of a weird singing chant carried up to us. Suddenly a waving flag of the Rising Sun was unfurled. Movement grew more agitated, men started leaping into the sea, and the chanting gave way to startled cries, and with them the popping sound of detonating grenades. It was the handful of soldiers, determined to prevent the surrender or escape of their kinfolks, who tossed grenades into the milling throng of men, women, and children, and then dived into the sea from which escape was impossible. The exploding grenades cut up the mob into patches of dead, dying, and wounded, and for the first time we actually saw water that ran red with human blood.[32]

For most Americans like Stott, the scene defied explanation. But notions of honor, familial obligation, and fidelity were all at play. Private Takeo described the disturbing dilemma for Japanese troops on Saipan: "In those days, Japanese soldiers really accepted the idea that they must eventually die." Surrender was no option for the defenders. As a prisoner of war, he recounted, "You could never face your own family. They'd been sent off by their neighbors with cheers of 'Banzai!' How could they now go home?" The quandary was not specific to Japanese troops. Takeo described an equal fervor among the civilians: "The women and children had cyanide. Those who didn't jumped off cliffs. Ones like me, who from the beginning were thinking about how to become prisoners, were real exceptions."[33]

The gut-wrenching civilian deaths added to an already unsettling carnage on Saipan. In all, Holland Smith's joint Army-Marine landing force lost 3,100 killed in action, 13,099 wounded, and 326 missing. Daily medical reports from the campaign reveal that American deaths remained around one hundred per day throughout the campaign, with several isolated examples of heavy fighting and, consequently, bloody losses. The costliest single day of fighting came on June 16—D-day plus 1—when U.S. forces lost 201 killed in action as they established their beachhead ashore.[34]

Disturbing as the losses might have been for Smith and his subordinate commanders, they did not compare to the virtual annihilation of Saito's Japanese detachment. Enemy casualty estimates at the time from Vice Admiral Turner's staff showed that American forces buried 25,144 enemy bodies on Saipan and recorded another 797 dead but uninterred Japanese troops. Turner's staff initially categorized 1,810 Japanese as prisoners of war, a relatively massive contingent of prisoners when compared against the larger saga of the Pacific War.[35] However, in accounting for miscategorized civilians and forced Korean labor troops, more recent scholarship suggests that the number was much lower. While more than 25,000 Japanese troops gave their lives on Saipan, perhaps as few as 300 or 400 made the choice to surrender.[36] With the clarity of hindsight, Saito's detachment seems to have paralleled the ominous and well-established trend of the Pacific War. With little regard for practicality or preservation, soldiers of the Japanese empire planned to fight until the bitter end.

DISCERNIBLE PROGRESS, CONTINUED CRITIQUE: FIRE SUPPORT AT SAIPAN

The American landing force on Saipan fought with more responsive and effective air and naval fire support than that provided to U.S. troops in the Gilbert or Marshall Island offensives. Navy and Marine units evidenced obvious progress in fire control and coordination, as they learned to more carefully and effectively integrate the disparate efforts. Developmental initiatives, in fact, had started months before Turner ordered his landing force ashore. From personnel management to tactical communications to the cultural integration of American units, Navy and Marine troops alike worked toward battlefield harmony.

In preparing for and then executing the assault on Saipan, American units overhauled their approach to fire support communications. As in the earlier Marshalls attack, communications teams stressed two general principles: rapidity and reliability. Their efforts gave American ground forces near-immediate naval and aerial support. The swift communications support, often established just minutes after arriving on the beachhead, tied the triphibious team together and kept Marine and Army units ashore in the early hours of the landing.[37] Impressed by dependable communications on D-day and beyond, the landing force signal officer judged supporting arms communications "very satisfactory" throughout the battle.[38]

To strengthen information sharing and precision within the task force, communications technicians expanded the number of tactical frequencies available and reinforced the proper use of each net. With the additional frequencies, JASCO control parties on Saipan experimented with "common" nets for control teams, gunfire ships, and local aircraft to simultaneously synchronize their actions. The move produced tangible results. Immediately behind the final salvo of a supporting ship, JASCO units could integrate a timely air strike and sustain devastating fires against persistent enemy targets. The practice worked remarkably well on Saipan, and several veteran officers encouraged the continued development of common nets for follow-on campaigns.[39]

American forces also advanced fire control procedures and lines of authority to make air and naval strikes more efficient and complementary in the Marianas. Prior to the operation, commanders assigned a specific fire support ship or ships to each assault battalion headed ashore. Supporting JASCO units then released one trained and experienced naval gunfire liaison officer to each infantry regiment and division. These officers worked with the shore fire control parties to supervise and integrate fire support requests within each respective unit. In addition to advising their regimental commanders on the appropriate use and integration of naval support, the liaison specialists assisted in prioritizing and coordinating the fire requests from subordinate battalions.[40]

Control and coordination teams on Saipan also streamlined procedures in order to provide more timely air and naval fires. Naval gunfire liaison officers (NGLOs) for each unit submitted twice-daily reports at 4:00 a.m. and 3:00 p.m. that included specific requests for fire support and general estimates of future requirements. Immediate requests—those labeled "call fires"—were transmitted and submitted by the shore fire control parties that fought alongside the infantry. After confirming target positions via their unit's intelligence staff and ensuring the safety of friendly troops, the control parties passed their requests through the successive NGLOs from the battalion to the regiment to the division representatives. The naval gunfire liaison officers, "at all times in closest cooperation with artillery and air support sections," then consolidated, prioritized, and confirmed the firing missions before passing target data and firing directions to the assigned vessels.[41] The practice was both methodical and thorough. The advanced procedures allowed for flexibility at each level and allowed American units to effectively manage an enormous demand for naval gunfire support in the Marianas. At the peak of operations, forty NGLOs, twenty-seven SFCPs, and sixty-six individual warships worked together to achieve their desired effects ashore.[42]

Troops coordinated air support in a similar manner but with slightly more centralization from the nucleus of the task force. During the Marianas assault, carrier pilots flew daily preplanned strike missions as assigned by the CSA, Captain Richard F. Whitehead, aboard Vice Admiral Turner's flagship, USS *Rocky Mount*. Whitehead communicated with each squadron's "air coordinator," the pilot specifically tasked with integrating his unit's flight into the general scheme of maneuver. As with naval gunfire procedures, immediate requests for air support were handled more informally by necessity, and could be given priority under certain circumstances. Underneath the JASCO construct, air liaison parties ashore operated alongside their assigned infantry units to collect, filter, and submit requests for support from above. Qualified air liaison officers collected and approved these inputs before passing them along to the CSA. Following the Americans' initial landing, immediate aviation support remained in high demand—with as many as forty-one air liaison parties requesting aircraft simultaneously—until Marine and Army artillery battalions could establish themselves ashore and begin playing their part in the symphony of fires.[43]

The recently unveiled JASCOs—and the continued refinement of their role in the firepower apparatus—played a significant part in the

American triumph. Serving as a unifying force between the land, sea, and air forces, the JASCOs established a newfound reputation through their actions on Saipan. Several NGLOs who fought in the battle and served within the novel companies praised the JASCOs' collective ability to process and coordinate a multitude of fire support requests throughout the campaign. In particular, the JASCOs' unique training background and distinctive skill set, built around an appreciation for triphibious operations, contributed to battlefield harmony among the American components. After observing the JASCOs direct naval and air support around the clock for twenty-six days straight on Saipan, Navy lieutenant Charles Corben commended the companies' effectiveness and utility: "Throughout the operation, [their] spirit, ingenuity, and teamwork was deserving of the highest commendation."[44]

The JASCOs on Saipan became a reliable channel of communication and coordination during the attack, allowing the various components to share and exchange timely battlefield information. Gunfire ships, aircraft squadrons, and artillery units all learned to share target data, intelligence updates, and enemy activity reports regularly. In facilitating this integration, the JASCOs promoted a more integrated attack and a more efficient use of supporting arms, especially as the operation wore on and naval shells and aviation ordnance became scarce. The close cooperation allowed the various components—afloat, ashore, and overhead—to collectively determine the most appropriate weapon for each target and curb redundancy in successive strikes.[45] "The value and necessity of the duties accomplished by these units," wrote an American signal officer, "cannot be over emphasized."[46] As another observer later acknowledged, the JASCOs reflected the fundamental advantage of a combined arms approach: "Coordinated use of these weapons made them far more effective than they would have been if used separately."[47]

Control procedures and force coordination were not the only advances on display in the Marianas. American maps also received a comprehensive overhaul. While the separate land, sea, and air entities of the task force had previously relied upon disparate maps or charts peculiar to their specialized unit, U.S. forces on Saipan planned with and fought from common, grid-based maps. The new design utilized one-thousand-yard squares sliced into two-hundred-yard subsections. Contour lines depicting critical elevation differences (for aviators in particular) overlaid the general grid system. The result was a simplified pattern that made target identification and recognition of friendly units both more efficient and more accurate. Ship and aircraft commanders alike praised the new charts, one labeling them "of great value" and another calling the improvement "highly successful."[48]

Throughout the battle for the Marianas, and representative of the increasing demand for their fire support, American ships and aircraft requested and then begged for more shells, bombs, and ammunition. The acute shortages revealed just how indispensable sea- and air-based fire support had become to the Americans' brand of amphibious warfare. Just as the landing force began to break out of its beachhead on the second and third days ashore at Saipan, naval commanders began to worry about severe ordnance shortages. Turner himself requested that USS *Mazama*, laden with explosives, depart the Americans' rear base at Enewetak to help fill the void. Additionally, Turner ordered all American ships departing the Marianas theater—whether for escort duty or reassignment—to transfer all surplus 5-inch shells to the vessels remaining behind. He permitted the offgoing ships to retain just sixty rounds per gun for protection during their voyage. He similarly directed "all types of craft" stopping in Saipan waters to offload their excess ammunition. Turner's superior and commander of the Fifth Fleet, Admiral Raymond Spruance, ordered U.S. carriers in the region to undertake similar efforts. He stripped the flattops of all excess ordnance before authorizing their departure and directed an emergency resupply of aerial bombs from Enewetak. In barely one month's time, American warships offloaded a total of 10,948 tons of naval shells and 2,233 tons of bombs and rockets in 195 impromptu ordnance transfers in the waters surrounding Saipan.[49]

The Americans' many advances in supporting arms coordination at Saipan delivered the most effective offshore fire support of the Pacific War to date. The improved processes and accurate supporting fires convinced more infantry units to not only integrate but also rely upon naval and air support as they fought ashore. Especially in the early days of the assault, when field artillery and tanks were still making their way to the beach, commanders acknowledged the critical role of offshore firepower.[50] Following the battle, the commander of Task Group 53.5, Rear Admiral Walden Ainsworth, wrote that naval gunfire in the Marianas was "deliberate and carefully controlled" and that the close cooperation of the task force allowed "our aviators to step up their dive bombing and strafing attacks to a furious intensity from low [altitude] levels." In a "beautifully coordinated" action, he noted, "naval gunfire of all calibers pounded enemy objectives unceasingly and swept the landing beaches continuously, interrupted only by our perfectly-timed air strikes."[51] Such glowing assessments were not to be found in the postbattle appraisals at Tarawa and the Marshall Islands.

A skeptic might question the objectivity of American naval officers evaluating their own performance at Saipan but could hardly challenge the authenticity of Japanese accounts. Following the battle, dozens of testimonies from enemy prisoners of war (POWs) and several captured Japanese reports revealed a common verdict: air and naval firepower was the decisive ingredient in the U.S. victory. Just days into the struggle for Saipan, one Japanese document acknowledged the Americans' advantage and their own consequent dilemma: "The fight on Saipan as things stand now is progressing one-sidedly, since, along with tremendous power of his barrages, the enemy holds control of sea and air. . . . Moreover, we are menaced by brazenly low-flying planes, and the enemy blasts at us from all sides with fierce naval and artillery crossfire." A separate midbattle summary emphasized the same reality: "The enemy is gradually advancing under cover of fierce naval gunfire and bombing and strafing. . . . the southern half of this island is generally under the subjugation of the enemy."[52]

The words of Japanese POWs echoed the formal battlefield reports. One soldier stated that "the greatest single factor in the American success . . . [was] naval gunfire." Another prisoner concluded after the battle that "the most feared of [American] weapons was the naval shelling which managed to reach the obscure mountain caves where [our] command posts were located. Second in effectiveness," he continued, were "the aerial bombings and lastly artillery."[53] A captured message from a

Japanese command bunker corroborated the spirit of the prisoners' statements: "If there just were no naval gunfire, we feel with determination that we could fight it out with the enemy in a decisive battle."[54]

Prisoner of war accounts revealed the practical role of American firepower in the Marianas, but the shellings were as much a psychological weapon as they were a vehicle of physical destruction. One POW admitted that he "was horrified by the number of deaths on our side due to the naval gunfire which continued every day."[55] A fellow prisoner shared his trepidation: "Caught in the concentration of naval gunfire the wounded and dead continued to increase." One soldier labeled the American shelling "terrible," while another recalled that it "was just too much for [us] to take." Yet another survivor remembered the trauma of the American bombardment on Saipan, wondering to himself of the outcome "if they would only stop the naval shelling."[56]

From the front lines in Saipan to the upper echelons of U.S. Navy Department leadership, observers recognized the critical role of naval gunfire and air support in both putting the landing force ashore and sustaining its advance throughout the operation. Chief of Naval Operations Ernest King himself, in reflecting on the landings of 1944, wrote that naval fire support had been "carried out on a scale not contemplated in the past."[57] Vice Admiral Turner, as he considered the American performance in the Marianas, acknowledged both the success and the delicate interdependency of triphibious operations: "Whether we employ ships' gunfire, airplane weapons, or field artillery to accomplish these ends is a matter of indifference, so far as the purpose is concerned. Each category of fire has its own points of excellence and weakness. All categories, however, are working to the same end. They are, in fact, complementary to each other, and all ought to be used in conjunction with each other for the solution of the same problem."[58]

THE MARIANAS: PRELUDE TO 1945

The struggle in the Marianas introduced, yet again, a heightened intensity to the Pacific War. The American armada that steamed to the Marianas—composed of more than six hundred ships and some 300,000 men—was the largest and most technologically advanced amphibious fleet yet assembled in the war. That the United States could mount such overwhelming martial strength in the same month that massive Allied landings unfolded across the beaches of Normandy was, in the words of historian Ian Toll, "a supreme demonstration of American military-industrial hegemony."[59]

Defeat at Saipan stole the final semblance of hope from Japan in World War II. In light of the American triumph and at the behest of the emperor himself, the prime minister, General Tojo Hideki, and his entire cabinet stepped down. Yet even the complete resignation of the Tojo administration did not compel a strategic reassessment. New leadership in Tokyo, led by the little-known but resolute Kuniaki Koiso, doubled down, promising an even more fervent defense of Japan's disintegrating perimeter. As American ships, tanks, planes, and munitions rolled off of assembly lines, the Imperial Japanese Army shifted its approach. No longer would Japanese soldiers contest the landing beach or launch impractical banzai assaults. Instead, they would fight across a series of inland positions, methodically organized and thoroughly fortified. Though outright victory for Tokyo had become little more than a pipe dream, spirited military and political leaders intended to draw out the American advance and bleed its armies white. Perhaps then the Japanese might eschew unconditional surrender and secure a tolerable peace with the United States.[60]

For the Marines and soldiers on the ground as well—both American and Japanese—the Marianas injected a newfound ferocity to the conflict. The immediate, significant presence of civilians on Saipan had done little to curb the trend. The intensity of Pacific combat had been well established by 1944, yet Saipan, Guam, and Tinian seemed to inject yet another measure of fury. As firepower surged, humanity faded. By the end of the struggle on Saipan, Captain Stott recorded a familiar but amplified tenor: "Death and destruction came to be the natural order. Wounded comrades were given little sympathy unless the wound was critical. Mostly they were envied for being out of it. No pangs of conscience were felt over civilian death, for dead people and wrecked buildings had become commonplace."[61] His remarks provided a grim foretaste of the final twelve months of the Pacific War.

CHAPTER 6

APPROACHING THE CRESCENDO

INTRAWAR ADJUSTMENTS, SAIPAN TO IWO JIMA

By 2013 Paul Kennedy had spent more than forty years as an academic historian. Having served as a research assistant for the renowned military strategist and scholar Sir Basil Liddell Hart, Kennedy received his PhD from the University of Oxford in 1970. Joining Yale University's department of history in 1983, he spent the next thirty years covering sweeping topics in diplomacy, statecraft, and grand strategy, best exemplified by his 1988 classic, *The Rise and Fall of the Great Powers*. Yet after decades of studying generals and policymakers, Kennedy called for a careful reassessment of history's largest conflict. In place of World War II's traditional actors and conventional explanations, his 2013 *Engineers of Victory* turned attention to the "problem solvers"—those who experimented, tinkered, and labored with the Allies' wartime methods and tools. While scholars and readers alike are often drawn to epic narratives and spectacular technologies, Kennedy argued that "what transpires at the middle level, or the level of practical implementation is often taken for granted."[1] The tedious and mundane efforts of these crucial players in the Allied victory, he continued, deserve renewed attention: "We have rarely if ever stepped back and understood how their work surfaced, was cultivated, and then was connected to the problems at hand, or appreciated how these various, eccentric pieces of the jigsaw puzzle fitted into the whole."[2]

The Americans' evolution of triphibious fire control and coordination in the Pacific perfectly illustrates Kennedy's historiographical shift and revisionary focus on the "problem solvers" of the Allied war effort. In addition to Kennedy's central themes covering Atlantic convoys, control of the skies, and the logistical challenges of fighting across the Pacific Ocean, we must acknowledge the diligent and resourceful work that advanced the use of

American firepower in 1944 and 1945. In doing so, we gain a fuller understanding of Allied victory and the Pacific War. By recognizing the nameless intermediaries who toiled to strengthen triphibious coordination, we restore a proper balance to the narrative of World War II.

Existing scholarship on the war, while paying great fanfare to the officers who wore stars, fails to properly credit the "middlemen," the grassroots leaders and creative tacticians who wrestled their way across the Central Pacific. These neglected specialists observed and fought alongside American ships, planes, and infantry battalions. As they advanced, they made far-reaching adjustments in the control and coordination of American triphibious firepower. The generals and admirals certainly did their part to effect success. But these specialists—many of them company- and field-grade officers[3]—bore equally critical responsibility in orchestrating American victory.

DONALD WELLER: SAVANT OF NAVAL GUNFIRE

Donald M. Weller was born on May 1, 1908, in Connecticut's capital city of Hartford. The son of a reserve chaplain in the U.S Army, he completed public schooling in Rhode Island and Pittsburgh, Pennsylvania. Following one year of study at Carnegie Tech, he earned an appointment to the U.S. Naval Academy in 1926. Weller found his four years at Annapolis rewarding and agreeable, even if he himself acknowledged his "great propensity for demerits."[4] Commissioned a Marine second lieutenant on June 5, 1930, Weller subsequently completed Marine officers' basic school and the infantry basic course before reporting to the Marine Barracks at the Norfolk Navy Yard.[5]

Almost from the moment he donned Marine blues, Weller's career prepared him to serve as an expert in amphibious fire support—in particular, to improve coordination between a Marine landing force and its naval gunfire ships. In 1933–34 he served as a detachment officer in USS *Arkansas*, a *Wyoming*-class battleship with a main battery of one dozen 12-inch guns. The Marines of *Arkansas* participated in a number of modest landing exercises during Weller's tenure, though he found the Americans' 1930s brand of amphibious warfare "rudimentary" and "unsophisticated" in nature.[6] Nonetheless, he emerged with an introductory appreciation for naval fires.

From *Arkansas*, with hard experience in hand, Weller attended the Army's field artillery school at Fort Sill, Oklahoma, where he spent nine months studying field artillery while sustaining his theoretical education in naval gunnery. As war with Japan became increasingly likely, Weller's topical focus appeared all the more pressing. At Fort Sill, Weller completed a thesis addressing the complications and shortcomings of the Allied landing at Gallipoli, to include careful study of the operation's supporting firepower. He emerged from his investigation not cynical of naval gunfire support, as so many of his contemporaries were, but instead optimistic: "I became convinced that there was a role for the naval gun—and a big one—in any future amphibious operation."[7] His growing conviction caused him, on his next assignment in command of the cruiser *Tuscaloosa*'s Marine detachment, to volunteer as an assistant fire control officer for the ship's 5-inch antiaircraft guns. In a display of initiative that few contemporaries contemplated, Captain Weller volunteered to serve as an assistant fire control officer under a more junior Navy lieutenant junior grade. In addition to commanding his forty-two-man Marine detachment, Weller would help control fire from *Tuscaloosa*'s eight 5-inch antiaircraft guns.[8]

The elective duty was calculated on Weller's part, that he might familiarize himself with naval gunnery and the challenges of firing from the sea. More generally, he intended to gather the "naval side of the shore bombardment picture" while assigned to the *New Orleans*–class cruiser. "I absorbed myself," Weller said, "and always in the back of my mind was how this fire control system—battery and ammunition—could be applied to the business of support of amphibious operations."[9] Following his tour with *Tuscaloosa*, Weller served as an artillery and naval gunfire advisor first with the 1st Marine Brigade, then with the Amphibious Corps, Atlantic Fleet, and finally with the Amphibious Corps, Pacific Fleet. His billet progression took him closer and closer, in both a professional and a geographical sense, to war in the Pacific. Following these advisory positions, Weller took command of the 12th Marine Regiment's 2d Battalion. He led his 75-mm howitzer batteries in combat on Bougainville in the South Pacific and the Mariana Islands, earning a Bronze Star with Combat "V" in each campaign.[10]

In August 1944, having established a firm technical background in both field artillery and naval gunnery, Weller took the post that would vault him to pioneer status in the art of amphibious fire support. Based on his emergence as a reliable expert in the field, Weller became the naval gunfire officer for the entire Fleet Marine Force, Pacific. Additionally—and in fact based upon his own recommendation that the position be created—Weller assumed the role of naval gunfire officer for the V Corps. From these influential positions, and based upon his wealth of experience in both practical experience and careful theoretical study, Donald Weller would orchestrate one of the most significant naval gunfire support efforts in the history of amphibious warfare.[11]

REST, REFIT, AND REFINEMENT

During the V Corps' operational pause between the attack on the Marianas (June–August 1944) and the assault on Iwo Jima (February–March 1945), Weller and his staff revolutionized the control and integration of American naval fire support in the Pacific. In a string of official correspondence throughout the autumn of 1944, Weller's subordinate naval gunfire and air support representatives constructed an imaginative and intricate proposal for the coordination of triphibious firepower. Weller himself both cultivated and supervised the effort, and then exchanged thoughts on the concept with the V Corps chief of staff, Colonel Joseph L. Stewart; the corps' assistant chief of staff and operations officer, Colonel Edward A. Craig; and the 3d Marine Division's chief of staff, Colonel Robert E. Hogaboom. Emerging from the Marianas, the group collectively understood that coordination among firing agencies and the troops they supported would become a crucial if not decisive determinant of American success. As both the geographical scale of operations and the number of units involved expanded in the prospective attacks of 1945, the necessity for effective teamwork surged. The enemy, too, promised a heightened challenge: future objectives in the Pacific were sure to present the most formidable targets yet encountered in the war.[12]

The staff's proposition built upon an informal coordination arrangement that had emerged organically during the Marines' midsummer battle for Saipan. Unlike previous operations, when control teams and liaison officers positioned themselves ashore according to either their own assessment or directions from their commander, the V Corps placed its primary naval gunfire, air support, and artillery representatives at one of the landing force command posts. For the first time in the Pacific, the senior fire control and coordination liaison officers were deliberately (even if spontaneously) collocated. The working arrangement "was the best ever realized before," assistant chief of staff Edward Craig wrote, even if it "was not completely adequate."[13]

The support was not unique to the team of Marine colonels. Navy lieutenant Charles S. Corben—who himself had served as the landing force's primary naval gunfire officer on Saipan—commended the collocation idea and encouraged its development in his own after-action report. With the landing force naval gunfire officer, air officer, and artillery officer "set up ashore in close proximity," Corben reasoned, the cohort was able to pass friendly unit updates, share enemy target information, and request immediate support from a fellow entity.[14] In a timely fashion, a naval gunfire ship could take over primary support for a target that suited its ammunition load, flat firing trajectory, or seaborne mobility. Likewise, the artillery officer could direct his units to assume responsibility for targets that matched their battlefield position or firing characteristics. Here, information and awareness were the coin of the realm. On Saipan, the informal arrangement worked to great effect. "By reason of the coordination with artillery and air," Corben wrote, "duplication and waste of ammunition was [*sic*] avoided." In the final analysis, he continued, "the combined and coordinated use of these supporting weapons made them far more effective than they would have been if used separately."[15]

The proximity of coordination personnel not only enabled the prompt exchange of information on Saipan; it also permitted greater flexibility in the application of triphibious fires. As they worked together to arrange the most efficient and effective fire support solution, the air, artillery, and naval gunfire liaison officers learned to switch their radios to a common frequency during simultaneous attacks, rather than remain on their primary (and inherently saturated) general channels. The technique—simple as it may have seemed—made for a "highly effective team" capable of near-immediate flexibility according to the tactical situation.[16] On more than one occasion, the measure allowed the coordination team to bring offshore fire support "as close as fifty yards in front of our own troops"—by far the sharpest recorded instance of naval gunfire coordination to date in the Pacific War. The high degree of precision delivered impressive barrages just in front of friendly American lines, and it played a critical role in repelling several Japanese counterattacks on Saipan. More importantly, it set a theoretical precedent for U.S. operations to come.[17]

Weller's staff, aware of the size and scope of future Allied objectives and buoyed by Lieutenant Corben's detailed analysis, determined to improve upon this Marianas model. After careful consideration in the late summer of 1944, they put forward a theoretical "AAG [air, artillery, and (naval) gunfire] center" that would control American triphibious firepower in a prospective three-division assault.[18] Essentially, the concept was a reinforced version of the Saipan embryo, now intensified and appropriately resourced. Under the AAG concept, and in accordance with recommendations emerging from U.S. after-action reports from the Marianas, the senior naval gunfire officer would stay in constant radio contact with each fire support ship, the air support liaison officer with each air control agency (though understandably not each individual aircraft), and the artillery representative with the fire direction center of each artillery battalion.[19]

One of the AAG center's primary responsibilities would be to supervise the radio traffic on American fire support frequencies. At Saipan, a tidal wave of fire support requests coupled with incidental radio transmissions flooded the net and threatened the entire coordination apparatus. Units wrestled with one another to send their transmissions, and some radiomen blatantly disregarded (whether consciously or not) the channel's purpose.[20] One commander estimated that twenty-five percent of traffic on the "support air request" frequency—the single frequency through which a unit could arrange air support—was irrelevant administrative information. The "dangerous overcrowding" of the frequency wasted precious radio time and inevitably delayed the arrival of friendly aircraft.[21]

The V Corps intended to curb this deluge of radio traffic in future operations. To limit extraneous radio transmissions, the AAG center's frequencies would only handle information related to the control and coordination of active and archived firing missions. Affected units were encouraged to listen in for battlefield awareness but were prohibited from interjecting with irrelevant chatter. In short, the AAG hub promised disciplined awareness and increased efficiency: "to know where and when all fires are being executed" and "to make the most effective use" of those fires.[22] Distraction from those priorities was not only discouraged; it was outlawed. The following month, V Corps General Order 70-44 turned the theory into practice. The aggressive order declared frequency management a "most important consideration" and, since the principle was only as effective as the radio monitors responsible for enforcing it, directed the relief of "all operators incapable of firm and forceful control of radio circuits."[23]

Perhaps the most innovative aspect of the AAG concept, and its most tangible supplement to the Saipan precedent, was a "central fire status board." As with the communications adjustments, this too was a battlefield lesson pulled forward from the Marianas campaign, where air officer Lieutenant Colonel B. F. Prewitt had recommended a "running" status board that might inform both staff and commanders with the latest firing data. The goal was to establish a "clear picture for all."[24] The AAG advocates picked up Prewitt's proposition and matured it. On their board, supporting arms personnel would track and manage each fire mission in support of the landing force. The common status board would indicate which missions were in active execution, which fire missions had "gone cold" (were terminated), and which units (ships, aircraft, or artillery batteries) were assigned to each objective. It would also record the grid location of each target ashore as well as the final results of the attack: target harassed, suppressed, neutralized, destroyed, etc.[25] The status board not only promised the most reliable real-time picture for senior leaders of the unit; it also informed the AAG center's authoritative veto power. With a comprehensive appreciation for the battlefield picture and all relevant fire missions from the sea, air, and land, the center could order a cease fire for select units or all supporting arms in order to deconflict efforts and prosecute an urgent target. Though the veto was intended as a tool of last resort, the prerogative represented the AAG center's theoretically superior picture of the battlefield.[26]

Increased personnel and equipment were to complement the AAG center plan. While the same tasks had been carried out by just a few overwhelmed officers and enlisted personnel under the earlier "distributed" operations, the new plan envisioned one primary officer and three assistant officers each for air, naval gunfire, and artillery support. Twelve enlisted communications specialists would complement the commissioned ranks. With similar prioritization, the center was to receive one principal and one standby radio set for each control frequency.[27] These changes, too, found their roots in Prewitt's post-Saipan reflections, where the air officer judged that coordination ashore "functioned very well" but was "handicapped by shortage of personnel and by radio equipment."[28]

The staff correspondence reflected some disagreement over the proper location of the novel coordination center, but each representative expressed their enthusiastic support. Some advocates called for the AAG center to reside next to the corps artillery headquarters. Others encouraged its placement within the corps commanding general's post. Prewitt threw his support behind the latter option, calling it the "ideal agency" through which to build the "closest possible conjunction" with forces afloat.[29] But dissent over positioning—they all agreed—should not thwart the broader development of the concept. Craig, Stewart, and Hogaboom all hoped to "expedite action" and advance the idea.[30] Based on the "considerable merit" of the AAG construct, staff representatives from the 3d Marine Division, 12th Marine Regiment, III Corps Artillery, and XXIV Corps Artillery recommended approval as well. Momentum was building, and the cadre of colonels urged Weller to develop the AAG construct further.[31]

As Weller and his team polished their proposal in the fall of 1944, they also turned attention to a persistent shortfall in coordination efforts during the battle for Saipan. American units, for the first time in the Pacific, acknowledged that their JASCO coordination teams were insufficiently manned and incapable of replacing their own casualties. Although the JASCOs' task organization[32] had not changed significantly since late 1943—and thus their personnel shortages had always been present—the V Corps' rapid assaults in the Marshall Islands had not tested the unit's depth chart. In operations lasting less than one week, casualty replacement procedures went untested; units made do with what they had. But in the month-long struggle for Saipan, the deficiency surfaced in spades. As JASCO teams turned to nearby communications technicians and even artillerymen to replace their losses, the substitutes revealed their inadequacy. Devoid of even elementary training in the characteristics of naval gunfire and air support, the replacements struggled to execute their specialized duties. One wounded naval gunfire liaison officer heroically refused evacuation, aware that his departure would leave the infantrymen without a knowledgeable expert and a dependable link to offshore fire support. Other liaison officers assigned to units waiting in reserve filled temporary coordination billets until their assigned unit joined the front lines. The casualty replacement void became the most widely recognized flaw in coordination efforts on Saipan.[33]

The solution was rather obvious. Those critical of the deficiency, to include Weller and Corben themselves, petitioned for more JASCO troops on the unit's task organization, in particular trained replacements that would stand ready to fill casualty voids in battle. They also recommended the creation of assistant liaison officers for both the air and naval liaison positions to familiarize secondary personnel with procedures and provide crucial experience prior to a casualty-induced promotion. Their call paralleled the V Corps' AAG center proposal, which uncoincidentally recommended a primary air, naval, and artillery liaison officer flanked by three assistants each. The larger teams, in addition to casualty protection, would help reduce battlefield fatigue. Whereas primary liaison officers might endure several days of demanding combat, such as that experienced in the Gilbert and Marshall islands, they could not sustain twenty-four-hour operations for weeks on end, as in the case of Saipan. Only with a deep bench, the advocates reasoned, could the American coordination effort tackle more daunting objectives ahead.[34]

Their casualty replacement critique notwithstanding, American officers hoped to sustain the JASCOs' 1944 momentum for the approaching operations of 1945. Lieutenant Colonel Harry Vadnais, the V Corps signal officer, left the Marianas certain that coordination efforts would prove decisive in the final campaigns of the war: "The value and necessity of the duties accomplished by these [JASCO] units cannot be over-emphasized."[35] Corben shared a similar conviction, proud that the remarkable "spirit, ingenuity, and teamwork" of his shore fire control parties helped deliver victory in the Marianas.[36] The naval gunfire officer for Task Force 56, having overseen all naval fire support in the Mariana Islands, was even more convinced of his team's contribution. In his remarks to Holland Smith, he wrote that "personnel of these [JASCO] organizations were enthusiastic, untiring, and resourceful in directing a continuous and well-executed program of close support throughout this long and unremitting operation."[37] All were convinced that fire support enabled success in the Marianas. They were equally sure that it would remain decisive in the months ahead.

Weller himself, the man who would be most responsible for linking the naval gunfire lessons of the Marianas and applying them to the V Corps' future objectives, acknowledged the significance of the moment. Writing several years after the war and reflecting on the story of naval gunfire support in the Pacific, Weller declared the autumn of 1944 to be the Americans' true moment of adoption. In the Marianas, he wrote, "the naval gun had become a full partner in the landing force effort, beginning with preliminary operations and continuing by night and day until the objective was secured. Doubting Thomas's [*sic*] in the Navy and in the Landing Forces were now convinced that here was an arm that paid its way."[38]

AMERICAN AIR SUPPORT: LAGGING BUT PROCEEDING

By late 1944 the wartime evolution of U.S. naval gunfire support had proven reliably linear. Commanders, staff officers, and practitioners had patiently fine-tuned fire control and coordination procedures while also retooling the specialized units that directed offshore bombardment. The development of American close air support in the Central Pacific was both more complicated and less triumphant. The contrast lent itself to several enduring themes in the story of mid-century naval aviation: obstructive interservice politics, a rapid pace of technological change, and an unaccommodating culture within the naval aviation community—namely, an unquenchable focus on pitched surface battles and spectacular carrier strikes to the exclusion of landing operations.

Quantitatively, the Marine Corps air component initiated and then sustained a meteoric growth in the months following the attack on Pearl Harbor. While the service had just thirteen aircraft squadrons when Yamamoto's *kido butai*—or combined carrier battle group—struck Hawaii, the Corps' air arm tripled in size during the first twelve months of war. Two years later, in 1944, Marine Corps aviation had grown to 118,000 personnel and 145 operational squadrons, more than eleven times its prewar size.[39]

Yet in spite of the obvious practical and cultural logic that Marine aviators could best support their own ground troops, even this explosive numerical growth did not make Corps aviation a centerpiece of the Central Pacific campaigns.[40] The disconnect was structural and geographical, for Marine pilots had not received sufficient carrier training (many having received none at all), and Nimitz's Central Pacific objectives lay well outside the range of land-based aircraft. Furthermore, the Navy was loath to free up precious carriers for Marine squadrons. As one historian captured it, the two services "were caught in a bind."[41] Thus, from 1942 through mid-1944 Marine squadrons assisted the American advance on Rabaul and then the Philippines, almost exclusively U.S. Army landings, while the Navy flew close support missions for Marine amphibious assaults in the Gilbert, Marshall, and Mariana islands.[42] But proud Marine aviators could not abide the arrangement, particularly men such as Brigadier General Louis Woods, who had commanded the legendary "Cactus Air Force" on Guadalcanal in 1942. "The Marine aviator and the Marine footsoldier," Woods petitioned two years later, "must be a team."[43]

In the late summer of 1944 the institutional winds began to shift. Following the American victory in the Marianas, Marine support for the integration of their own Leatherneck pilots solidified. The commanding officer of the 24th Marine Regiment and veteran of the battles for Saipan and Tinian, Colonel Franklin Hart, offered an impassioned plea: that "every possible effort be made to have Marine pilots supply the air support for Marine ground units." If the Navy would acquiesce, Hart anticipated "a higher degree of efficiency" from his common air arm, since "it is doctrine for Marine pilots to have training in close support maneuvers."[44]

Marine Commandant Lieutenant General Alexander Archer Vandegrift hardly needed the nudge. Vandegrift made his case to Nimitz at a series of joint Navy-Marine conferences in Pearl Harbor the same month that American forces declared the Marianas secure. Among the topics discussed was a general reassessment of Marine aviation's role in the Pacific War. Flanked by his commander of Marine air wings and director of Marine aviation, Ross Rowell and Brigadier General Field Harris, Vandegrift brokered a compromise. In the resulting agreement, Nimitz authorized six *Commencement Bay*–class escort carriers exclusively for Marine fighter (VMF) and dive bomber (VMSB) squadrons. Marine leadership was content, and Nimitz himself was pleased with the arrangement. The Navy's top Pacific commander wrote that the shuffling would "more firmly integrate [Marine] aviation within the Marine Corps" and would be "in the interest of [the entire] naval service."[45]

But despite contemporary estimates, it was not the conference's carrier settlement that would prove most beneficial for the Marines and their future, both in the Pacific War and beyond. The discussions in fact delivered much more; in exchange for retiring one of the Marine Corps' five standing aircraft wings—which appeased Chief of Naval Operations Ernest King by loosening the Navy Department's purse strings—the Marine Corps would also assume control[46] of all aircraft operating in support of amphibious landings. No longer would a displaced, blue-clad Sailor aboard an offshore Navy flagship exercise command and control of Allied aircraft in support of a Marine landing force. According to the new model, Marine infantry would make the attack, Marine (as well as Navy) airmen would support overhead, and Marine liaison teams would direct the show from the beach.[47]

The arrangement was revolutionary, even if only appreciated by select Marines at the time. Future experience in both World War II and beyond would evidence the wisdom of localized aircraft control as a landing force fought its way ashore. Indeed, visionary Marines had mentioned the possibility during the early campaigns of 1942 and 1943; those fighting across the beaches of the Mariana Islands in 1944 began to encourage the transfer of authority in earnest. The senior air officer for the Marianas assault, Lieutenant Colonel B. F. Prewitt, argued that proximity ashore between an air controller and the ground troops he supported enabled a degree of coordination that was simply unachievable with the same control authority afloat. Without ready access to the troop commanders ashore and the tactical situation as it unfolded, an offshore controller could not provide the most effective and efficient support.[48] The commanding general of the 4th Marine Division, in reflecting on the Saipan operation, shared Prewitt's conviction, arguing that air liaison personnel ashore should exercise complete authority over "air operations affecting the ground troops."[49] But even if the consensus was in, the unproven moment of 1944 was just that. American officers awaited their first opportunity to test the principle in battle.

ORGANIZING, TRAINING, AND TRUSTING: HONING THE JASCO

While their subordinate shore fire control parties and air liaison parties furthered their internal procedures and coordination measures in late 1944, so too did the JASCOs push their own capabilities and refine their approach. For JASCO commanders, the most pressing issue was the transitory and rotational nature of their specialized units. Since the JASCOs' introduction in 1943, the companies had been assigned to a particular corps in preparation for a specific assault. Once American forces secured the objective, the JASCOs were reassigned according to operational demands. The arrangement left them in a persistent cycle of assignment and reassignment, like nomads of the vast Pacific. The V Corps signal officer, among others, labeled the concept "impracticable" and called for its revision.[50]

The solution seemed feasible enough: make the JASCOs a vested unit, permanently assigned to each landing force division. Though a shortage of trained personnel and efficiency concerns dictated the units' rotational arrangement, the proposed adjustment promised benefits for each party. The move would bring increased stability as well as greater resources and funding for the JASCOs themselves, and the supported divisions could now enjoy the enduring presence of their coordination teams. Perhaps the most appealing benefit, however, was the one that responded directly to the JASCOs' casualty replacement issues on Saipan, where inexperienced and untrained troops were thrust into JASCO billets out of pure necessity. With a permanent footing in the organization of each division, the JASCOs could adequately and systematically replace their own battlefield losses with proficient specialists.[51]

The units' standing designation allowed them to control their personnel and equipment consistently. Furthermore, they could work alongside the landing force throughout the preparation, execution, and recovery phases of an amphibious assault. In less than fifteen months, the specialized companies had grown from little more than a theoretical embryo to a full and permanent partner of the Marine division.[52] Though their early struggles had reflected their novelty, the JASCOs' persistence and careful reflection improved their utility and earned them the support of the infantry divisions they served.

Even while the JASCOs petitioned for permanence in late 1944 and early 1945, they also embarked on a program of internal improvement. Victory in the Marianas could not lead to complacency, Weller and his naval gunfire staff reasoned.[53] Beginning in November, and while his subordinates revised and updated the Americans' gunnery training manuals, Weller ordered each shore fire control party back to Kahoolawe for an advanced round of live gunfire exercises and simulated landing drills. It was a unique opportunity, Weller recognized, in that the control teams could flow easily across the Pacific between combat operations and the U.S. training installation in Hawaii. "We were able to immediately translate the results," Weller recalled, "from the operators to the trainers."[54] As the various JASCOs rotated through Kahoolawe, Weller was also able to transfer experienced personnel between units, thereby distributing the wealth of accumulated knowledge and protecting against the risk of fresh, unversed coordination teams.[55]

But Kahoolawe was as much about practical, live-fire experience as it was about capturing conceptual lessons and reshuffling combat experience. In less than two months, Weller's control parties coordinated and delivered more than two thousand naval shells onto the training beaches (a paltry figure compared to the astounding combat expenditures of the Pacific, but a significant investment for a training command).[56] The refresher curriculum ran daily from noon until midnight. And it was not merely an evaluation for the shore fire control parties; it was every bit "a tough and rugged workout" for the gunnery personnel on each participating warship.[57] The drills tested shipboard crews in direct fire missions, indirect fire missions, and "reverse slope"[58] targets. Evaluators even mixed in course and drift adjustments to mimic the unavoidable challenges of an uncooperative sea state. Weller gave as much attention to the ships as he did the coordination teams, eventually qualifying more than six hundred ships on Kahoolawe's range before they steamed across the ocean to their combat assignments.[59]

The JASCOs' air liaison parties similarly reinforced their live-fire exercises and advanced new techniques at newly minted training ranges on Saipan and Tinian islands. American pilots, working hand in hand with their air liaisons, learned to execute beach strafing runs on a parallel axis to the front lines of their landing force. The method maximized the safety of friendly troops and lengthened the time window that attack aircraft could strike at enemy units. The air liaison teams, as they had noted during the Marianas campaign, learned that colored smoke signals and panel markers rather than radio communications were the most effective and reliable means of marking friendly positions ashore. Eighty-one-millimeter smoke mortars, on the other hand, clearly distinguished important enemy targets worthy of special attention from the American aviators aloft. The Saipan and Tinian ranges trained 181 aircraft in more than 158 close support missions in the final weeks of December alone. Just as with the naval guns back at Kahoolawe, live-fire training led to dramatic improvements and valuable experience in the art of firepower coordination.[60]

At virtually every level, the control and coordination of American firepower in the amphibious assault was maturing into superior form. Yet amid the many substantial and quite practical U.S. advancements in the months after the battle for the Marianas, the most significant development was neither revolutionary nor dramatic, neither technological nor procedural. In fact, the most important initiative for the coordination teams of late 1944 was an impassioned effort to build personal rapport and shared understanding across the task force. The effort, officers believed, would build trust across the sand, surf, and skies of Pacific battlefields. That trust would then advance the effectiveness of their collective efforts.

The idea was not new; it had emerged in the earliest after-action reports at Tarawa in late 1943. But following the struggle on Saipan, American officers intensified their initiative. They recognized that only through mutual appreciation and a shared sense of dependency could American naval guns, attack aircraft, field artillery howitzers, and infantry units achieve complete harmony. The various specialists needed a more comprehensive appreciation of combined arms and a fuller indoctrination into the experiences, challenges, and frustrations of their counterparts.

In his role as senior air officer during the Marianas campaign, Prewitt emphasized the divergence in perspective between an airborne pilot and his air liaison officer ashore. Without mutual understanding, Prewitt wrote, the pair could hardly succeed: "The air liaison officer has the difficult problem of orienting his location in battle torn terrain with few reference points and the further task of target orientation from his estimated positions. The pilot has the task of determining from information received the location of the target and the location of nearest friendly troops; the pilot's problem is further complicated by the small scale and sometimes inaccurate maps with which he must work."[61] Without constant and clear directions from the air liaison officer, who himself must acknowledge the challenges and constraints of the pilot's situation, the team could hardly approach effectiveness. The key was in relative appreciation and close cooperation.

Prewitt and the air coordinators were hardly alone; the 24th Marine Regiment, which had faced some of the stiffest Japanese resistance on Saipan and subsequently led the first landing wave onto Tinian, echoed the call for greater awareness in their postbattle analysis. The regiment called for each of its infantry officers to receive specialized training in the characteristics, procedures, and limitations of naval gunfire support. With such a background, they hoped to more effectively communicate with their naval gunfire liaison officers and, in the specialists' possible absence, to coordinate their own offshore fire support.[62] The 24th Marines' higher headquarters, the 4th Marine Division, took the idea one step further: petitioning for all JASCO personnel to receive advanced training on infantry tactics, methods, weapons, and integration of field artillery. The goal, again, was a fuller awareness across the entire task force, ensuring "that naval liaison officers [would] be better equipped to advise the infantry commander in the proper employment of naval gunfire in conformity with the tactical plan and in coordination with artillery fires."[63]

In its organizational adjustments, enhanced training curriculums, and reinforced planning initiatives from October to December 1944, the V Corps prepared for its most formidable work of the war. Well aware that the size, scope, and intensity of its 1945 objectives would dwarf its earlier operations, the unit determined to hone, yet again, its approach to the control and coordination of supporting firepower. All hands hove to in the corps' collective pursuit of improvement. Most importantly, by indoctrinating each entity—land, sea, and air—with a conscious appreciation for and understanding of their counterparts, American forces labored to perfect the synergy of their triphibious team.

MAPPING THE NEXT COURSE: IWO JIMA

As the officers and troops of the V Corps developed their approach to both naval gunfire and air support in the amphibious arena, their next objective of the Pacific War began to crystallize. Indeed, the final months of 1944 delivered clarity at several levels. Following the joint chiefs' autumn decision to discard the Formosa option and instead focus Douglas MacArthur's advancing army on Luzon and the Philippines, the senior leadership circle directed Nimitz to advance on the Nanpo Shoto, a string of island chains that extended south from Japan's largest island of Honshu. The joint chiefs' order was—geographically speaking—a natural one. The Nanpo Shoto strand encompassed the Izut Shoto, Bonin, and Volcano island groups along a linear axis that extended from the American-held Marianas to the enemy's home islands. Pressure here would tighten the noose around the Japanese perimeter and edge Allied forces ever closer to their ultimate target.

It fell to Nimitz and his staff to develop the Nanpo Shoto offensive. But as his intelligence officers quickly determined, the accomplished admiral "had no freedom of selection" in the matter, his autonomy curbed by geographical reality.[64] The volcanic island of Iwo Jima was the only fitting candidate, for Iwo alone offered the features that suited the Allies' plan. First, and of paramount importance, the island presented adequate landing beaches. Second, and of equally critical strategic significance, Iwo's terrain and composition allowed for airfield construction, the consistent holy grail of Nimitz's Central Pacific attacks.[65]

In American hands, the outpost would serve two vital purposes. First, it would provide a welcome emergency landing strip for B-29 Superfortresses then making the impending three-thousand-mile round-trip bombing flights from the Marianas to the Japanese home islands. Rather than ditching into the waves of the Pacific, B-29 crews—whether for mechanical, meteorological, or miscellaneous difficulties—could employ Iwo as a forward air base. Second, Iwo Jima would provide those same B-29 missions with fighter escorts in the skies over Tokyo. Though the escort planes could hardly dream of joining the B-29s' take-off in the Marianas (model-dependent, the P-51 Mustang's range peaked at roughly 1,500 miles), they could join the sorties mid-flight at Iwo Jima and protect the heavy bombers en route to their targets. Each benefit, as it were, validated the postwar conclusion of military historians Isely and Crowl that "a well-trained amphibious arm was as essential to the United States Army Air Forces as to the Navy."[66] As an added—though delayed—spoil, the seizure of Iwo's eight square miles would protect the right flank of a prospective American assault against the next link in the landing chain: the attack on Okinawa.[67]

Having found the right island candidate in the Nanpo Shoto, Navy and Marine planners of the V Corps turned to their staff work in late 1944, just as American coordination teams focused on improving their techniques, organization, and integration. Raking aerial photographs and intelligence assessments and building on battle-hardened concepts refined over more than two years of campaigning in the South and Central Pacific, Nimitz's staff resolved to orchestrate the largest Marine landing of the Pacific War to date. Their scheme—in accordance with the conflict's trendline—would employ the greatest concentration of air and naval firepower yet seen in the war. But the next contest, as so many before it, would not be solely dictated by American plans. As U.S. officers designed their assault, Lieutenant General Tadamichi Kuribayashi of the Imperial Japanese Army awaited the Allies' arrival. And he, too, had a plan in the making—a plan meant to challenge American triphibious warfare to the limit.

Battle damage from the American naval bombardment on Tarawa
Marine Corps History Division

Images such as this one from the Tarawa landing beaches captured the intensity and human cost of the Pacific War. *Marine Corps History Division*

A U.S. Marine shares water with a kitten underneath a wrecked Japanese tank on Tarawa, November 1943. *Marine Corps History Division*

The American task force bombs and shells Japanese positions on Saipan, June 14, 1944. *Marine Corps History Division*

A heavy cruiser provides fire support as American landing craft move toward the Saipan landing beaches on June 16, 1944. *Marine Corps History Division*

An American carrier off of Iwo Jima on D-day, February 19, 1945 *Marine Corps History Division*

Navy carrier planes attack Iwo Jima before the American landing on February 19, 1945. *Marine Corps History Division*

American landing craft and amphibious tanks advance toward Iwo Jima under the guns of USS *Halligan* (DD 584). *Marine Corps History Division*

Marine artillerymen of the V Amphibious Corps entrenched on Iwo Jima
Marine Corps History Division

U.S. ships fire in support of the American landing on Iwo Jima.
Marine Corps History Division

At Iwo Jima, Japanese commander Tadamichi Kuribayashi forbade local banzai attacks and ordered his Japanese troops to fight from their prepared underground shelters. *Marine Corps History Division*

A division of American F6F Hellcats attacks Japanese targets in support of Marine ground forces on Iwo Jima. *Marine Corps History Division*

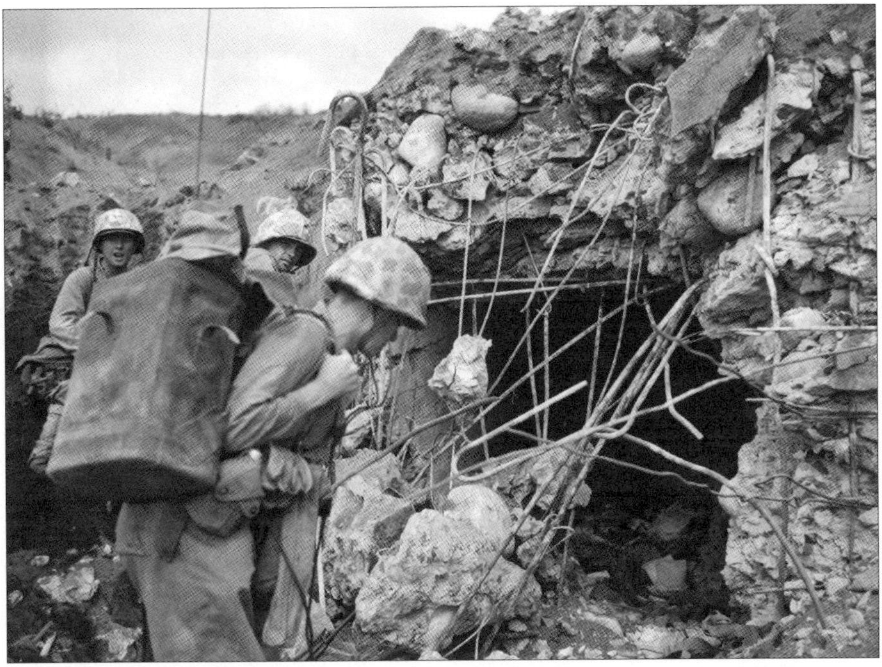

An American patrol of the 5th Marine Division prepares to clear a Japanese bunker previously demolished by air and naval bombardment. *Marine Corps History Division*

U.S. ships and field artillery damaged these Japanese water storage tanks during the battle of Iwo Jima. *Marine Corps History Division*

A Marine tank crew employs some dark humor on Iwo Jima.
Marine Corps History Division

An American destroyer provides fire support as the Marines clear the northern sector of Iwo Jima in March 1945. *Marine Corps History Division*

CHAPTER 7

PINNACLE IN THE PACIFIC

THE BATTLE FOR IWO JIMA AND THE APEX OF AMERICAN TRIPHIBIOUS FIREPOWER COORDINATION

On the morning of June 8, 1944, Lieutenant General Tadamichi Kuribayashi dined with his family for the last time. His wife, Yoshii, prepared one of his favorite dishes: herring wrapped in seaweed complemented by rice and red beans. That day, Kuribayashi departed for what would be his final defense of the Japanese empire. He was chosen for the command by the prime minister himself and departed with the emperor's personal blessing. The selection honored Kuribayashi, his wife, and his three children. Committed equally to both his family and his nation, the resolute commander arrived on Iwo Jima and assumed his responsibility with unfettered diligence.

Japan's recent collapse in the Marianas discouraged Kuribayashi deeply. But the seemingly doomed fate of the Japanese empire did little to curb his determination and fighting spirit. Immediately upon his arrival, Kuribayashi personally inspected the island by foot, building a thorough and personal knowledge of Iwo Jima's characteristics. With a metal canteen draped over his shoulder and walking stick in hand, Kuribayashi looked more like a sentry than a prestigious general. The act symbolized his leadership style as much as it did his thoroughness. The former cavalry officer, devoted father, and amateur poet would spare no effort on Iwo.[1] In time, Kuribayashi would develop his fortress into its fullest potential. From a consolidated defense-in-depth—founded on Iwo's elaborate network of obstacles, tunnels, and concrete fighting positions—the Japanese commander hoped to impose the highest of human costs upon the American attackers.

As Kuribayashi turned to his work with feverish intensity, U.S. Navy and Marine officers advanced their own plans for Iwo Jima. It was to be a two-division assault across the island's southern beaches. A third division would act as a "floating reserve," joining the attack on order. The assault was to include a dizzying list of specialized fire control and coordination teams in support: from the recently established 1st, 3d, and 5th Joint Assault Signal Companies—each composed of their subordinate shore fire control parties, air liaison parties, and shore party communications sections—to the war's first landing force air support control unit, established to manage U.S. aviation support from the front lines of the operation.[2] Each entity was a distinct product of American wartime adaptation in the Pacific—spawned, developed, and refined during the vicious campaigns for the Solomon, Gilbert, Marshall, and Mariana Islands. In short, the V Corps would land on Iwo Jima with the most advanced and deliberate system of triphibious fire control and coordination seen in the Pacific War. From that highly evolved network of specialists, the Americans would leverage their firepower advantage with crushing effect. In doing so, U.S. troops helped to produce one of the fiercest contests in military history.

PLANNING ARMAGEDDON: JAPANESE AND AMERICAN PREPARATIONS

As Imperial Japanese Army reinforcements made their way to Iwo Jima in the summer of 1944, the island's inhospitality greeted them. Major Yoshitaka Horie found a landscape "with no water, no sparrow, and no swallow."[3] With neither natural springs nor streams, the defenders were forced to construct elaborate cisterns and carefully ration their water supply. The island was covered in volcanic ash, rocks, and scrub vegetation, and natural food sources were scarce. Even the simplest of foot marches felt like a test of endurance. The island's aura itself seemed to forecast the bitter experience to come.

Upon their arrival, the Japanese had little reason to believe they could defend Iwo Jima. In those early days, Horie judged Iwo "as hazardous as a pile of eggs" and estimated that the Americans would take the island in just two or three days. In fact, in light of the Allies' material superiority, he saw little hope in defending Iwo Jima at all. "The best plan," he surmised in 1944, "is to sink the island into the sea or cut the island in half."[4] His proposal found at least some traction; a staff officer senior to Horie asked him to estimate the explosives necessary to "sink" the problematic outpost. But further investigation revealed the folly of the plan.

Unable to sink Iwo, Kuribayashi determined to fortify it handsomely. His men quickly and convincingly improved their odds. Concrete pillboxes and blockhouses became an early priority; by February 1945 the island boasted 642 of them. Bunker walls ranged from three to five feet in thickness. Troops emplaced and then protected naval guns and field artillery pieces of various calibers throughout the island: 120 large naval guns, 300 antiaircraft guns, 130 howitzers, 70 rocket launchers, 20 mortar tubes, 60 antitank guns, and 20,000 small arms (including heavy and light machine guns). Ammunition was in abundant supply as well. The detachment stockpiled more than 620,000 rounds of large caliber ammunition and an astounding twenty-two million rounds for their smaller guns. Twenty-three thousand troops manned Kuribayashi's island citadel.[5]

Japanese officers on Iwo Jima were well aware of the Americans' growing advantage in both men and firepower. Few of them expected to survive the battle, but they nonetheless embraced their mission with zeal. The detachment was to stand and fight, extracting the greatest possible blood toll from the American task force. Even while he surged his material strength on Iwo, Kuribayashi sharpened his soldiers mentally and morally for the struggle. By late 1944 the island commander heightened his rhetoric and prepared his detachment for both utter annihilation and unconditional fidelity. He stressed the value of "bodily attacks on enemy tanks" and directed the creation of special badges to honor the sacrifice.[6] In January, the general distributed his "oaths of combat" to each defender on Iwo Jima. The six loyal pledges emphasized the Japanese warrior code, championed the spiritual over the material, and instructed each soldier to take ten American lives before his final breath.[7] Horie recalled how the general's guidance intensified as the American attack neared: "Each man should think of his defense position as his graveyard," Kuribayashi instructed. "Fight until the last and give many damages to the enemy."[8]

Kuribayashi's defense of Iwo Jima, however, was to be as practical as it was spiritual. Rather than defend at the water's edge—the traditional Japanese defensive approach of the war—Kuribayashi planned an elaborate defense-in-depth on Iwo. As early as June 1944 the general labeled the beach defense "ineffective" and instructed his subordinate commanders to cease construction efforts on the shoreline. "However firm, stout pill-boxes you may build," he insisted, "they will be destroyed by bombardments of main armament of the [American] battleships."[9] Instead, Kuribayashi's forces were to focus their efforts inland in the hope of prolonging the struggle and maximizing American losses. The general directed the construction of extensive tunnels—eventually totaling several miles—to connect Japanese fighting positions, living quarters, and ammunition dumps. Forbidding the much celebrated but piecemeal banzai attacks, he directed his men to fight with maximum effectiveness: dying loyally in their hardened bunkers one by one. In recognition of the catastrophic affair that was to come, Kuribayashi's own command post lay seventy-five feet below the surface.[10]

In light of the evidence, the general's midsummer guidance made him the first Japanese commander to direct such a pivot. Although historians widely recognize Japan's 1944 defensive shift from the beach to the interior, they designate the revision a lesson of the Marianas campaign. Overcome by American mass and firepower on Saipan, Guam, and Tinian, these accounts conclude, Japanese strategists acknowledged the futility of shoreline resistance.[11] But Kuribayashi unveiled his plan while the American landing on Saipan was just beginning. The timing reveals that at least some attentive Japanese officers drew the conclusion well before their defeat in the Marianas. This planning lends further credence to Kuribayashi's industrious preparation and impressive generalship. As one Marine remarked of Kuribayashi after the grisly battle, "Let's hope the Japs don't have any more like him."[12]

As Kuribayashi's men readied their fortress in the months preceding the assault, Allied intelligence confirmed Iwo Jima's increasingly formidable posture. Although the island's terrain allowed for landing operations and promised airfield spoils to the victor, it favored the Japanese defenders. Steep gradients on the landing beaches presented the attackers with an immediate obstacle, and the enemy's visibility was unobstructed. The soft volcanic ash would impede vehicles and infantrymen alike. "The geographical situation," Holland Smith explained to a reporter, "is as difficult as any assaulting force has ever faced. . . . There was no possibility of surprise."[13] Historian Joseph Alexander put it more succinctly: the Marines' "first enemy in the campaign would prove to be the island itself."[14]

If surprise was unfeasible, the Americans meant to compensate with mass. Rear Admiral Marc Mitscher's Task Force 58, comprising sixteen total carriers, would provide aviation support. Rear Admiral B. J. Rodgers' Task Force 54, composed of three battleship divisions, three destroyer divisions, and one cruiser division, would assume shore bombardment responsibilities. The 71,000 Marines slated to take Iwo's beaches belonged to Major General Harry Schmidt, now in command of the V Corps. Subordinate divisions included the 3d Marine Division (under Major General Graves Erskine), the 4th Marine Division (Major General Clifton Cates), and the 5th Marine Division (Major General Keller Rockey). Holland Smith, promoted to commanding general of the Fleet Marine Force, Pacific, assumed the ceremonial title of commanding general, Expeditionary Forces. The combined outfit totaled an astounding 111,308 troops and 495 ships. As had become customary by 1945, the United States would fight from a position of quantitative supremacy.[15]

To offset Kuribayashi's elaborate scheme and accommodating terrain, American officers turned to their dependable advantage: firepower. Destruction from surf and sky was to deliver the landing force ashore. The Americans' bombardment against Kuribayashi and his men represented the increased intensity of the century's second global conflict. Following their barrage of November 11–12, American gunships fired subsequent missions on December 8, 25, and 27 as well as January 5 and 24. All told, in the weeks leading up to the ground assault, American Sailors pummeled Iwo Jima and its surrounding islands with no fewer than 8,891 8-inch shells and 22,107 5-inch shells, as well an array of smaller 40- and 20-mm projectiles.[16] To this shelling, as had become tradition in the Pacific, U.S. bomber and fighter aircraft added their own destruction throughout the months of November, December, and January.[17]

MAP 4. IWO JIMA

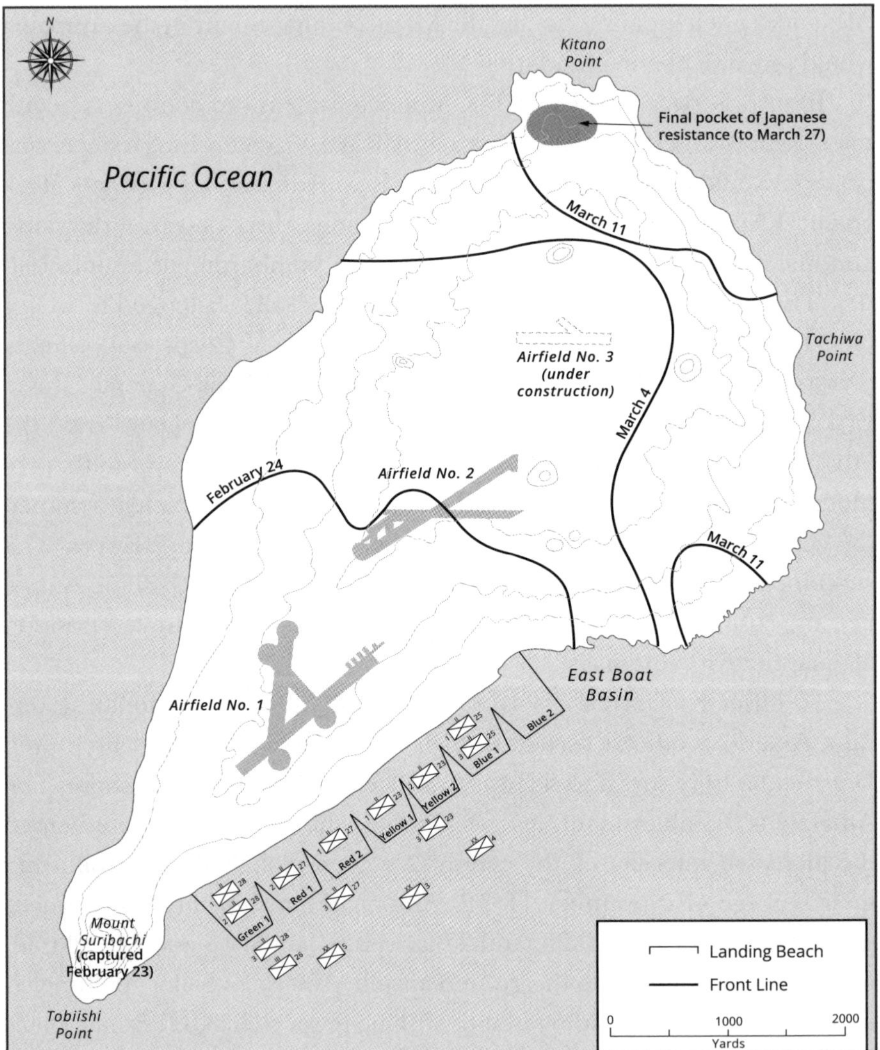

Prepared by Chris Robinson

On February 16, three days before the Marines were to fight their way onto the beaches of Iwo Jima, these intermittent preparatory fires gave way to a massive and near-continuous prelanding barrage. The heightened bombardment had been an issue of acute disagreement for American officers. The Marines, aware of Iwo's natural obstacles as well as Kuribayashi's formidable posture, petitioned for a lengthy final bombardment. Holland Smith, among others, requested ten full days of shelling. But Navy representatives worried that too long a preamble might tip the Americans' hand and endanger simultaneous carrier raids scheduled to strike Tokyo. After passionate staff debate, the Navy agreed to a three-day barrage. By 1945 the tradeoff had become nearly habitual. With or without their consent, the Marines would assume increased risk at the beachhead to preserve the larger strategic surprise of the U.S. fleet.[18]

INNOVATING NAVAL FIRE SUPPORT: THE ROLLING BARRAGE

In the early morning hours of February 19, 1945, the Marines of the V Corps donned their combat gear and climbed aboard the amphibian tractors that would ferry them to the black sand beaches of Iwo Jima. Although disrupted by poor weather and visibility, the final three-day barrage from Admiral William Blandy's task force was impressive nonetheless. Seven battleships, seven heavy cruisers, seventeen destroyers, and sixty-eight gunboats saturated the island with naval shells, mortars, and rockets of all stripes. Ranging in diameter from sixteen inches down to twenty millimeters, more than 65,000 rounds in all struck Iwo Jima in less than three days.[19]

In the early hours of D-day on Iwo Jima, American units mounted their most ambitious fire support coordination effort of the Pacific War. Before the attack of the landing force, battleships and aircraft worked from a carefully choreographed timeline (with H-hour constituting the moment of the Marines' arrival on the beach) that deconflicted efforts and maximized destructive fire over the landing zones. From dawn until H-55, each warship attacked specific objectives ashore. Several concentrated their sights on Mount Suribachi, the towering 550-foot peak at Iwo's southern tip. USS *New York* took aim at the center landing beaches, while USS *Tuscaloosa*—the ship on which the V Corps' naval gunfire officer, Donald Weller, cut his teeth as a young Marine lieutenant—targeted the Japanese airfield on the island's central plateau. All gunfire efforts focused on neutralizing the landing beaches prior to the infantry's imminent arrival.[20] It was, in the words of Samuel Eliot Morison, "the heaviest pre-H-hour bombardment of World War II."[21]

The naval deluge then gave way to a flurry of aerial activity. Precisely fifty-five minutes before the infantry was scheduled to wade ashore, thirty-six fighter planes, eighteen torpedo bombers, and eighteen dive bombers struck Iwo Jima from above. The aviators focused their bombs and strafing fire on the immediate landing beaches as well as the east and northeast slopes of Mount Suribachi—in complementary fashion, those positions most difficult to reach with naval ordnance. At the same time, forty-eight U.S. fighters arrived overhead. Flying just above the surf, the fighter pilots split into corresponding sections and put on a performance for the troops bobbing their way ashore. While one section flew north to south and trained its strafing fire on the center of the landing beach, another section flew south to north, targeting the very same coordinates. In the final moment before collision, the converging aircraft peeled off and prepared for another pass. The technique resembled a majestic air show as much as a martial attack. For twenty minutes, as the American LVTs (landing vehicles, tracked) and assorted landing craft edged closer to the shore, the aircraft battered the landing beaches. Though the maneuver's practical effect was hard to measure amid the cacophony of fires, its psychological impact was powerful, providing a jolt of confidence to the Marines making their final approach to the shoreline. Then, at precisely H-35, the planes concluded their barrage and passed the fire support baton back to the Sailors offshore.[22]

On cue, the U.S. warships resumed their blitz. Several battleships closed their distance to the shoreline, some coming within two thousand yards of Iwo's black sand. USS *California* focused its 5- and 14-inch steel projectiles on the eastern landing beaches while battleships *Mississippi*, *New York*, and *Nevada* alongside cruisers *Indianapolis* and *Louisville* took to their own fire sectors.[23] Other vessels crept in as close as one thousand yards from the beach.[24] The decision to place American gunfire ships so close to the shoreline was a bold move, not only because the shallow water threatened to ground the vessels (which carried a draft of more than thirty feet), but also because the ships' close proximity left them vulnerable to Japanese artillery fire. Yet in the technique's very risk lay its handsome reward. With more reliable communications, better direct observation for the Sailors themselves, and shorter firing trajectories, the nearby firing positions allowed U.S. ships to deliver both more accurate and more responsive support. Weller later praised the courage of the ship captains and the "unremitting, close destructive fires" that their proximity enabled.[25]

Impressive as this initial synchronization might have been, the Americans' next move represented the most innovative fire support tactic of the battle and, arguably, of the entire war. For several weeks, Weller had drafted and refined an audacious plan to protect the infantrymen through the most vulnerable stage of their attack. While the Marines bobbed ashore and prepared to touch the beach, Weller's shore fire control teams (of the larger JASCO outfits) attempted a naval "rolling barrage," one of the first of its kind in the history of amphibious warfare. Through the bold gamble, Weller intended to "wring the last ounce of potential out of the naval gun" and provide the Marines a timely antidote against Kuribayashi's fortress.[26]

The rolling barrage concept initially appeared on the bloody Western Front battlefields of World War I. Military historian Paddy Griffith noted its first use in 1915 by the British 15th Division, but the scheme was quickly adopted by other European combatants. Searching for tactical solutions to the hellish stalemate of the Great War, British, French, and German officers attempted to precede their infantry assaults with a mobile curtain of "neutralizing" firepower. The focus, in this case, lay on disrupting the enemy rather than killing him. If applied properly, the creeping artillery fire would allow friendly infantry units to advance across the vulnerable planes of "no man's land."[27]

Without radio communications, however, artillery and infantry units on the Western Front coordinated their actions through prescriptive timetables. But timetables rarely work in war. Thus, when the pace of an infantry attack accelerated or stalled, the rolling barrage derailed. In some cases, the barrage continued deeper and deeper into enemy territory, with diminishing returns. In the worst cases, artillery rounds threatened and then killed friendly troops in the attack. Reacting to the dilemma, some fire directors added more safety buffers into their calculations, hoping to protect their front-line peers. But caution only reduced the utility of their support. European artillerymen labored to overcome these challenges, but to no enduring solution. Transformative in concept, the Great War's "rolling barrage" remained elemental—if not disastrous—in practice.[28]

The proposal to take this Great War precedent and adapt it for use in the triphibious assault on Iwo Jima did not come from the V Corps' naval gunfire pioneer himself, but from a fellow artillery officer of the same staff: William "Bucky" Buchanan. Nonetheless, the concept earned Weller's immediate enthusiasm, and he assumed responsibility for the development of the creeping naval bombardment. For weeks leading up to the battle, Weller and his staff matured the idea from embryo to final form. As their landing craft came within four hundred yards of Iwo Jima's beaches, American naval gunfire would methodically crawl its way up the beach in a mobile umbrella of protection. Aerial observers were to mark the progress of the landing force and arrange coordination in real time over assigned radio channels. As the Marines advanced through successive hundred-yard blocks, the overhead conductors would direct the American men-of-war to shift their fire accordingly.[29]

The calibrated fire coverage was sure to buttress the Marines' attack, but it also carried acute risk, as the Great War had shown. In the naval application, the battleships' sheer destructiveness raised the stakes. A single projectile from a 16-inch naval gun weighed the same as a standard passenger car.[30] Should coordination fail at the beachhead, Weller later acknowledged, "you might just cream the hell out of some of your own troops." As the task force steamed for Iwo Jima and his staff put the finishing touches on their plan, Weller wrestled with the scheme's danger: "I had a lot of sleepless nights, I can tell you that. Because it had never been done before."[31] Sharing Weller's concern in the weeks before the attack, Lieutenant Colonel Louis B. Blissard emphasized the importance of the barrage in an updated instruction to his First Battalion of the 23rd Regiment. The commander assured his men of the concept's careful design and its potential value on the beachhead. Trust between the naval gunners, the shore fire control parties, and the attacking infantry had to prevail. He even took careful time to caution his Marines against enemy deception. His directive reveals both the V Corps' diligent preparation for the innovative bombardment and the enemy's clever attempts to negate American fire superiority in the Pacific:

> All hands are cautioned that this rolling barrage is planned with great detail, and, once it is ordered to cease, probably will not be able to get back on schedule. Because of this fact, Japanese mortar or artillery fire must not be mistaken for friendly Naval Gunfire. It is an old Jap trick to fire at the same time our guns are firing and it is reasonable to expect that the Japs will try to fool us into thinking we are being hit by our own fire in this case. *REMEMBER*—Naval Gunfire falls in salvos of 4 or 5 rounds; Japs usually fire 1 or 2 pieces at a time. DO NOT BE RESPONSIBLE FOR DEPRIVING YOUR BATTALION OF VALUABLE NAVAL SUPPORT BY REQUESTING NAVAL GUNFIRE TO CEASE BECAUSE YOU THINK IT IS FALLING SHORT. PROBABLY ENEMY ARTILLERY OR MORTARS ARE HITTING YOU.[32]

Risk, uncertainty, deception, and all, officers of the V Corps knew that the rolling barrage would play an instrumental role against the menacing target of Iwo Jima.

IWO: THE ASSAULT

As American ships and aircraft rained their final preparatory fires, the Marines of the V Corps enjoyed—as best their circumstances could allow—a traditional prelanding breakfast of steak and eggs. At 7:30, Marine amphibian tractors of the 4th and 5th Marine Divisions began plunging from the well decks of their LSTs (landing ships, tank) and turned their bows toward Iwo's coast. The assault force was scheduled to touch the beach at precisely 9:00 a.m. Navy coxswains organized their craft according to unit integrity and their assigned wave position within the landing plan. Just as the first wave of Marine LVTs came within four hundred yards of the beach, the V Corps triggered its dramatic rolling barrage. As the landing force neared the beach, the airborne observers transmitted updates to the fire control centers of each warship, and the Americans' curtain of naval gunfire crept two hundred yards up the beach. At precisely 9:02—matching the progress of the landing force with choreographed precision—the American warships rolled their fires another two hundred yards inland.[33]

As they reached their assigned beaches, a surprising and even disconcerting peace greeted the Marines. Kuribayashi's plan to cede the shoreline provided at least momentary relief for the troops toiling their way up Iwo's steep black slopes, hoping to establish the critical momentum that separated a successful amphibious assault from a futile prod at the beach. In the words of five Marine veterans, "The island was strangely, frighteningly quiet."[34] The result was surprising early progress for the V Corps: by 9:30 initial waves had advanced some two hundred yards inland, and secondary units found their own inertia. Some outfits advanced to three hundred and even four hundred yards across the beach.[35] Tsuruji Akikusa, a Japanese radioman, recalled his anticipation from his foxhole ashore: "The Marines were digging in down at the water's edge. There were so many of them. . . . It reminded me of a crowd of baseball fans waiting for the stadium to open. I saw their numbers swell from several hundred to a few thousand."[36]

As a few Marine intelligence officers had feared, however, the island's natural composition impeded progress. Iwo's volcanic ash ensnared wheeled vehicles and even hampered tracked machines.[37] Terrace grades proved equally difficult, some as steep as forty percent. As troops summited the first beach shelf, Japanese machine guns erupted along preregistered azimuths. According to one official report, in a matter of minutes, "a trail of wreckage marked the way" for subsequent landing waves.[38] Marine Captain Earl Stearns, riding ashore with the regimental weapons company of the 27th Marines, reported the early challenges. As the American battleships delivered an "unceasing rain of steel on the eastern beach," Stearns' men encountered a twelve-foot-high sand terrace blocking their advance. Neither American M3 "half-tracks" nor M29 "weasel" trucks could navigate the volcanic ash, and the weapons company struggled to mount momentum.[39]

As successive landing waves delivered American fire support ashore, however, the Marines' capacity for destruction grew and helped to provide both the time and space necessary to negotiate the troublesome terrace. At 9:30 a.m., M-4 Sherman medium tanks of the 5th Tank Battalion began arriving. By nightfall, the encouraged infantrymen could count some forty tanks ashore. Several hours later, elements of the 14th Marine Artillery Regiment set foot on Iwo. The howitzers' arrival was encouraging, but the gun teams would not complete their registration process until 6:00 that evening. For D-day, naval gunfire and aviation support remained the Marines' primary tools of fire support.[40] For the moment, at least, they were enough. Stearns proudly recalled his unit's achievement that evening: "A toehold had been established on one of Japan's prize outposts."[41]

As the V Corps' firepower built up ashore, so too did its capacity to control, coordinate, and apply that destruction. The firepower surge at Iwo Jima, in fact, demanded the most elaborate shore-based system of fire control and coordination of the Pacific War. Along with the arriving tanks and artillery pieces came an expert team of forward observers, liaison officers, and control elements of the now-accomplished JASCOs. Evolved through and matured by nearly three years of offensive landing operations, the American coordination apparatus had reached its pinnacle.

Upon their arrival, the JASCOs' shore fire control parties assumed responsibility for adjusting and controlling the rolling naval barrage. Block by block, the teams nudged the curtain of American shells forward, several hundred yards in front of the advancing troops. Just as the innovative bombardment helped to put the Marines ashore, so too did it propel their attack forward. Immediately upon their arrival, the observers from each shore fire control party established radio communications with their assigned firing ships and adjusted the naval rounds according to the advance of the corresponding infantry unit. The result was a tailored and responsive application of sea-based shelling.[42] Navy Yeoman James Orvill Raines, on the destroyer USS *Howorth*, proudly recorded his personal satisfaction with the rolling barrage in a late-night letter to his wife:

> When we started firing in the morning we were shooting about the middle of the island. Later, [we] shifted more to the left and then again. We kept moving left all day, stopping several times while our Marines moved up closer to the front. It was like playing checkers. We kept jumping ahead all the time. At nightfall our forces were fighting well past where we had been shooting in the morning. It was gratifying to know we had helped.[43]

Two other postbattle synopses of a more official variety acknowledged the control parties' remarkable coordination efforts, calling the rolling barrage and its execution "excellent supporting gunfire" and a "vital continuation of support" as the V Corps fought its way from surf to sand.[44]

By the time of the battle for Iwo Jima, the Americans had advanced their naval gunfire coordination process to a high degree of both accuracy and efficiency. As Raines described a typical request on Iwo, the Marine radio operator of the shore fire control party used an assigned frequency to alert the ship's command center of a fire request. After receiving the target data, the shipboard gunnery officer—typically a junior lieutenant or ensign—computed the firing trajectory and approved the mission before directing his gunners to proceed. Approval gave way to immediate shelling, and the coordination party ashore used a team of forward observers to record and transmit results back to the supporting vessel. The Sailors were utterly reliant on the radio reports to distinguish their direct hits from their complete misses. Raines noted that during a particularly feverish firing sequence, his gunnery officer, Lieutenant Patrick Arnold, "didn't see daylight" for fourteen hours. Instead, he remained in his shipboard plotting room surrounded by firing diagrams and maps. "Through a series of very complicated instruments and radar business," Raines recalled, Arnold "put them [shells] right where the marine called for them."[45]

As they lent support to the infantrymen ashore, the shipboard gunners waited anxiously to receive their marks. In one particular case, Raines remembered the pride of a job well done when the forward observer reported: "It might interest you to know your shooting is very good. The results are very gratifying." Perhaps by design, the Marine's compliment stirred the gunners' motivation and diligence. Hoping to replicate the result, "we redoubled our efforts to shoot perfectly," Raines recalled.[46] Even in the throes of one of the Pacific War's most intense battles, self-esteem and a competitive streak remained at play.

As the coordination teams and gunners afloat executed their firing missions, staff representatives of the V Corps monitored the various radio frequencies and passively screened the requests from a unified command tent ashore. If the Corps' air, artillery, or naval gunfire representative deemed the request unsafe or redundant, he intervened and adjusted the mission accordingly. The nerve center became a one-stop shop for fire support management and picked up the colloquial title "supporting arms tent."[47] Throughout the campaign on Iwo Jima, close personal liaison and mutual trust drove the effectiveness of American triphibious fire support.[48] If by no other metric, the informally labeled supporting arms tent was a major milestone on account of the concept's longevity. In subsequent months, the tent became known as the fire support coordination center, a Marine fire control feature that remains in existence even today.[49]

In spite of highly advanced coordination procedures, Japanese resistance on Iwo Jima remained fierce. Added to air and naval gunfire efforts, the Marines slowly accumulated combat power ashore—including organic fire support—that would begin to turn the tide of the battle. By sunset on February 19, Navy coxswains had delivered both the 4th and 5th Marine Divisions onto Iwo Jima. As night approached, the Americans dug in to protect their progress. In line with his defensive philosophy, Kuribayashi, too, restrained his efforts. Prohibited from counterattacking, Japanese troops preserved their energy and waited for General Schmidt to resume his attack.[50]

Awaking to a gloomy drizzle on February 20, the divisions renewed their offensive to the north under intense air and naval fire support. The landed artillerymen added their own weight while U.S. tanks cleared suspected mine fields and provided protection to the advancing infantry. Reflective of the initial bombardment and landing, JASCO fire control teams ensured precise coordination between the American entities. The display was stunning, and war correspondent Robert Sherrod—a veteran journalist from the Battle of Tarawa and no stranger to amphibious bombardments—called the February 21 barrage "the greatest concentration of fire I had ever seen."[51] But naval shells and air-delivered bombs could only do so much on Iwo Jima. As Kuribayashi's men maintained their disciplined posture and fought from their reinforced positions, Marine infantry teams leveraged a concoction of hand grenades, flame throwers, satchel charges, and bayonets to clear each individual bunker.[52]

The next few days of combat revealed—as if any American required the reminder—that Iwo Jima would be the toughest objective of the Pacific War. Yet even as the V Corps reckoned with that realization, it enjoyed a monumental moment on February 23, 1945. After four days ashore, a patrol from the 28th Marine Regiment climbed Mount Suribachi under close fire support from the offshore battleships.[53] Intent on publicizing their achievement, the men lashed an American flag to a nearby discarded iron pipe and threw the ensign to the sky. Moments later, they replaced the colors with an even larger standard. Joe Rosenthal's iconic photograph of this second act became one of the most famous images in American military history, representative of the U.S. Marine Corps itself.[54] Despite the stirring achievement, the battle raged on in Suribachi's shadow. A photograph could lift spirits on the home front, even help solidify the reputation of an entire military institution, but it could not clear the remaining bunkers of Iwo Jima. That task remained for the Marines.

Having established a foothold ashore and taken the island's highest peak, the Marines settled into a monotonous daily routine of violence and destruction. As the V Corps slogged its way forward, naval shells, aerial bombs, and field cannons propelled the attack.[55] On February 24, Sherrod described what had become the Americans' morning routine: "At 0800 our heavy naval barrage signaled the beginning of a new offensive against the hard-to-crack center of the Jap line. The battleships joined the destroyers and cruisers, the 105's and 155's [howitzers] from the southern end of the island, the infantry mortars." Within minutes, dozens of U.S. aircraft joined the scuffle, "dropping bombs, strafing Jap positions, and firing their sizzling rockets." The resulting scene, he recorded, was "a haze of black smoke, billowing topsoil, and flying debris" that consumed the northern half of the island. "On Iwo," Sherrod concluded, "we really had the power."[56]

The destruction wrought by American combined arms on Iwo Jima—coupled with the combatants' utter determination and Kuribayashi's masterful defensive plan—created some of the most savage combat conditions in the history of warfare. Since the conflict's opening blows, the tone of battle in the Pacific had been particularly vicious, with neither Japanese nor Allied forces giving quarter. But on Iwo Jima—where the supreme tactics, tools, and tenacity of the Pacific War seemed to coalesce—the contest reached new heights. Sherrod reported the horrifying crescendo:

> Whether the dead were Japs or Americans, they had one thing in common; they had died with the greatest possible violence. Nowhere in the Pacific war had I seen such badly mangled bodies. Many were cut squarely in half. Legs and arms lay fifty feet away from any body. In one spot on the sand, far from the nearest cluster of dead, I saw a string of guts 15 feet long. Only legs were easy to identify; they were Jap if wrapped in khaki puttees, American if covered by canvas leggings.[57]

Others not only acknowledged, but also participated in, the war's surging inhumanity. Yeoman Raines described his own pride and satisfaction in a letter to his wife, confident that his *Fletcher*-class destroyer did its part in delivering destruction ashore: "I'm glad, in spite of the sacrifice I feel that you and I are making, that I had something to do with killing some of them. I feel really grand about it. I get a special kick out of killing them. I only wish I were in close enough to see their bodies and parts of their bodies go sky high when our shells hit."[58]

Ashore, Japanese lieutenant Satoru Omagari endured the harrowing barrage from Raines and his fellow naval gunners as he grappled with the harrowing reality of combat. Omagari's account was equally emotional, if less triumphant: "Men didn't just die on Iwo Jima, they were ripped apart, torn to shreds and scattered. I saw torsos with no limbs, dismembered legs, arms and hands, and internal organs splashed onto the rocks."[59] In short, on Iwo Jima, the two belligerents mastered their respective tasks: for the Americans, assaulting an enemy-held island from the sea; for the Japanese, defending against that very attack. In perfecting their work, many of the combatants jettisoned their humanity. The result was annihilation of the highest order.

The war's intensification—founded primarily on the marked proficiency of the combatants—was also a product of proximity. As the battlefields crept ever closer to the Japanese home islands, the war's ferocity escalated. Japanese troops fortified their already-strong resolve to defend their homeland unconditionally. American forces, though much more attentive to their own physical survival, yearned to settle the contest and return home. Racism, though not formative, amplified the intensity of the struggle. The intersection of these dynamics produced combat rarely matched in the history of armed conflict. It was total war of an extraordinary variety.

BOMBS FROM ABOVE: AIR SUPPORT AT IWO JIMA

Destruction on Iwo Jima was not solely the result of American naval gunfire and infantry action. Air support played a substantive, if secondary, role in the initial seizure of Iwo's beaches and the Marines' early advance. In a torrent of .50-caliber rounds, 5-inch rockets, and napalm bombs, aerial fires helped to neutralize stubborn Japanese positions and provide brief respites under which American ground troops could maneuver and advance. It was an eclectic but effective overhead display, with Grumman F6F Hellcats, Vought F4U Corsairs, and Curtiss SB2C Helldivers each playing their part aloft.

Perhaps in an attempt to match the naval gunners' imaginative rolling barrage, Marine air coordinators introduced their own revolutionary approach in the control of supporting aircraft at Iwo Jima. Led by the diligent and pioneering Vernon E. Megee, the Corps created an experimental control team to accompany the infantry units ashore and direct close air support missions from the front lines.[60] Previously, all aviation support had been arranged and controlled from Navy command centers afloat.

Although the JASCOs' air liaison parties managed requests for air support, advised ground commanders on aviation capabilities, and provided pilots with important updates from the ground, they did not direct the aircraft in-flight. That "control" authority, prior to Iwo Jima, remained at sea. Relying solely on radio communications, the displaced Navy control teams enjoyed the centralized information resident in their well-informed nerve centers but lacked an acute appreciation for the tactical situation on the beach and the progress of the landing force. Megee's outfit, rather awkwardly labeled the landing force air support control unit (LFASCU, in the equally awkward military acronym), intended to bridge the gap and strengthen both the accessibility and flexibility of Navy and Marine air support.

Megee, a native of Tulsa, Oklahoma, emerged as a determined proponent of Marine aviation during the interwar lull. Enlisting in the Marines in 1919 and securing an officer's commission three years later, Megee served on expeditionary duty in Haiti and China before battling Sandinista rebels in Nicaragua. After completing Navy flight training in Pensacola, Florida and the Army Air Corps' Tactical School at Maxwell Field, Alabama, Megee spent two years as a military instructor in Quantico, Virginia. The posting allowed him to study and help develop both the Corps' amphibious doctrine and its integration of air support. By the late 1930s Megee was a recognized and aggressive advocate of close air support, particularly for its use in landing operations.[61]

In his endeavor to promote aviation, Megee argued that air-delivered fire support could account for the intrinsic gaps of naval gunnery. In particular, he reasoned, attack aircraft and dive bombers could strike targets with greater precision, wear down reinforced enemy bunkers, and prosecute reverse-slope defensive positions (that most elusive of objectives for a naval cannon). Furthermore, Megee envisioned a fleet of aircraft trained in the critical importance of flexibility and responsiveness. Able to attack, reload, and stand by on their proximate carriers, Navy and Marine pilots could deliver a crucial and renewable umbrella of protection to the landing force ashore.[62]

For aviation support to achieve its fullest potential, however, Megee envisioned a novel method of aircraft control. Instead of relying on the Navy's sea-based air control team (labeled the close air support control unit),

Megee insisted that Marine-led teams manage their own aircraft support from the beach. Amid the dynamic circumstances of an amphibious assault, he argued, aircraft control could not reside "out on some ship."[63] The Navy air controllers afloat, Megee reasoned, "couldn't see what was going on. All they had were maps and most everything they were running was pre-planned. They would send in so many strikes whether [the Marines] needed them or not. And the poor devil up there on the front line that needed air support for a given problem now couldn't get it."[64]

Having recognized the limitations of offshore aviation management in the early campaigns of the Pacific War, particularly on Peleliu, Megee championed his concept of shore-based air control for the assault on Iwo Jima. His logic fell on sympathetic ears, and he secured brisk approval for his plan. As the V Corps rehearsed its operation and loaded its transport shipping for Iwo Jima, Megee's enterprise grew to a team of seventeen officers (primarily Marines, but supplemented with Navy representatives) and fifty-six enlisted technicians. Lacking sufficient radios, signaling gear, and jeeps—as well as the time necessary to acquire them—Megee's men brokered and begged their unit into existence, even as the assault on Iwo Jima began. In the final days of February, with a sufficient beachhead secured behind the infantry divisions, the men, maps, radios, and jeeps of LFASCU 1 charged ashore and prepared for the next great development in American triphibious war.

At 10:00 a.m. local time on March 1, 1945, Megee's pioneer outfit secured radio communications with its offshore headquarters and assumed control of all close air support operations in the skies above Iwo Jima. As with many monumental moments in military history, the raging combat ashore precluded ample celebration and kept the control team's focus on the situation at hand. Immediately adjacent to the landing force command post, Megee's LFASCU began directing all strike missions, combat air patrols, tactical air observer and air coordinator flights, and miscellaneous aircraft.[65]

When his men accepted authority for aircraft control, Megee, already serving as commander, LFASCU, added the more senior (and more daunting) title of commander air, Iwo Jima. In the service of both roles, he introduced an array of procedural modifications to improve the precision, safety, and effectiveness of American air support on Iwo. Immediately, Megee's coordinators initiated an updated briefing procedure. For each approaching air strike, LFASCU radio operators announced the aircraft's mission number, target coordinates, attack timeline, heading, and minimum strike altitude over the V Corps' artillery fire direction control net. The broadcast—heard by every subordinate artillery element on Iwo Jima—allowed howitzer batteries and mortar teams to tailor their own fire missions to accommodate the American air strikes. Artillery fire directors subsequently reported their own "maximum ordinate" (highest shell altitude) so that nearby aircraft could remain comfortably clear of the danger. If necessary, the firing batteries, according to the details of each individual brief, adjusted their own supporting fires on the ground. In the most critical circumstances, the LFASCU radioman ordered a complete cease-fire for all subordinate gun teams, to allow the pilots to make a risky pass over a difficult Japanese target.[66] This general radio transmission proved effective on Iwo Jima, but the adjustment was, by most any definition, an elementary one. It was Megee's additional air control adjustments that proved both more audacious and more helpful in the Americans' search for a first-rate system of fire integration.

Building on an impromptu technique that American fire control teams experimented with on Saipan some six months earlier, LFASCU 1 instituted two novel coordination measures to deconflict air and naval support efforts on Iwo Jima. The first, dubbed Plan Victor, stipulated that when mortar, artillery, and rocket units were firing on a Japanese position within 2,500 yards of an aircraft's target, all land-based fires would keep their ordnance below 1,100 feet.[67] The artificial ceiling allowed American pilots to execute their bombing and strafing runs with impunity, at least from friendly munitions. Though scripted and centralized in nature (the measure took effect upon command, and without exception), Plan Victor ensured an aircraft's safety during heightened moments of fire support activity.[68]

Alternatively, air coordinators on Iwo Jima could invoke Plan Mike, which called for an immediate cease-fire from all naval guns prosecuting shore targets. In this case, the measure guaranteed safety for the attacking pilots, so long as American warships both received and complied with the order. As an alternative or a complement, the LFASCU had Plan Negat at its disposal—a carbon copy cease-fire order that applied to all field artillery and mortar units. Taken in sum, plans Victor, Mike, and Negat armed Megee's control unit and complementary JASCOs with a robust spread of pinpoint coordination measures on Iwo Jima.[69] The standardized techniques added a substantial and immediate control lever to the V Corps' otherwise flexible and decentralized system of fire coordination. The techniques enabled, to a "full extent," Megee later wrote, "the terrific firepower of the air and sea arms."[70]

In the final days of February and the first days of March 1945, the Marine LFASCU earned, and then sustained, resounding approval from the units and commanders that it supported on Iwo Jima. One Navy officer concluded that Megee's system "far surpassed anything that has ever gone before in air support operations" and observed that the LFASCU's coordination techniques enabled highly responsive air strikes. For this officer at least, the unit's debut performance was enough to establish its utility: "for the control of troop support missions," he continued, "a Landing Force Air Support Control Unit is an absolute necessity."[71]

SUSTAINING THE ATTACK ON IWO

American planes, ships, and field artillery continued to support the Marines' attack as a monotonous cycle of violence continued ashore through early March. The U.S. advantage in firepower remained both apparent and overwhelming, but the veterans of the V Corps had long since learned that even the greatest of firepower exhibitions had its limits. Though disrupted, frightened, and even jumbled by American fires from the sea and air, most Japanese troops on Iwo Jima survived the punishment intact.[72] As the battle for Peleliu demonstrated six months earlier, bombardment was inextricably followed by infantry assault. Complementary warfare worked, and U.S. forces maximized its utility. But the American Marine on foot and the vicious flame-throwing M4A3 Sherman tank seemed the only tools capable of clearing a Japanese bunker.[73]

For the Marines, the month of March became a broken record—one defined by near-constant explosions, frightening bunker-clearing duties, and an inescapable longing for the whole bloody nightmare to end. Corporal Arthur J. Kiely captured the simultaneous horror and wonder, writing that "[Iwo Jima] looks like a Fourth of July celebration . . . only here there is more at stake than the amusement of the public."[74] The Americans continued to play to their strengths by relying on abundant firepower, whatever its source. One infantry company expended four hundred hand grenades in a single thirty-minute attack.[75] The Fourth Tank Battalion reported equally staggering munitions counts throughout the operation. In one particular skirmish on the twelfth day of battle, tankers fired one thousand gallons of flamethrower fuel on a single Japanese blockhouse.[76]

The reality of bunker-clearing and savage combat notwithstanding, Marine units clung to American air and naval fire support to ease their demanding task on Iwo Jima. In several instances, field commanders made conscious choices to incur the risk of friendly fire in exchange for one final moment of coverage. Though Megee cautioned his air coordinators to use a "one-yard–one-pound" ratio on Iwo Jima (whereby pilots were to drop a 500-pound bomb five hundred yards from the nearest Marine), infantry officers often discarded the very measure intended to protect their front lines. Megee emphasized caution, telling one battalion commander that "a thousand-pound bomb going off two or three hundred yards in front of you is no toy."[77]

Megee's message was received, but rejected nonetheless. For the Marines on Iwo Jima, air support became indispensable, even when it threatened friendly units and violated the wisest of procedures. Assaulting a honeycombed cave network north of the Motoyama Plateau in early March, one battalion commander petitioned for exception to Megee's guideline. "You can't hurt us any worse than we're being hurt. We'll keep everybody's head down in the fox holes," the officer exclaimed. Concerned but sympathetic, Megee approved the request. "We jarred the back teeth of a lot of people," he later recalled, "but we didn't hurt anybody but Japs."[78]

Throughout the assault on Iwo Jima, air support proved especially valuable in exposing hardened, underground, and reverse slope enemy positions. Army P-51 Mustang pilots of the Fifteenth Fighter Group proved particularly adept at attacking elevated Japanese holdouts. The airmen would swoop in from a high-altitude approach, release their ordnance, and enter a steep, evasive climb to clear the radius of the subsequent blast. The result was equal parts effective and spectacular, Megee recalled. As the plane escaped danger and the bomb detonated, "the whole damn face of the bluff would fall off into the sea" as the American pilots searched for their next target.[79]

Howitzers, too, played their part in the crescendo of firepower on Iwo. One coordinated offensive on March 6 included the heaviest artillery support of the entire campaign. Assisted by fires from the sea, General Schmidt ordered each and every available field cannon to join the line. In just one day, the V Corps expended 2,500 155-mm rounds and 20,000 75- and 105-mm rounds. The U.S. warships contributed another 22,000 shells to the deluge. As with Megee's air support, infantry commanders invited unprecedented risk in order to drain the last drop of fire support from the warships offshore. In several cases, JASCO units coordinated (and nearby Marines encouraged) friendly naval rounds as close as seventy-five yards to their own unit positions.[80]

On the back of this unprecedented triphibious fire support, the Marines eventually secured Iwo Jima. The final weeks of combat represented a painstaking repetition of coordinated destruction, modest advance, and more coordinated destruction. American tools behind the front lines sustained the attack—indeed, were indispensable in the grisly assault. Umbrellas of firepower—including field artillery, naval gunfire, and air support—preceded every major ground offensive. The preparatory bombardments typically lasted thirty minutes and, in some cases, extended for sixty minutes. When the infantrymen moved forward, the ships, planes, and howitzers shifted their sights, at the direction of their respective control teams ashore, to individual Japanese targets.[81] Behind this curtain of firepower, Marine units crawled forward with flamethrowers, tanks, dynamite, and amphibious tractors. Kuribayashi's men—for their part—maintained their discipline and fought to the death. Holland Smith, himself inclined to emphasize the contribution of the courageous front-line infantryman, offered careful recognition of the supporting gunners: "Artillery barrages, poundings by naval guns, and air strikes were maintained as a matter of routine."[82] Finally, in the evening hours of March 16, 1945, the V Corps secured complete control of Iwo Jima. In an unqualified display of loyalty to their emperor and island commander, isolated pockets of Japanese troops fought on for another two weeks but failed to reverse the reality of the situation. On March 17, the Japanese government acknowledged the unthinkable. The island belonged to the Allies.[83]

Kuribayashi's own death seemed to encapsulate the battle in which it was spent. Though his remains were never identified, and some skeptics suggest suicide, Japanese sources indicate that the brilliant general died directing a final coordinated attack on March 26. Committed both to his fate and his purpose on Iwo Jima, Kuribayashi and his withering detachment extracted another 170 American casualties before the general gave his final breath. Much in contrast to the fanatical Japanese banzai attacks of 1942 and 1943, Kuribayashi coldly and adeptly drew a final sacrifice from his American attackers.[84]

The battle for Iwo Jima was, by nearly any gauge, the Marines' most difficult objective of the Pacific War. Arguably, it was the most difficult objective of the Corps' entire combat history. On the eve of the attack, Donald Weller labeled it the Marines' "toughest nut to crack."[85] Six days into the struggle, Holland Smith told a reporter that "this probably would be the most difficult mission the Marine Corps had ever been assigned in its 168 years of service."[86] Time only deepened Smith's conviction. Writing three years after the war, Iwo Jima became, for him, "the most terrific battle in the history of the Marine Corps" with "few parallels in military annals."[87]

Few could challenge Smith's pronouncement, then or now. Kuribayashi roused complete and fervent loyalty from his men. He ordered them to fight and die on their island outpost. Fight and die they did; American forces took only 216 prisoners. The remainder of Kuribayashi's 22,000-man detachment perished amid the shells and flames of battle. For their sacrifice, the Japanese extracted—for the first time in the Pacific War—a higher total casualty count from the American attackers. Nearly 26,000 Marines fell on Iwo; more than 5,000 of them lost their lives.[88] When considering the savage fighting, challenging terrain, and near-complete extermination of Kuribayashi's detachment, Iwo Jima deserves comparison with the most ferocious and brutal encounters in the history of armed conflict.

Only the finest display of triphibious firepower coordination could have seized the historic fortress that was Kuribayashi's Iwo Jima. And for the Americans, there was plenty of firepower to coordinate. Even by the standards of the Pacific War, U.S. ordnance expenditures on the island were truly astonishing. In thirty-six total days of combat—including "mopping up" operations that extended through March 26—Marine artillery fired some 450,000 rounds. Even within individual units, the amounts were astounding. One howitzer battalion expended 19,187 high-explosive shells on Iwo Jima. In proving the norm, a second battalion averaged 973 rounds per day throughout the month-long operation.[89] Kuribayashi's staff itself estimated that American ships delivered 30,000 rounds per day.[90] In arguably the most advanced display of close air support to date in the war, Navy and Marine pilots contributed 1,315 tons of bombs and rockets as well as 456 napalm incendiaries from the sky.[91]

But howitzer shells, naval munitions, and aerial bombs cannot coordinate themselves in battle. The staggering deluge of American ordnance on Iwo Jima required careful application and integration. American JASCOs—including both shore fire control and air liaison parties—alongside Vernon Megee's trailblazing air support control unit arranged, calibrated, and adjusted the avalanche of U.S. firepower. When front-line Marines such as Stearns concluded that "close coordination between air, ground, and sea units was excellent throughout the entire campaign," the credit primarily belonged to American coordination teams.[92] In organization, training, and tactics, the specialized parties matured through two years of brutal and unforgiving combat against an unwavering opponent in the South and Central Pacific. The battle for Iwo Jima was the pinnacle of their wartime evolution. Against Kuribayashi's extraordinary defensive scheme, these specialists proved their value and solidified their reputation as a critical component of Allied warmaking.[93] Without them, the American assault on Iwo Jima could not have prevailed.

General Kuribayashi himself acknowledged the overwhelming role of air and naval fires during the struggle for Iwo. Having spent months preparing his citadel, and having observed the opening days of battle ashore, few were positioned to analyze American military power as well as Kuribayashi.

From his underground command bunker, Kuribayashi's staff recorded the general's candid admission: "I am not afraid of the fighting power of only three American Marine Divisions if there are no bombardments from aircraft and warships. This is the only reason why we have to see such a miserable situation."[94] One of Kuribayashi's principal staff officers and one of the few Japanese survivors from Iwo Jima, Major Yoshitaka Horie, recalled a similar realization, writing, "When I look back at the Japanese defense plan and battle of Iwo Jima, I must pay many respects to the overwhelming material quantity and skillful operations of American forces."[95]

The U.S. success in both aerial and naval fire support at Iwo Jima was founded upon an exceptional degree of triphibious cooperation. American commanders, from the task force and corps level down to the front-line company, were quick to acknowledge that achievement. "No operation," Admiral Turner stated in a mid-battle interview aboard his flagship, "has ever shown a more close and sincere cooperation among all the services—the army, the navy, the marines, the coast guard . . . whether they operate in the air on the surface or under the surface. All of these elements have played vital parts in this offensive."[96] Turner's Marine counterpart, Holland Smith—himself habitually guilty of service parochialism—reinforced the reflection: "In fact, I think we have one of the finest fighting teams in the world right here in the Fifth Amphibious Force, which includes men in all the services. Credit belongs to all of them as American fighting men—not to any one branch of the service."[97] Captain Stearns concluded much the same: "Close cooperation between air, ground, and sea units was excellent throughout the entire campaign."[98] In recognizing the extraordinary harmony of American combined operations at Iwo Jima, Turner, Smith, and Stearns were paying respect to the highly evolved system of triphibious fire control and coordination. The island demanded the highest degree of cooperation from U.S. aircraft, battleships, artillery battalions, and infantry units. On the back of their triphibious coordination teams, the Americans seized Iwo Jima.

CHAPTER 8

EXAMINING SUCCESS

THE LEGACY OF AMERICAN FIRE CONTROL AND COORDINATION

Bloody as it was, victory on Iwo Jima delivered the very spoils that had lured American commanders there in the first place. The Allies secured their emergency landing strip, emplaced their forward fighter base, and tightened their strategic noose around Tokyo. Along the way, the Marines' flag raising on Mount Suribachi provided a jolt to the war-weary American public.[1] Though criticism would develop over time, the benefits of seizing Iwo Jima were, in 1945, both tangible and compelling.[2] Taken in sum, the Battle of Iwo Jima confirmed the conflict's irreversible trends: American gains on the ground promised eventual if costly triumph as Japan's ability to make war approached the point of collapse.

Though it could not have known it at the time, the V Corps would not have to fight again in the Pacific. In the ensuing months, the unit prepared diligently for its next grisly assignment—an amphibious assault on the Japanese home island of Kyushu. In support of Operation Olympic, Major General Harry Schmidt was to put his corps ashore on southwestern Kyushu, flanked to its right by the U.S. Army's XI Corps and I Corps. Olympic called for a staggering 300,000 combat troops, with an ever-extending train of Army, Navy, and Marine combat support personnel that brought the operation's total troop count to 693,295.[3] It was to be, without question, the largest amphibious operation in American history. But the attack never came. As history would have it, Iwo Jima marked the V Corps' final battle.

Even as Schmidt's Marines escaped the misery of a home island invasion, the war dragged on in other ways and for other troops. The conflict's final outcome was clearly decided, but its ultimate price in human life and length in calendar days remained under passionate dispute through the late spring and summer of 1945. In fact, the war's destruction had only begun to climax as the Marines cleared the last of Kuribayashi's bunkers on Iwo Jima. Just days before Holland Smith declared the island secure, U.S. Army Air Forces General Curtis LeMay initiated one of the war's most destructive urban bombing campaigns. With a fleet of more than three hundred B-29 Superfortresses loaded with the Americans' recently developed M69 incendiary bombs, LeMay targeted Tokyo's industrial center on the night of March 9–10, 1945. The results were equal parts spectacular and horrific. The bombers leveled some fifteen square miles of the city, killed nearly 100,000 Japanese, and displaced hundreds of thousands of civilians. The raids continued throughout the spring, spreading their flames to Nagoya, Osaka, Yokohama, Kobe, and Kawasaki.[4] By historian Richard B. Franks' count, the incendiary bombing campaign razed more than 105 square miles, destroyed 1.4 million homes, and killed at least 126,000.[5]

The Allies' assault on Okinawa the following month may have lacked the flair of LeMay's firebombing revolution, but it promised comparable destruction for the American servicemen, Japanese troops, and local civilians that endured it. The success of the initial landing encouraged U.S. commanders, and Simon Buckner's Tenth Army (composed of one corps each of Army and Marine forces) made welcome progress for the first week. But Japanese General Mitsuru Ushijima had not intended to resist the initial landings; he planned all along to fight from the island's rugged interior. Aided by Okinawa's springtime monsoon rains, Ushijima carried out a punishing and methodical defense of the outpost. American units drove their attack forward in fits and starts, and the battle deteriorated into a three-month slog defined by mud, artillery shells, and nervous breakdowns.[6] In the end, peace on Okinawa came at a terrible cost: more than 110,000 Japanese soldiers and 12,000 American troops lost their lives. The island's native community suffered 120,000 deaths, an astounding one-third of its recorded population. Yet even here, the conflict had not reached its apogee. As historian Joseph Wheelan points out, even the Okinawa struggle "was neither the climax nor the resolution of the Pacific War."[7]

It took the introduction of the Americans' newly developed atomic bombs in early August 1945, alongside the threat of Soviet entry into the war, to wring peace from Japan's government.[8] Understandably, the weapons became a spectacle of unlimited proportion. And historians have spared little ink debating the justification, decisions, and historical circumstances surrounding the bombs' use. In their proper context, however, the atomic weapons that annihilated Hiroshima and Nagasaki in the summer of 1945 were far more representative of the Pacific War than any observer—then or now—would care to acknowledge. The weapons were certainly revolutionary in their technological achievement and grandeur, but their effect was an all-too-familiar reminder of a war that had offered little mercy for four years. The violence, tenacity, and barbarity of the contest were defined not only by nuclear weapons, but also by naval shellings, aircraft bombings, and hand-to-hand fighting.

PLACING AMERICAN SUCCESS: COMBINED OPERATIONS ASHORE AND AFLOAT

In 1907, well before the outbreak of World War I, British major Gerald Gilbert of the British Indian army chastised his peers for their professional introversion: "We have gotten into the fashion of talking of cavalry tactics, artillery tactics, and infantry tactics. This distinction is nothing but a mere abstraction. . . . There is but one art, and that is the tactics of the combined arms."[9] Though Gilbert focused almost exclusively on the integration of foot soldiers, cavalry units, and cumbersome field artillery pieces, his conclusion captured the essence of war in the twentieth century. The challenge of the combined arms approach—particularly in an age of rapid technological change—defined the battlefields of both world wars and often determined an army's success. Gilbert may not have predicted the integration of motorized military vehicles, tanks, or airplanes, but the spirit of his critique remained germane for decades to come.

If land-based operations were difficult enough to combine and coordinate, the open ocean aggravated the martial challenge. Accordingly, throughout the interwar period, reengineering the amphibious assault remained an unsettled—and neglected—military chore. The ocean itself was problematic for a litany of reasons, and the vulnerable transition from sea to shore made the exercise all the more daunting. Even for the accomplished and self-assured Germans, who seemed to have mastered the combination of arms ashore in the opening blows of World War II, the task gave serious cause for concern. At the pinnacle of Nazi supremacy in 1940, Berlin's plan to attack Britain from the sea remained—at best—a dubious proposal. With insufficient naval strength of his own and a still-capable British fleet in defense, Operation Sea Lion was little short of a pipe dream for Hitler.[10]

For the Americans, the development of amphibious warfare had fallen to the U.S. Marine Corps. In concert with the U.S. Navy, and initially driven by a string of visionary commandants in the 1920s and 1930s, the Marines studied, wrestled with, and refined their approach to the amphibious assault. The early years of World War II gave the Corps much-needed experience that allowed it to mature its interwar theory into practical wisdom. By the end of the war, the Marines had transformed a previously inconceivable operation into a cornerstone of Allied strategy. None other than Chief of Naval Operations Ernest King remarked that "the outstanding development of this war, in the field of joint undertakings, was the perfection of amphibious operations, the most difficult of all operations in modern warfare."[11] Combat journalist Robert Sherrod gave the Marines similar marks, designating their advance in the Central Pacific "a campaign which has no precedent in history."[12] Even when the contemporary hyperbole receded, the service's accomplishment remained. As one military historian summarized it, the Corps' work in the amphibious assault was "a major contribution (perhaps the major contribution)" in the Allies' operational success of World War II.[13]

Just as Marine proficiency in amphibious warfare was essential to Allied victory, the effective control and coordination of air and naval gunfire support were essential to the Marines' operational success. American infantry—aided by flamethrowers, tanks, and hand grenades—may have finished the tactical jobs in places such as Saipan, Peleliu, Iwo Jima, and Okinawa, but it was U.S. naval gunfire, air support, and field artillery that sustained the assaults from ship to shore and contributed to their final success. As evidenced by the story of the V Corps, these supporting arms directly enabled the Americans' initial landing and then buttressed their continued assault across Japanese-held beaches and island interiors. The supporting gunfire was indispensable, and the coordination teams that directed it were equally critical.

The Americans' ability to mount tremendous synchronized triphibious firepower at the beachhead demands recognition, and the U.S. Navy and Marine Corps' ability to seize any fortified Japanese island of its choice by 1945 deserves similar acknowledgment. What had begun as an intellectual exercise in the interwar lull became a finely tuned and unprecedented application of combat power. And the V Corps achieved it through a gradual and determined process of wartime adaptation.

THE WARTIME EVOLUTION OF TRIPHIBIOUS FIRES IN THE PACIFIC WAR

The United States' operational achievements in the Pacific have gone underrecognized, in part because they lacked the Germans' immediate and conspicuous expertise. Marine and Navy planners of the interwar period recognized but did not rectify the challenges of delivering and integrating supporting firepower during a triphibious operation. In many cases, their attention was simply absorbed by more pressing concerns (as they perceived them at the time), such as logistics, shipping, communications, intelligence, and equipment.[14] Generally, the staff officers that did contemplate the coordination of supporting arms felt confident in their theoretical solutions. Certainly, they believed, American naval shells and air-delivered bombs would find their targets. Certainly, they said, those shells and bombs would provide the support necessary to place men ashore. And of course, such supporting efforts would complement, not impede or endanger, the attacking infantry. Just as the soldiers and Marines of World War I learned to creep behind a protective wall of artillery fire, so too would American troops storm ashore behind effective air and naval fire support. But as war so often reveals, theoretical solutions devoid of practical experience are only part of the puzzle.

The Marines' misplaced confidence resulted in both insufficient doctrine and artificial training exercises throughout the 1930s. In spite of its many outstanding contributions to the theory of amphibious warfare, the Marines' 1934 *Tentative Manual for Landing Operations* was too prescriptive, too formulaic, and too optimistic. The manual acknowledged but did not elaborate on the need for mutual understanding across the dissimilar components of a triphibious force. While the authors dedicated more than eleven pages to discussions on ship firing positions, targeting techniques, ammunition characteristics, and fuze combinations, they committed just two pages to fire control parties and the coordination of naval gunfire.[15] As in their earlier assessments, planners assumed that coordination would come naturally. Their doctrine, untested in combat, presumed a degree of familiarity and trust among American forces and military specialties. In reality, American forces in the Pacific would spend the first two years of the war building, strengthening, and finally enjoying effective integration and complementary confidence across its many disparate units.

Guadalcanal provided important lessons ashore, but the landing itself was unopposed, thus delaying the Americans' true reckoning with the coordination of triphibious fires. The pilots, artillerymen, and infantry forces learned to cooperate at the tactical level, but they were not tested at the seam of the surf and the sand, nor were they challenged with a capable, equipped, and premeditated beach defense. Tarawa, instead, served as the first true crucible. In that operation, U.S. troops utterly failed to calibrate and coordinate their offshore fire support: the Marines' umbrella of firepower ended nearly half an hour before the infantrymen waded ashore; U.S. air support floundered through several paralyzing delays and disruptions; and the ground units of the V Corps labored to apply their supporting fires.[16] Though the Marines secured Tarawa's Betio Island, it came at a harrowing price—3,400 casualties in just three days of combat for a meager outpost less than one square mile in size.[17] As the British diplomat Lord William Eden wondered after the Crown's costly triumph on Bunker Hill in 1775: "If we have eight more such victories, there will be nobody left to bring the news of them."[18]

In the subsequent campaigns of the war, American officers created a number of imaginative fire control and coordination solutions that enabled the Allies' advance across the Central Pacific. Their efforts spanned the military spectrum, from the structural and administrative to the technological and tactical. In most cases, the efforts complemented one another and contributed to the holistic progress of the Navy–Marine Corps task forces.

In October 1943 the V Corps' christening of the naval gunfire training section at Kahoolawe, Hawaii, provided a structural upgrade that returned dividends for the remainder of the conflict. Led at first by the tenacious Donald Weller, the center aimed to improve unit skills in naval gunnery, communications, and cross-unit cooperation. Within months, the school established itself as a linchpin of American operational success in the Pacific. The island's veteran cadre of instructors built a baseline curriculum for coordination teams and then integrated combat lessons from their peers on the front lines, creating a nerve center for wartime adaptation. As it indoctrinated fresh troops traveling west from the United States and refined battlefield experiences traveling east from the war, Kahoolawe trained an astonishing eight hundred ships along with their respective control teams between 1943 and 1945.[19]

The joint assault signal companies that emerged in late 1943 played an equally critical role in the V Corps' success. As evidenced in the struggle for Tarawa, the disparate components of the American task force lacked both familiarity with and confidence in one another. In particular, fire control and coordination teams needed to share battlefield information more freely, communicate progress and objectives more reliably, and otherwise blend their efforts into polished, comprehensive action.[20] Despite their unique responsibilities, victory depended upon the efficient integration and careful coordination of subordinate air, naval, and land components. In Tarawa's wake, that ambitious charge fell to the novel JASCOs. They became—in fact if not in title—the conductors of the American assaults through the Marshall, Mariana, and Bonin islands. As the record later proved, only cooperative and responsive triphibious fire support could enable the V Corps' seizure of the Japanese island fortresses that spanned the Central Pacific.

By the end of 1944 the JASCOs had convincingly established their worth in the Allied war effort. In line with their charter, the companies initiated shipboard visits between amphibious landings, allowing air, ground, and naval representatives to generate cohesion and share combat lessons. Though their focus lay primarily on the coordination of supporting arms, the practice helped to spur cooperation of a more general nature. The JASCOs began to root themselves within both the purpose and the culture of the landing force while they established a personal rapport that facilitated collaboration in combat.[21] In subsequent attacks against Roi-Namur, Saipan, and Iwo Jima, these human networks permitted effective and responsive fires. Even at war, as the cliche has it, cooperation and coordination remained a "people business."

In their campaign for the Marshalls in the summer and fall of 1944, the V Corps advanced underneath a dependable synergy of triphibious fire support. The shipboard conferences helped sustain success, and battlefield coordination techniques continued to improve. By prioritizing requests more efficiently and curbing redundancy within the task force, JASCO shore fire control and air liaison parties produced responsive coverage ashore. American control teams initiated a common coordination frequency for urgent missions, and ground commanders enjoyed more flexible support from the ships offshore and planes overhead.[22] At the same time, Kahoolawe's naval gunfire training section intensified both its training curriculum and its standards for naval gunnery crews, aviators, and fire control teams, ensuring that American amphibious forces received the most capable and experienced troops available.[23]

In the contest for Iwo Jima, the V Corps displayed its most advanced approach to the control and coordination of air and naval support. Their use of a "rolling" naval barrage carefully coordinated through mobile shore fire control parties deserves recognition as one of the most daring, and ultimately successful, undertakings in modern military history. As so often is the case in war, it was the action's great risk that delivered its considerable profit. Underneath what the commanding general termed the "vital continuation" of naval fire support, the Marines first secured a foothold and then expanded their grasp on the fortified island.[24]

Vernon Megee's front-line air control team (the LFASCU) was a comparable tactical gamble on Iwo Jima. Based on their experience in the

Central Pacific, Megee's men insisted that localized, shore-based control of close air support planes would deliver more flexible and effective aviation fires. By battle's end, Megee's team convinced its fellow Marines, with one troop calling the local air control an "absolute necessity" in amphibious warfare.[25] Megee's arrangement was sound, and shore-based aircraft control teams became a staple of American amphibious units following the war. The LFASCU's footprint has only grown in the twenty-first century, where a dizzying repertoire of shore-based teams to include the tactical air command center, the direct air support center, and the tactical air control party, integrates U.S. air support on the modern battlefield.[26]

The assault on Iwo Jima both symbolized and validated the V Corps' wartime mastery of the amphibious assault. In particular, the unit's ability to mass coordinated fire support through creative battlefield techniques captured the very essence of its story over the preceding two and a half years. Aided by greater and greater amounts of more effectively coordinated air and naval firepower, the Americans seized increasingly difficult objectives across the Pacific between 1942 and 1945. Though the bullets, bombs, and shells were significant in their own right, it was the coordination teams—the very conductors of firepower—that enabled success.

The months and years following the V Corps' assault on Iwo Jima confirmed the wisdom of the unit's fire support concepts and coordination teams. Navy and Marine authors alike flooded the service journal *Marine Corps Gazette* with fourteen articles professing confidence in the wartime techniques and outfits. Writers complemented the JASCOs' adaptive nature, encouraged the unified spirit of the coordination teams, and applauded the audacious "creeping" naval barrage executed on Iwo Jima.[27] Though the majority of Marine officers entered the war unsure or even dismissive of naval gunfire capabilities, they learned to rely upon sea-based fires as the "artillery of the landing force."[28] Weller himself acknowledged his own surprise, declaring that "naval gunfire support achieved results which nobody could have ever really thought back in the [interwar] days when we were fiddling around in the Caribbean and trying to develop the capability. It outscored anything I ever had in mind by a quantum amount."[29] Marine colonel Robert Heinl emerged with the same conviction, writing that "an untried and obscure specialty, had, by 1945, become a sine qua non of amphibious assault."[30]

But combat effectiveness should not be the only metric of achievement. In his classic study of the U.S. Marine Corps, Allan R. Millett argued that "operational [military] history should be evaluated for its impact on the service and not solely its impact on the course of the war."[31] Applying his logic, the postwar growth and continued development of the JASCOs and their subordinate outfits evidenced their broader success and enduring utility within the Marine Corps. For a brief period following the war, the JASCOs dropped their joint designation and became merely assault signal companies. Before long, service leaders recast them again under a novel title, this time air-naval gunfire liaison companies (ANGLICOs). In spite of the dizzying rotation of titles, the companies sustained their primary purpose throughout the brief years of peace and into the United States' war on the Korean peninsula. The ANGLICOs' task organization changed little in that time—assigned in support of one Marine division, the companies provided a naval gunfire and air support section to each of the division's three regiments and nine battalions, along with one senior advisory team attached to the ground commander's staff. In battle, they retained their commission to "control, coordinate, and advise" naval and air assets in support of the landing force.[32]

Whether serendipitous or calculated, the ANGLICOs helped the Marine Corps to strengthen its institutional claim on amphibious capabilities in the immediate postwar years. As the Army drew back from its amphibious operations of World War II to accommodate a focus on large-scale land operations, the Joint Chiefs of Staff turned to the Marine Corps to maintain its proficiency in amphibious operations and in fact lead the fellow services in that sphere. Provisions went so far to include a Marine-organized ANGLICO designed to serve with U.S. Army infantry forces as necessary in wartime. Better to let the Marines apply the triphibious fires, the joint chiefs seemed to say.[33] Through its recognized achievements in the Pacific and its sharp sense of institutional purpose, the Marine Corps protected its existence and its health. Though both natural and appropriate at the time, the move complemented Marine parochialism and buttressed its twentieth-century efforts at bureaucratic survival.

EXPLAINING AMERICAN EXPERTISE AND TRIUMPH

What conditions, then, allowed the V Corps to successfully adapt its firing techniques, coordination efforts, training priorities, and even task organization in the two and a half years of war between Guadalcanal and Iwo Jima? Theo Farrell succinctly summarized a conventional answer: "war forces states and their militaries to adapt."[34] In this narrative, the adaptor triumphs, and the stubborn traditionalist pays with the lives of his troops. But such general explanations fail to differentiate why some armies innovate and adapt well while others struggle, or why one combatant adapts more rapidly or more decisively than his opponent.

Scholar Adam Grissom moves us closer to an answer. In 2006 he summarized the field of military innovation studies by declaring four contemporary models: the civil-military school, the interservice school, the intraservice model, and the cultural model. Though the categories are not rigid, the four schools are defined primarily by their innovation catalyst—Grissom's civil-military school is driven by external civilian initiative, the interservice school by competition among branches, the intraservice school by competition between a single service's various communities, and the cultural school by an army's distinctive organizational culture.[35] As Grissom himself acknowledged, the four existing models focused primarily on top-down theory, where senior uniformed leaders or policy makers forced change upon their institutions. Instead, Grissom petitioned more scholars to investigate bottom-up adaptation and innovation. How do troops on the front lines devise and incorporate new methods? And what conditions allow for successful battlefield adaptation?

The wartime innovation and adaptation of the joint assault signal companies, shore fire control parties, air liaison parties, and landing force air support control units represented Grissom's organizational culture school, where a blend of identity, purpose, and wartime pressures enabled successful progress. And the Marine Corps' understanding of warfare—to include the significance of flexibility—provided particularly fertile ground for wartime change.[36] It was, in fact, the Corps' enduring focus on the human elements of war that made the problem of triphibious firepower coordination a manageable task. As military historian Aaron O'Connell argued in his study on the twentieth-century Marine Corps, "They were the service least enamored with machines and computers and most committed to intimate, spiritual, and transcendent themes."[37] Their outlook on war championed teamwork over material solutions. Supportive but skeptical of new technology, the Marines pursued practical, human-focused solutions.

The V Corps itself elevated the human element of warfare as it strove for practical solutions in the Central Pacific. Setting aside grand theories and formulaic models, the V Corps understood that war was a dynamic and disordered affair best solved by art rather than science. The unit pursued a culture of understanding across its disparate components, hopeful that it would enable success. Whether in organizing shipboard conferences for fire support planning between campaigns, directing the careful cross-unit management of a rolling naval barrage on Iwo Jima, or shifting aircraft control authority ashore to better serve the landing force, the Marines placed a premium on flexibility, human relationships, and practical battlefield solutions.

Bottom-up adaptation drove much of the Americans' progress, and the efforts of junior and mid-level American officers compel recognition. Naval gunnery experts such as Lieutenant Charles Corben provided candid critique—and deserved praise—following each Central Pacific landing. Whether commenting on ship positioning, targeting techniques, communications procedures, or cross-unit cooperation, men like Corben championed the ideas that worked, doctored the concepts that needed attention, and dismissed the faulty practices. Others, such as Weller and Megee, complemented Corben's reflections by proposing bold new measures to improve the effectiveness and efficiency of American fire support. They operated in a constant feedback loop of battle, reflection, and refinement, what scholar James Russell labeled "tactical, ad hoc adaptation."[38]

In addition to confirming Russell's version of adaptation, Corben, Weller, and Megee fall under scholar Paul Kennedy's 2013 label: the "engineers of victory."[39] These were the officers—so often excluded from the historical narrative—who worked out practical solutions in the field and refined American methods between campaigns. Neither lauded commanders nor front-line riflemen, much of their work has gone unrecognized in the voluminous literature of World War II. Hollywood's motion pictures—ranging from the 1949 movie *Sands of Iwo Jima* to the 2010 miniseries *The Pacific*—sustain a relentless focus on the gallant Marine infantry. However, Marine and Navy lieutenants, captains, majors, and commanders accountable for triphibious fire support contributed novel solutions, supplied forthright critique, and worked out some of the war's most pressing tactical challenges. These men were the "in-between" managers responsible for the messy business of producing battlefield results.

Structure also played a decisive role in the V Corps' advance across the Central Pacific. In his classic 1972 study of the U.S. failure in Vietnam, Robert "Blowtorch Bob" Komer argued that the constraints inherent in American institutions "made it more difficult for them to cope with an unfamiliar conflict environment" in Southeast Asia.[40] It was, he argued, the bureaucratic "weight" of the American armed services that guaranteed an "overly militarized response" in Vietnam. In Komer's caustic but compelling rendering, the Americans' decisive limitation was their "institutional inertia—the built-in reluctance of organizations to change preferred ways of functioning except slowly and incrementally."[41] His catchphrase became both an accurate and a tragic description of the American fiasco: the bureaucracy simply "did its thing."

But if Komer's theory captured the American tragedy in South Vietnam, it also helps account for the United States' success on the far more conventional battlefields of the Pacific War. In the latter case, credit is due to the bureaucratic nature of American military organizations. The V Corps' progress in triphibious fire control and coordination is in fact a tale of modest bureaucratic adaptation and innovation. The unit's developments in triphibious warfare match what scholars Williamson Murray and Allan R. Millett have labeled "evolutionary innovation": a process whereby organizations evolve over time, and one in which "tactics, equipment, and conceptions change on a gradual basis."[42] For the V Corps, the path to final success depended upon persistent, deliberate administrative work. Each wartime operation of the V Corps produced after-action reports averaging more than one thousand pages each.[43] Before the next campaign, staff officers tinkered with manning solutions and coordination networks in the hopes of realizing the most effective path forward. Prior to its official adoption, the JASCO proposal, meant to address glaring deficiencies in triphibious coordination, travelled to the highest uniformed leaders of the American military, the Joint Chiefs of Staff themselves. It was in fact their blessing that guaranteed sufficient resources and appropriate visibility for the JASCO concept.[44] In sum, the incremental, painstaking process that Komer rightfully lamented in Vietnam helped to produce common and comprehensive solutions in the Central Pacific.

Certainly, the V Corps' progress in triphibious fire control and coordination contributed to the Allies' success in the Pacific. The island landings of 1944 and 1945 in particular were utterly dependent upon overwhelming fire support from American ships and planes. But the fire support itself—the mere presence of bombs and shells—was of little value without precise and timely coordination. Arriving to the battlefield with more pallets of ammunition than your opponent does not guarantee conquest. Alongside overwhelming industrial production, American triumph required careful human adaptation and patient but determined institutional learning. Only well-coordinated and highly flexible air and naval support could put the landing force ashore and then sustain its advance across the objective.

The story of American fire control and coordination in the Pacific War suggests that irrespective of technological advancement, war requires fundamentally human solutions. Combat is, after all, a deeply interactive and dynamic process. Of course, material advantage is preferable, often necessary. But in the case of the V Corps, the aircraft, ships, and artillery pieces were never enough on their own. Triphibious war in the Central Pacific demanded relational, artistic solutions that no device could provide. Military mass aided the Americans, but their advance across the Gilberts, Marshalls, Marianas, and Bonins also depended upon their ability to produce flexible solutions and fight as a cohesive team.

American efforts to coordinate air, naval, and land actions in the Pacific War reflect scholar Stephen Biddle's understated observation that "combined arms tactics impose high orders of complexity."[45] For the V Corps, the challenge of calibrating and harmonizing disparate ships, planes, landing craft, and infantry units in the heat of battle was no simple charge. Legendary U.S. Army general George Patton might have captured the challenge best in 1941, on the eve of American entry into World War II:

> There is still a tendency in each separate unit . . . to be a onehanded puncher. By that I mean that the rifleman wants to shoot, the tanker to charge, the artilleryman to fire. . . . That is not the way to win battles. If the band played a piece first with the piccolo, then with the brass horn, then with the clarinet, and then with the trumpet, there would be a hell of a lot of noise but no music. To get harmony in music each instrument must support the others. To get harmony in battle, each weapon must support the other. Team play wins.[46]

Though the Army officer did not share a common uniform with the V Corps, his remarks struck at the very core of its task in the Central Pacific, where team play won indeed.

TRIPHIBIOUS WAR BEYOND THE CENTRAL PACIFIC

In a fitting conclusion to his 2001 *Combined Arms Warfare in the Twentieth Century*, historian Jonathan M. House wrote that "individual weapons, however powerful, do not win wars."[47] His maxim cannot be overstated. In the experience of the V Corps, it was the effective combination of military power that enabled victory for the United States. Though naval gunfire, air support, field artillery, and tank-infantry assaults all proved essential, not one of these capabilities was sufficient on its own. Rather, the synergy of triphibious operations and firepower permitted American success on the battlefields of the Central Pacific.

The Navy and Marine Corps' development of triphibious war did not begin with Yamamoto's startling attack at Pearl Harbor in late 1941, nor did it end with the official Japanese surrender aboard the battleship *Missouri* in the autumn of 1945. As this study reveals, the story was more prolonged, more dynamic, and more interesting. The services' interwar doctrine and fleet exercises of the 1930s provided an insufficient but critical foundation for this novel brand of warfare prior to the opening salvos of World War

II. In the Americans' ensuing twentieth-century military ventures on the Korean Peninsula and in Southeast Asia, they furthered their mastery of the triphibious approach. Despite challenging and eventually insurmountable political hurdles in these subsequent conflicts, American units continued to display marked proficiency in the coordination of fire support from land, sea, and air. And that proficiency sustained U.S. operational success.

During the Marines' famed landing at Inchon in September 1950, Army General Douglas MacArthur relied upon both prelanding and accompanying naval and aerial fire support to place his troops ashore. Cruisers and destroyers of Joint Task Force 7 and aircraft from Fast Carrier Task Force 77 supported the landing with preparatory fires and sustained on-call support. On the peninsula, American forces benefitted from many of the operational lessons that the V Corps had drawn from the Pacific War, including the use of tactical fire control parties (now organized within ANGLICOs rather than JASCOs), fire coordination "ceilings" that enabled simultaneous air attacks by American Corsairs, and deliberate on-call targeting procedures for increased safety and responsiveness.[48]

Throughout the assault, U.S. ships and aircraft protected and sustained the landing force. In one particular attack on the afternoon of D-day, September 15, Marine and Navy Corsairs and Skyraiders flew above and beyond the fire of American ships, orchestrating an expert umbrella of fire support for the landed Marines. At another vulnerable moment with allied troops advancing beyond Inchon's urban area on September 21, heavy cruisers *Toledo* and *Rochester* delivered more than five hundred 8-inch shells onto enemy positions and allowed South Korean marines to annihilate a company of North Korean fighters.[49] Just as in the Central Pacific five years earlier, American triphibious fires enabled the advance of the landing party.

A decade and a half later—this time in South Vietnam—the Americans again displayed impressive coordination in a joint land, sea, and air attack when U.S. Marines engaged in their opening bout of the Vietnam War. In August 1965 offshore firepower and aviation support played critical roles in the III Marine Amphibious Force's attack south of Chu Lai on the Vietnamese coast during Operation Starlite, an assault meant to disrupt the threat from Viet Cong forces in the region. This time, American Sailors and Marines integrated their destruction with friendly helicopters inserting troops ashore. The short-fused planning, the complexity of the attack, and the proximity to nearby civilian villages all presented significant challenges for the coordination of U.S. firepower; but much as in the closing bouts of the Pacific War, Marine commanders were both impressed and thankful for effective and timely coordination throughout the operation.[50]

With the added challenge of vertical envelopment operations, American fire support specialists in Vietnam continued to ensure effective and timely integration. Two U.S. destroyers and one cruiser alone fired 1,562 high-explosive and illumination rounds during Starlite, and close air support teams—building on the accomplishments of American JASCOs in the Pacific—arranged air strikes within fifty yards of friendly lines. Lewis "Lew" Walt, commanding general of the III Marine Amphibious Force, later determined that Starlite was "one of the most fantastic demonstrations of close air support that I have ever seen."[51] Though American proficiency in triphibious operations could not account for the political hurdles of the war in Vietnam, operational effectiveness remained just the same.

Just as Marine landings of the twentieth century required triphibious support, so too will future combat demand integrated fires from land, sea, air, and even space. As nearly any careful observer will conclude in the present day, the integration of warfare domains will remain a more—not less—relevant military task well into the future. As a result, integrated firepower in all its varieties will remain a central factor of those coinciding domains. And if militaries are to effectively adapt to the circumstances of future war, they must depend upon the collective reformers within the ranks, such as Charles Corben, Donald Weller, and Vernon Megee.[52] Just as American forces learned to fuse the three arms of triphibious war in their bout against Japan, U.S. troops of the twenty-first century will be called upon to effectively and efficiently arrange, integrate, and execute fires from an increasing number of sources. The task will remain challenging; it will also remain decisive.

The apparent omnipotence of technology in the present day can lead military professionals to believe that the combatant with the most advanced jets, most capable submarines, most survivable tanks, and most disruptive cyber tools will dominate the battlefield of tomorrow. But as the record of the V Corps makes clear, the problem of firepower coordination is a human art, not a formulaic science. While technological capabilities and competency matter, the effective combination and delivery of fires depends upon flexibility, creativity, trust, and other intangible elements. In such an environment, faulty concepts and defective teamwork can easily negate material advantages and perfect firing equations. As military historian John Lynn argued nearly twenty years ago in his classic study *Battle: A History of Combat and Culture*, military technology is a "tide that raises all boats." With comparable weapons at the disposal of each adversary, he concluded: "It is, indeed, the conceptual choices that matter most."[53] Certainly, the United States should labor to equip its troops with the most powerful weapons for future combat. But its armed services must—in parallel—master the practical application of those weapons: the inescapable art of controlling, coordinating, and delivering fires.

Particularly as the U.S. Navy and Marine Corps pivot to address peer threats around the world, a renewed focus on the conceptual and human aspects of both firepower coordination and warfare more generally is a valuable investment. The commandant of the U.S. Marine Corps, General David H. Berger, highlighted these fundamental themes in a March 2022 message to his Marines, emphasizing the essential, timeless elements of warfare: "The power of the human will and spirit, the ever-present influence of fog, friction, and chaos; and the likely futility of any approach to warfare that seeks an unattainable certainty or prioritizes a single element of the combined arms equation over the integrated application of the whole."[54] The fire control and coordination specialists that helped deliver victory in the Central Pacific would welcome Berger's nuance and insight, which in many ways acknowledged their own remarkable story of wartime adaptation, combined arms integration, and a relentless focus on waging triphibious war.

NOTES

INTRODUCTION

1. Joseph H. Alexander, *Closing In: Marines in the Seizure of Iwo Jima* (Washington, DC: Marine Corps Historical Center, 1994), 52.
2. Samuel Eliot Morison, *History of United States Naval Operations in World War II*, vol. 14, *Victory in the Pacific: 1945* (Boston: Little, Brown and Company, 1964), 35; Alexander, *Closing In*, 12–17.
3. Ronald H. Spector, *Eagle against the Sun: The American War with Japan* (New York: Vintage Books, 1985); Waldo Heinrichs and Marc Gallicchio, *Implacable Foes: War in the Pacific, 1944–1945* (New York: Oxford University Press, 2017); Allan R. Millett and Williamson Murray, *A War To Be Won: Fighting the Second World War* (Cambridge, MA: Belknap Press, 2000); Gerhard L. Weinberg, *A World at Arms: A Global History of World War II* (New York: Cambridge University Press, 1994).
4. Richard B. Frank, *Tower of Skulls: A History of the Asia-Pacific War, July 1937–May 1942* (New York: W. W. Norton, 2020); John C. McManus, *Fire and Fortitude: The U.S. Army in the Pacific War, 1941–1943* (New York: Dutton Caliber, 2019); Ian W. Toll, *The Conquering Tide: War in the Pacific Islands, 1942–1944* (New York: W. W. Norton, 2016).
5. Phillips Payson O'Brien, *How the War Was Won: Air-Sea Power and Allied Victory in World War II* (Cambridge: Cambridge University Press, 2015).
6. For example, see John Ellis, *Brute Force: Allied Strategy and Tactics in the Second World War* (New York: Viking, 1990), and Max Hastings, *Overlord: D-Day and the Battle for Normandy* (New York: Simon and Schuster, 1984).
7. Allan R. Millett, *Semper Fidelis: The History of the United States Marine Corps*, rev. ed. (New York: The Free Press, 1991); Robert Debs Heinl Jr., *Soldiers of the Sea: The United States Marine Corps, 1775–1962*, 2nd ed. (Baltimore: Nautical and Aviation Publishing Company of America, 1991); Allan R. Millett, "Assault from the Sea: The Development of Amphibious Warfare Between the Wars," in *Military Innovation in the Interwar Period*, ed. Allan R. Millett and Williamson Murray (New York: Cambridge University Press, 1996), 50–95. See also Paul

Kennedy, *Engineers of Victory: The Problem Solvers Who Turned the Tide in the Second World War* (New York: Random House Trade Paperbacks, 2013), 303–13.

8. Jeter A. Isely and Philip A. Crowl, *The U.S. Marines and Amphibious War: Its Theory, and Its Practice in the Pacific* (Princeton, NJ: Princeton University Press, 1951). Additional studies on the Marines' application of amphibious war in the Pacific include John A. Lorelli, *To Foreign Shores: U.S. Amphibious Operations in World War II* (Annapolis, MD: Naval Institute Press, 1995), and Richard Wheeler, *A Special Valor: The U.S. Marines and the Pacific War* (1983; repr. Annapolis, MD: Bluejacket Books, 2006).
9. Sharon Tosi Lacey, *Pacific Blitzkrieg: World War II in the Central Pacific* (Denton: University of North Texas Press, 2013), xvi.
10. Wheeler, *Special Valor*; Joseph H. Alexander, *Storm Landings: Epic Amphibious Battles in the Central Pacific* (Annapolis, MD: Naval Institute Press, 1997).
11. For example, see *Sands of Iwo Jima* (1949) and HBO's miniseries *The Pacific* (2010). The Marine Corps itself, with the support of sympathetic journalists, played a central role in furthering the heroic image of the Marine infantryman. See Aaron B. O'Connell, *Underdogs: The Making of the Modern Marine Corps* (Cambridge, MA: Harvard University Press, 2012), 73–77.
12. John W. Dower, *War without Mercy: Race and Power in the Pacific War* (New York: Pantheon Books, 1986); Peter Schrijvers, *The GI War against Japan: American Soldiers in Asia and the Pacific during World War II* (New York: New York University Press, 2005); and Michael C. C. Adams, *The Best War Ever: America and World War II* (Baltimore: Johns Hopkins University Press, 1994). Historian Craig M. Cameron added notions of mythology and imagery to the theme of racism; see Cameron, *American Samurai: Myth, Imagination, and the Conduct of Battle in the First Marine Division, 1941–1951* (New York: Cambridge University Press, 1994), 1–20.
13. This study joins a growing body of scholarship that counters Dower's thesis by arguing that the ferocious combat conditions of the Pacific

were in fact due to the intense nature of the combat rather than an underlying ideology. See John A. Lynn, *Battle: A History of Combat and Culture, from Ancient Greece to Modern America* (Boulder, CO: Westview, 2003), 219–80; and Cathal J. Nolan, *The Allure of Battle: A History of How Wars Have Been Won and Lost* (New York: Oxford University Press, 2017), 547–48.

14. Michael D. Doubler, *Closing with the Enemy: How GIs Fought the War in Europe, 1944–1945* (Lawrence: University Press of Kansas, 1994); James S. Powell, *Learning Under Fire: The 112th Cavalry Regiment in World War II* (College Station: Texas A&M University Press, 2010); James Jay Carafano, *GI Ingenuity: Improvisation, Technology, and Winning World War II* (Mechanicsburg, PA: Stackpole Books, 2006); Adam Grissom, "The Future of Military Innovation Studies," *Journal of Strategic Studies* 29, no. 5 (October 2006): 905–34; James A. Russell, *Innovation, Transformation, and War: Counterinsurgency Operations in Anbar and Ninewa, Iraq, 2005–2007* (Stanford, CA: Stanford Security Studies, 2011), 30. While overarching theories lag behind, several studies recognize bottom-up military innovation. See Russell, *Innovation, Transformation, and War*; Bruce I. Gudmundsson, *Stormtroop Tactics: Innovation in the German Army, 1914–1918* (1989; repr., Westport, CT: Praeger Publishers, 1995); John A. Nagl, *Learning to Eat Soup with a Knife: Counterinsurgency Lessons from Malaya and Vietnam* (2002; repr., Chicago: University of Chicago Press, 2005); and Keith B. Bickel, *Mars Learning: The Marine Corps' Development of Small Wars Doctrine, 1915–1940* (Boulder, CO: Westview Press, 2001).
15. For notable examples, see Stephen Peter Rosen, *Winning the Next War: Innovation and the Modern Military* (Ithaca, NY: Cornell University Press, 1991); Allan R. Millett and Williamson Murray, eds., *Military Innovation in the Interwar Period* (New York: Cambridge University Press, 1996); and Geoffrey Parker, *The Military Revolution: Military Innovation and the Rise of the West, 1500–1800*, 2nd ed. (New York: Cambridge University Press, 1996).
16. Frank G. Hoffman, *Mars Adapting: Military Change during War* (Annapolis, MD: Naval Institute Press, 2021), 2–3.

17. See book one, particularly chapter eight, of Carl von Clausewitz, *On War*, trans. Michael Howard and Peter Paret (Princeton, NJ: Princeton University Press, 1976).
18. In addition to Hoffman's excellent study, see James A. Russell, Frans Osinga, and Theo Farrell, eds., *Military Adaptation in Afghanistan* (Palo Alto, CA: Stanford Security Studies, 2013); and David Barno and Nora Bensahel, *Adaptation Under Fire: How Militaries Change in Wartime* (New York: Oxford University Press, 2020).
19. Shelford Bidwell and Dominick Graham, *Fire-Power: The British Army Weapons and Theories of War, 1904–1945* (1982; repr., South Yorkshire: Pen and Sword Military Classics, 2004); Stephen Biddle, *Military Power: Explaining Victory and Defeat in Modern Battle* (Princeton, NJ: Princeton University Press, 2004); and Tim Travers, *How the War Was Won: Command and Technology in the British Army on the Western Front, 1917–1918* (New York: Routledge, 1992).
20. Jeremy Black, *Combined Operations: A Global History of Amphibious and Airborne Warfare* (Lanham, MD: Rowman and Littlefield, 2018), ix.
21. Black, 211.

CHAPTER 1. "GETTING THE SHELLS TO FALL WHERE YOU WANT THEM"

This chapter is reprinted with permission from *Marine Corps History*. Chris K. Hemler, "'Getting the Shells to Fall Where You Want Them': Coordinating U.S. Naval Gunfire and Air Support in the Interwar Period," *Marine Corps History* 6, no. 1 (Summer 2020): 5–17, https://doi.org/10.35318/mch.2020060101.

1. For representative interpretations, see Wheeler, "Prologue: The Corps Finds a Mission," in *Special Valor*, 1–3; Victor H. Krulak, *First to Fight: An Inside View of the U.S. Marine Corps* (Annapolis, MD: Naval Institute Press, 1984), 71–87; Dirk Anthony Ballendorf and Merrill Lewis Bartlett, *Pete Ellis: An Amphibious Warfare Prophet, 1880–1923* (Annapolis, MD: Naval Institute Press, 1997), 159–62; David J. Ulbrich, *Preparing for Victory: Thomas Holcomb and the Making of the Modern Marine Corps, 1936–1943* (Annapolis, MD: Naval Institute Press, 2011), 43–70.

2. See Craig C. Felker, *Testing American Sea Power: U.S. Navy Strategic Exercises, 1923–1940* (College Station: Texas A&M University Press, 2007), 88–109; Millett, *Semper Fidelis*, 332–33.
3. Triphibious refers to concurrent land, sea, and air actions.
4. Quoted in Arthur J. Marder, *The Anatomy of British Sea Power: A History of British Naval Policy in the Pre-Dreadnought Era, 1880–1905* (New York: Alfred A. Knopf, 1940), 495.
5. Gunther E. Rothenberg, "From Gallipoli to Guadalcanal," in *Assault from the Sea: Essays on the History of Amphibious Warfare*, ed. Merrill L. Bartlett (Annapolis, MD: Naval Institute Press, 1983).
6. Rothenberg; Isely and Crowl, *Marines and Amphibious War*, 17–21.
7. Theodore L. Gatchel, *At the Water's Edge: Defending against the Modern Amphibious Assault* (Annapolis, MD: Naval Institute Press, 1996), 10.
8. Roger Keyes, *Amphibious Warfare and Combined Operations* (Cambridge: Cambridge University Press, 1943), 53.
9. William G. Haan, "A Positive System of Coast Defense (Army)," *Journal of United States Artillery* 53 (December 1920): 569. Historian Brian Linn labels Haan one of the foremost military thinkers of the post–World War I period. See Brian McAllister Linn, *The Echo of Battle: The Army's Way of War* (Cambridge, MA: Harvard University Press, 2007), 125–26.
10. Angus Murray, "The U.S. Marine Corps and Gallipoli," in *On Contested Shores: The Evolving Role of Amphibious Operations in the History of Warfare*, ed. Timothy Heck and B. A. Friedman (Quantico, VA: Marine Corps University Press, 2020).
11. Millett, *Semper Fidelis*, 303–18.
12. Heinl, *Soldiers of the Sea*, 231–32.
13. Isely and Crowl, *Marines and Amphibious War*, 23–24.
14. Millett, *Semper Fidelis*, 322–25.
15. Quoted in Ballendorf and Bartlett, *Pete Ellis*, 5.
16. Earl H. Ellis, "Advanced Base Operations in Micronesia," Operation Plan 712, Historical Amphibious File (HAF) 165, COLL/3634, Archives Branch, Marine Corps History Division (MCHD), Quantico, VA, 28.

17. See in particular Ballendorf and Bartlett, *Pete Ellis*, 140–1.
18. Isely and Crowl, *Marines and Amphibious War*, 24–26, 33–35; Frank O. Hough, Verle E. Ludwig, and Henry I. Shaw Jr., *History of U.S. Marine Corps Operations in World War II*, vol. 1, *Pearl Harbor to Guadalcanal* (Washington, DC: Government Printing Office, 1966), 11–14; Merwin H. Silverthorn, interview by Benis M. Frank, March 10, 1969, Marine Corps Oral History Collection, Archives Branch, MCHD, Quantico, VA.
19. Felker, *Testing American Sea Power*, 94–100; Heinl, *Soldiers of the Sea*, 258–59. For an inside look at the Marines' interwar development of landing craft, see chapter 5, "Ideas But No Boats," in Krulak, *First to Fight*, 88–99.
20. Murray, "U.S. Marine Corps and Gallipoli," 154.
21. Heinl, *Soldiers of the Sea*, 299–301; Millett, *Semper Fidelis*, 329–31; Isely and Crowl, *Marines and Amphibious War*, 35–36; Oliver Prince Smith, interview by Benis M. Frank, June 9, 1969, Marine Corps Oral History Collection, Archives Branch, MCHD; Bruce Gudmundsson, "Ambiguous Application: The Study of Amphibious Warfare at the Marine Corps Schools, 1920–33," in *On Contested Shores*, 179.
22. Isely and Crowl, 36.
23. Millett, *Semper Fidelis*, 322–43; Isely and Crowl, 34–44.
24. United States Marine Corps, *Tentative Manual for Landing Operations*, 1934, HAF 39, COLL/3634, Archives Branch, MCHD, para. 1-34.
25. USMC, "Chapter II: Employment of Naval Supporting Groups," in *Tentative Manual for Landing Operations*, para. 2-300–25; R. D. Heinl Jr., "Naval Gunfire Support in Landings," *Marine Corps Gazette* 29, no. 9 (September 1945): 40–43; Isely and Crowl, *Marines and Amphibious War*, 38–39, 50. On early twentieth-century naval gunnery, see Trent Hone, "The Gunnery System," in *Learning War: The Evolution of Fighting Doctrine in the U.S. Navy, 1898–1945* (Annapolis, MD: Naval Institute Press, 2018), 55–91.
26. On the Navy's interwar dismissal of naval gunfire and amphibious operations—what the author terms "a strategic afterthought"—see Felker, *Testing American Sea Power*, 88–109.

27. USMC, *Tentative Manual for Landing Operations.*
28. USMC, *Tentative Manual for Landing Operations*, 2-415–428.
29. USMC, *Tentative Manual for Landing Operations*, 2-318.
30. USMC, *Tentative Manual for Landing Operations*, 2-318.
31. Special Board, Marine Corps Schools, "Enclosure A: General Discussion of Landing Operations," in *Naval Gunfire Support of Landings*, February 18, 1931, HAF 66, COLL/3634, Archives Branch, MCHD, 5.
32. "Enclosure A: General Discussion of Landing Operations," 7.
33. "Enclosure A: General Discussion of Landing Operations," 4.
34. "Enclosure A: General Discussion of Landing Operations," 7.
35. Charles Barrett, "Correspondence: Major C. D. Barrett to CDR H. A. Flannigan," October 15, 1931, HAF 70, COLL/3634, Archives Branch, MCHD, 1–2.
36. Barrett, "Correspondence," 2–3.
37. Barrett, "Correspondence," 4.
38. James Breckinridge, "Remarks of General Breckinridge," in "Conference Proceedings Discussing, Approving, or Commenting on the Various Headings and Sub-Headings of the Tentative Manual for Landing Operations," 1934, HAF 41, COLL/3634, Archives Branch, MCHD, 1.
39. "Remarks by Captain Campbell, Aviation Committee, Landing Operations Manual," in "Conference Proceedings Discussing, Approving, or Commenting on the Various Headings and Sub-Headings of the Tentative Manual for Landing Operations," 1.
40. Felker, *Testing American Sea Power*, 100.
41. Felker, 100; Silverthorn interview.
42. U.S. Navy, "Report of the Major General Commandant of the United States Marine Corps," in *Annual Reports of the Navy Department for the Fiscal Year 1932* (Washington, DC: Government Printing Office, 1932), 1163.
43. U.S. Navy, *Annual Report of the Secretary of the Navy for the Fiscal Year 1937* (Washington, DC: Government Printing Office, 1937), 17; U.S. Navy, *Annual Report of the Secretary of the Navy for the Fiscal Year 1939*

(Washington, DC: Government Printing Office, 1939), 19; Millett, *Semper Fidelis*, 320, 335.

44. *Annual Report of the Secretary of the Navy 1937*, 17; *Annual Report of the Secretary of the Navy 1939*, 19; U.S. Navy, *Annual Report of the Secretary of the Navy for the Fiscal Year 1940* (Washington, DC: Government Printing Office, 1940), 18.
45. B. W. Gally, "A History of U.S. Fleet Landing Exercises," July 3, 1939, HAF 73, COLL/3634, Archives Branch, MCHD; Millett, *Semper Fidelis*, 338–40; Krulak, *First to Fight*, 88–99; David S. Nasca, *The Emergence of American Amphibious Warfare, 1898–1945* (Annapolis, MD: Naval Institute Press, 2020), 168–70.
46. Gally, 5–6; Millett, 337–41.
47. W. C. Lemly, "Lessons Learned by Aviation from Fleet Landing Exercise No. 3," 1938, HAF 118, COLL/3634, Archives Branch, MCHD, 1.
48. David L. Nutter, "Gunfire Support in Fleet Landing Exercises," 1939, HAF 73, COLL/3634, Archives Branch, MCHD; Rothenberg, 178; Millett, *Semper Fidelis*, 337–41.
49. Millett, 338.
50. Murray, "The U.S. Marine Corps and Gallipoli," 155–60.
51. "Admiral Ellis," quoted in Gally, "History of U.S. Fleet," 6.
52. Gally, 8.
53. "Report of Gunnery Exercises," in Fleet Training Publication 203–1, 1939, HAF 148, COLL/3634, Archives Branch, MCHD, 44, 46.
54. C. G. Richardson, "Naval Gunfire Support of Landing Operations," 1939, HAF 64, COLL/3634, Archives Branch, MCHD, 4, 33–34.

CHAPTER 2. THE FIRST TEST

1. Samuel Eliot Morison, *History of United States Naval Operations in World War II*, vol. I, *The Rising Sun in the Pacific: 1931–April 1942* (1948; repr., Boston: Little, Brown and Company, 1968), 58–62; Spector, *Eagle against the Sun*, 72–89.
2. Spector, 77.
3. Spector, 82–85.

4. Hough, Ludwig, and Shaw, *History of U.S. Marine Corps Operations*, 70–73.
5. Hough, Ludwig, and Shaw, 84; Spector, *Eagle against the Sun*, 106; John Keegan, *The Second World War* (New York: Penguin Books, 2005), 256–58. See also the classic account from Gordon W. Prange with Donald M. Goldstein and Katherine V. Dillon, *At Dawn We Slept: The Untold Story of Pearl Harbor* (1981; repr., New York: Penguin, 2001).
6. Winston S. Churchill, *The Second World War*, vol. IV, *The Hinge of Fate* (Boston: Houghton Mifflin, 1950), 92.
7. Contemporary military rations hovered around four thousand calories per day. Thus, in some cases, quarter-rations dropped below one thousand calories per day.
8. Spector, *Eagle against the Sun*, 101–6.
9. Spector, 168–76.
10. Spector, 185–86; Isely and Crowl, *Marines and Amphibious War*, 72–73.
11. A. A. Vandegrift and Robert B. Asprey, *Once a Marine: The Memoirs of General A. A. Vandegrift, Commandant of the U.S. Marines in World War II* (New York: Ballantine Books, 1964), 100.
12. Isely and Crowl, *Marines and Amphibious War*, 87; Spector, *Eagle against the Sun*, 186–87.
13. A. A. Vandegrift, "Phase II," in *1st Marine Division Commander's Final Report on Guadalcanal*, vol. I, July 1, 1943, HAF, COLL/3654, MCHD, 1–14; Vandegrift, "Phase III," in *1st Marine Division Commander's Final Report on Guadalcanal*, vol. I, July 1, 1943, HAF, COLL/3654, MCHD, 1–11; Millett, *Semper Fidelis*, 364–71.
14. William F. Halsey Jr., "Bombardment of Enemy Positions on Guadalcanal, October 17, 1942," December 1942, HAF, COLL/3654, MCHD, 1.
15. "Enclosure (A): Commander Task Unit 64.5.1 Secret Serial 021 of 18 October 1942," in Halsey, "Bombardment of Enemy Positions on Guadalcanal, October 17, 1942," 2.
16. U.S. Fleet, Headquarters of the Commander in Chief, *Battle Experience: Solomon Islands and Alaskan Actions, January–February 1943*, Bulletin no. 6 (Washington, DC: Headquarters of the Commander in Chief, U.S. Navy, 1944), 37-2–11.

17. "Interview of Major John Smith, USMC, VMF Squadron 223, Guadalcanal Island," November 10, 1942, HAF, COLL/3654, MCHD, 14.
18. "Notes on Conference with Brig. Gen. Pedro del Valle, USMC, Artillery Officer, 1st Marine Division," in *Interviews and Statements by Officers of the 1st Marine Division on the Guadalcanal Operations, December 5, 1942–January 19, 1943*, compiled by Colonel B. Q. Jones, G.S.C., January 19, 1943, https://cgsc.contentdm.oclc.org/digital/collection/p4013coll8/id/4338/rec/1, 3.
19. "Notes on Conference with Brig. Gen. Pedro del Valle, USMC," 2–4.
20. "Notes on Talk with Major Walt, 5th Marines," in Jones, 3.
21. Thomas B. Hughes, "Annex E: Artillery Phase IV," in *1st Marine Division Commander's Final Report on Guadalcanal*, vol. II, July 1, 1943, HAF, COLL/3654, MCHD, 1–3; Hughes, "Annex R: Artillery Phase V," in *1st Marine Division Commander's Final Report on Guadalcanal*, vol. II, 1–5.
22. A. A. Vandegrift, "Final Report on Guadalcanal Operation," in *1st Marine Division Commander's Final Report on Guadalcanal*, vol. II, 33; Vandegrift and Asprey, *Once a Marine*, 213–14.
23. "Cactus" served as the U.S. code name for the island of Guadalcanal. Millett, *Semper Fidelis*, 370–71; Isely and Crowl, *Marines and Amphibious War*, 165; Richard Frank, *Guadalcanal: The Definitive Account of the Landmark Battle* (New York: Penguin Books, 1990), 59–72, 596–98.
24. Hughes, "Annex R: Artillery Phase V," 4.
25. Vandegrift, "Final Report on Guadalcanal Operation," 6.
26. Vandegrift, 6.
27. "War in the Southwest Pacific," in Jones, 4.
28. "War in the Southwest Pacific," 7.
29. Hughes, "Annex R: Artillery Phase V," 4.
30. "Conference with Lt. Col. William Twining, U.S. Marines, G-3 of 1st Marine Division in Guadalcanal," in Jones, 3.
31. "Notes on Conference with Brig. Gen. Pedro del Valle," 2–3.
32. Hough, Ludwig, and Shaw, *History of U.S. Marine Corps Operations*, 371–74; Millett, *Semper Fidelis*, 369; Keegan, *Second World War*, 292.

33. Captain William J. McKennan account quoted in Marlin Groft, *Bloody Ridge and Beyond: A World War II Marine's Memoir of Edson's Raiders in the Pacific* (New York: Dutton Caliber, 2014),144; Keegan, 292.
34. Quoted in Herbert Christian Laing Merillat, *The Island: A History of the First Marine Division on Guadalcanal* (Yardley, PA: Westholme, 2010), 33.
35. Isely and Crowl, *Marines and Amphibious War*, 165.
36. Famously, after assuming office, King changed the latter position's acronym from CINCUS to COMINCH, believing that the pronunciation of the old abbreviation ("SINK US") was unbecoming of both his individual position and his beloved service.
37. Spector, *Eagle against the Sun*, 252–53; Millett, *Semper Fidelis*, 388–93; Isely and Crowl, *Marines and Amphibious War*, 192–203.
38. Many celebrate Holland Smith as the Marine Corps' "father" of amphibious warfare. For a balanced and succinct biography, see Anne Cipriano Venzon, *From Whaleboats to Amphibious Warfare: Lt. Gen. "Howling Mad" Smith and the U.S. Marine Corps* (Westport, CT: Praeger, 2003).
39. Quoted in Joseph H. Alexander, *Across the Reef: The Marine Assault of Tarawa* (Washington, DC: Marine Corps Historical Center, 1993), 4; Gatchel, *At the Water's Edge*, 119–20.
40. Millett, *Semper Fidelis*, 393–95.
41. Gatchel, *At the Water's Edge*, 121; Isely and Crowl, *Marines and Amphibious War*, 201; Alexander, *Across the Reef*, 6–7; James P. McGrath III, "Missing the Mark: Lessons in Naval Gunfire Support at Tarawa," in Heck and Friedman, *On Contested Shores*, 224–25.
42. Robert Sherrod, *Tarawa: The Incredible Story of One of World War II's Bloodiest Battles* (1944; repr., New York: Skyhorse Publishing, 2013), 62.
43. Arwin Bowden, interview by Floyd Cox and Becky Lindig, World War II Veterans Oral History Collection, Nimitz Education and Research Center (NERC), Fredericksburg, TX, March 9, 2000.
44. Samuel Eliot Morison, *History of United States Naval Operations in World War II*, vol. VII, *Aleutians, Gilberts, and Marshalls: June 1942–April 1944* (1951; repr., Edison, NJ: Castle Books, 2001), 156–61; Alexander, *Across the Reef*, 8–9. In the weeks before the attack, intelligence officers

labored to determine if the LCVPs would have enough clearance over the reef. One New Zealand naval reserve officer with fifteen years of sailing experience off Tarawa remained adamant that the Americans would not get their craft over the obstacle: "There won't be three feet of water on the reef!" See Alexander, *Across the Reef*, 4; Henry P. Jim Crowe, interview by Benis M. Frank, March 2, 1969, Marine Corps Oral History Collection, Archives Branch, MCHD, Quantico, VA.

45. "H-hour" refers to the hour when a military operation is set to begin—in this case, when the first wave of the landing force will arrive ashore.

46. Commanding Officer, USS *Schroeder*, "Transport Division Four Operational Report," December 4, 1943, COLL/3653, MCHD; Morison, *Aleutians, Gilberts, and Marshalls*, 161.

47. J. G. Busick, "Action Report in Connection with Capture of Tarawa," November 24, 1943, COLL/3653, MCHD, 2; Commanding Officer, USS *Schroeder*, "Transport Division Four Operational Report," 12; Roger M. Emmons, "Tarawa Bombardment," *Marine Corps Gazette* 32, no. 3 (March 1948): 43.

48. Quoted in Corps naval gunfire officer, "Report on Naval Gunfire during GALVANIC," in *Report by Special Staff Officers on Gilbert Islands*, January 6, 1944, COLL/3653, MCHD, 13.

49. Henry I. Shaw Jr., Bernard C. Nalty, and Edwin T. Turnbladh, *History of U.S. Marine Corps Operations in World War II*, vol. III, *Central Pacific Drive* (Washington, DC: Government Printing Office, 1966), 59–60.

50. I. E. McMillian, "Naval Gunfire at Roi-Namur," *Marine Corps Gazette* 32, no. 7 (July 1948): 51.

51. Corps air officer, "Air Officer Report of GALVANIC Operations," in *Report by Special Staff Officers on Gilbert Islands*, 1–4.

52. Holland M. Smith, "Report of GALVANIC Operation (GILBERT ISLANDS)," in *Headquarters Fifth Amphibious Corps Report on Gilbert Islands Operation*, January 11, 1944, COLL/3653, MCHD, 9–10, 17–18.

53. Corps signal officer, "Analysis of Communication Reports, Galvanic Operation," in *Report by Special Staff Officers on Gilbert Islands*; Corps air officer, "Air Officer Report," 4.

54. Corps naval gunfire officer, "Report on Naval Gunfire," 5; J. J. Reber, "The Evolution of Amphibious Communications," *Marine Corps Gazette* 40, no. 11 (November 1956): 39; Corps air officer, "Air Officer Report," 3–4.
55. Corps signal officer, "Analysis of Communication Reports," 5–8; Corps naval gunfire officer, "Report on Naval Gunfire," 4–7; Corps air officer, "Air Officer Report," 2–3.
56. Gatchel, *At the Water's Edge*, 125–27; Alexander, *Storm Landings*, 52–55.
57. Quoted in Alexander, *Across the Reef*, 23; Morison, *Aleutians, Gilberts, and Marshalls*, 168–69.
58. On Shibasaki's death, see Joseph H. Alexander, *Utmost Savagery: The Three Days of Tarawa* (New York: Ivy Books, 1995), 147–52.
59. Shaw, Nalty, and Turnbladh, *History of U.S. Marine Corps Operations*, 65.
60. Shoup, quoted in Shaw, Nalty, and Turnbladh, 79.
61. Alexander, *Storm Landings*, 54–55; Crowe interview.
62. Smith, quoted in Alexander, *Across the Reef*, 52; Sherrod, *Tarawa*, 136; Shaw, Nalty, and Turnbladh, *History of U.S. Marine Corps Operations*, 71–90.
63. Norman Hatch, interviewed by unknown, World War II Veterans Oral History Collection, NERC.
64. Sherrod, *Tarawa*, 123.
65. "Some Will Be Killed," *Time* 42, no. 26 (December 27, 1943): 26.
66. "Tarawa: The Marines Win New Glory in the Gilberts and Prove There Is No Cheap Way to Victory," *Life* 15 (December 6, 1943), 36.
67. The practice—dubbed an after-action report in military jargon—remains quite familiar to military officers today. Alexander, *Across the Reef*, 50–52; Isely and Crowl, *Marines and Amphibious War*, 251–52; Shaw, Nalty, and Turnbladh, *History of U.S. Marine Corps Operations*, 114.
68. *Headquarters Fifth Amphibious Corps Report on Gilbert Islands Operation*.
69. Roger M. Emmons, "Tarawa Bombardment," *Marine Corps Gazette* 32, no. 3 (March 1948): 43; McMillian, "Naval Gunfire at Roi-Namur," 51; Alexander, *Across the Reef*, 49; McGrath, "Missing the Mark," 234–36.

70. Smith, "Report of GALVANIC Operation (GILBERT ISLANDS)," 15.
71. Corps air officer, "Air Officer Report," 1–2.
72. Corps naval gunfire officer, "Report on Naval Gunfire," 7, 13.
73. Corps signal officer, "Analysis of Communication Reports," 4; Smith, "Report of GALVANIC Operation (GILBERT ISLANDS)," 11.
74. Corps naval gunfire officer, "Report on Naval Gunfire," 7–8, 10; Corps air officer, "Air Officer Report," 1.
75. Corps naval gunfire officer, "Report on Naval Gunfire," 7–10, 15; Corps signal officer, "Analysis of Communication Reports," 2–4; Thomas N. Greene, "Greater Coordination of Supporting Fires," *Marine Corps Gazette* 31, no. 4 (April 1947): 40.
76. Morison, *Aleutians, Gilberts, and Marshalls*, 182.
77. Smith, "Report of GALVANIC Operation (GILBERT ISLANDS)," 1.
78. Isely and Crowl, *Marines and Amphibious War*, 251–52.

CHAPTER 3. BUILDING A "SPIRIT OF COOPERATION"

1. Michael Howard, "Military Science in an Age of Peace," *RUSI Journal* 119, no. 1 (March 1974): 4.
2. Reber, "Evolution of Amphibious Communications," 43.
3. USMC, *Tentative Manual for Landing Operations*, 1934, HAF 39, COLL/3634, MCHD, para. 2-323–324.
4. USMC, *Tentative Manual for Landing Operations*, 2-323.
5. For a detailed study, see Wray R. Johnson, *Biplanes at War: U.S. Marine Corps Aviation in the Small Wars Era, 1913–1934* (Lexington: University Press of Kentucky, 2019).
6. Harold D. Campbell, "Aviation in Guerrilla Warfare," *Marine Corps Gazette* 15, no. 5 (May 1931).
7. USMC, *Tentative Manual for Landing Operations*, 2-418.
8. William B. Oldfield, "Shore Fire Control Parties," *Marine Corps Gazette* 29, no. 11 (November 1945): 53.
9. F. W. Rockwell, "Training Bulletin No. 2–43: Amphibious Force Landing Exercises—Feb. 21–March 9, 1943, and March 10–27, 1943," 1943, HAF, COLL/3634, MCHD, 16.

10. Rockwell, 21. Emphasis in original.
11. R. C. D. Hunt Jr., "Naval Gunfire Support of Landing Troops," *Field Artillery Journal* 32, no. 4 (April 1942): 286–88.
12. Hunt, 286–88.
13. Oldfield, "Shore Fire Control Parties," 53.
14. Donald M. Weller, "Salvo-Splash! The Development of Naval Gunfire Support in World War II," U.S. Naval Institute *Proceedings* 80, no. 8 (August 1954): 845.
15. Weller, "Salvo-Splash!," 845.
16. Oldfield, "Shore Fire Control Parties," 53.
17. Amphibious Warfare School Senior Course, *Naval Gunfire Support Handbook* (Quantico, VA: Marine Corps Schools, 1948–1950), 4–6; McMillian, "Naval Gunfire at Roi-Namur," 52.
18. Weller, "Salvo-Splash!," 842–43.
19. Hunt, "Naval Gunfire Support," 287.
20. Holland M. Smith, Corps General Order Number 6-43, *Naval Gunfire Support in Landing Operations*, 1943, HAF, MCHD, 1, 9.
21. Weller, "Salvo-Splash!," 843–44; Rockwell, "Training Bulletin No. 2–43," 22.
22. Hunt, "Naval Gunfire Support," 287.
23. Smith, Corps General Order Number 6-43, 53. Emphasis in original.
24. Holland M. Smith, Corps General Order Number 14-43, *Standard Operating Procedure for Employment of Direct Support Aircraft*, 1943, HAF, MCHD, 2–6; Reber, "Evolution of Amphibious Communications," 43.
25. McMillian, "Naval Gunfire at Roi-Namur," 52; Amphibious Warfare School Senior Course, *Naval Gunfire Support Handbook*, 4–6; Smith, "Report of GALVANIC Operation (GILBERT ISLANDS)."
26. Hunt, "Naval Gunfire Support," 287.
27. Weller, "Salvo-Splash!," 843.
28. Robert D. Heinl Jr., "Minority Report on (J)ASCO," *Marine Corps Gazette* 31, no. 7 (July 1947); Isely and Crowl, *Marines and Amphibious War*, 251–52.
29. John H. Ellis, interview by Richard Misenhimer, World War II Veterans Oral History Collection, NERC, November 26, 2002.

30. Robert D. Heinl Jr., "Naval Gunfire Training in the Pacific," *Marine Corps Gazette* 32, no. 6 (June 1948): 12; George Raynor Thompson and Dixie R. Harris, *The Signal Corps: The Outcome (Mid-1943 through 1945)* (Washington, DC: U.S. Army Center of Military History, 1991), 231–33; Gordon L. Rottman, *U.S. Marine Corps World War II Order of Battle: Ground and Air Units in the Pacific War, 1939–1945* (Westport, CT: Greenwood Press, 2002), 233.
31. Ellis interview.
32. A table of organization and equipment delineates the leadership, structure, and equipment of a particular military unit. Rottman, *U.S. Marine Corps World War II Order of Battle*, 233.
33. Thompson and Harris, *Signal Corps*, 231.
34. Heinl, "Naval Gunfire Support in Landings," 43.
35. Ellis interview; Gordon L. Rottman, *U.S. World War II Amphibious Tactics: Army and Marine Corps, Pacific Theater* (Long Island City, NY: Osprey Publishing, 2004), 22.
36. Heinl, "Naval Gunfire Support in Landings," 40–41; Robert D. Heinl Jr., "Naval Gunfire Support: A New Staff Function," *Military Review* 26, no. 9 (December 1946): 19–22; Robert Sherrod, *History of Marine Corps Aviation in World War II* (San Rafael, CA: Presidio Press, 1952), 292–93.
37. Reber, "Evolution of Amphibious Communications," 39, 43; Oldfield, "Shore Fire Control Parties," 54.
38. Amphibious Warfare School Senior Course, *Naval Gunfire Support Handbook*, 2.
39. Commander, Amphibious Forces, Pacific Fleet, "Retention of Shore Bombardment Range-Kahoolawe," November 27, 1945, HAF, COLL/3634, MCHD; Robert D. Heinl Jr., "The Most Shot-At Island in the Pacific," U.S. Naval Institute *Proceedings* 73, no. 4 (April 1947): 397–99; Heinl, "Naval Gunfire Training in the Pacific."
40. Attesting to Kahoolawe's remote location, thick vegetation, and graded landing beaches, nineteenth-century opium and pearl runners had trafficked their goods through the island long before the U.S. military set up camp, christening one inlet "Smugglers' Cove" on the western edge of the island.

41. Heinl, "Naval Gunfire Training in the Pacific," 12.
42. Commander, Fifth Amphibious Corps, Corps Training Memorandum Number 17-43, *Joint Assault Signal Company*, HAF, MCHD, 1; Heinl, "Naval Gunfire Training in the Pacific," 11–13; McGrath, "Missing the Mark," 236–37.
43. Heinl, "Most Shot-At Island in the Pacific," 397.
44. Commander, Fifth Amphibious Corps, *Joint Assault Signal Company, Training*, HAF, MCHD, 1943, 1–11.
45. James C. Fahey, *The Ships and Aircraft of the U.S. Fleet*, Second War Edition (New York: Gemsco, Inc., 1944), 4–5.
46. Bureau of Aeronautics, Navy Department, "NAVAER: Airplane Characteristics and Performance: Model F4F-4" (Washington, DC: Naval History and Heritage Command, July 1, 1943).
47. Bureau of Aeronautics, Navy Department, "Standard Aircraft Characteristics NAVAER 1335D: F6F-5 Hellcat" (Washington, DC: Naval History and Heritage Command, 1949); Fahey, *Ships and Aircraft*, 41–42; Ian W. Toll, *Twilight of the Gods: War in the Western Pacific, 1944–1945* (New York: W. W. Norton, 2020), 97.
48. Quoted in Robert Sherrod, *On to Westward: The Battles of Saipan and Iwo Jima* (1945; repr., Baltimore: Nautical and Aviation Publishing Company of America, 1990), 245.
49. Arthur Herman, *Freedom's Forge: How American Business Produced Victory in World War II* (New York: Random House, 2013), 247–48.

CHAPTER 4. ON TO THE MARSHALLS

1. The Marshall Islands of Roi and Namur were connected by a common sandspit. Consequently, historians have vacillated between identifying the entire mass as "Roi-Namur" and categorizing each component by its individual title. This study will use the joint Roi-Namur designation, since American planners "considered it one island." Headquarters of the Commander in Chief, U.S. Fleet, chapter 70 in Bulletin no. 17, *Battle Experience: Supporting Operations for the Occupation of the Marshall Islands Including the Westernmost Atoll, Eniwetok, February 1944*, October 16, 1944 (Washington, DC: Government Printing Office, 1944).

2. Isely and Crowl, *Marines and Amphibious War*, 278.
3. Commander Fifth Amphibious Corps, "Chapter IX: Miscellaneous: Artillery," in *Amphibious Operations: The Marshall Islands, January and February 1944* (Washington, DC: Headquarters of the Commander in Chief, U.S. Navy, May 20, 1944; Bulletin no. 17, 70-35.
4. "Area bombing" refers to aerial bombardment over broad, general target areas rather than individual, specified positions.
5. Bulletin no. 17, 70-141; Commander Carrier Air Group Nine, "Air Support–Roi-Namur," in *Amphibious Operations: The Marshall Islands*, 2-22.
6. Commander Carrier Air Group Nine, "Air Support–Roi-Namur," 2-24.
7. Bulletin no. 17, 70-147–148.
8. "CO USS Tennessee Comments," in Bulletin no. 17, 70-116.
9. Commander Destroyer Squadron One, "Naval Gunfire–Destroyers," in *Amphibious Operations: The Marshall Islands*, 3-25.
10. Morison, *History of United States Naval Operations in World War II*, vol. 7, *Aleutians, Gilberts, and Marshalls*, 243.
11. "Commander in Chief, U.S. Pacific Fleet Comments," in Bulletin no. 17, 70-152; "Chapter III: Naval Gunfire," in *Amphibious Operations: The Marshall Islands*.
12. Emphasis added. "CTU 53.5.5 Recommends," in Bulletin no. 17, 70-123.
13. Gatchel, *At the Water's Edge*, 131.
14. John C. Chapin, *Breaking the Outer Ring: Marine Landings in the Marshall Islands* (Washington, DC: Marine Corps Historical Center, 1994), 7–9; Isely and Crowl, *Marines and Amphibious War*, 263.
15. "Chapter I: Landing Operations" and "Chapter III: Naval Gunfire," in *Amphibious Operations: The Marshall Islands*.
16. "Chapter III: Naval Gunfire," 3-13–14.
17. "Chapter III: Naval Gunfire," 3-5.
18. "Call fires" are those fire missions requested by troops operating ashore as they encounter enemy targets in the attack.
19. "Chapter III: Naval Gunfire," in *Amphibious Operations: The Marshall Islands*, 3-5.

20. Air observer quoted in Robert D. Heinl Jr. and John A. Crown, *The Marshalls: Increasing the Tempo* (Quantico, VA: Historical Branch, G-3 Division, Headquarters, U.S. Marine Corps, 1954), 74–76.
21. "Chapter II: Air Support," in *Amphibious Operations: The Marshall Islands*, 2-5–6.
22. "Control" in this sense refers to the specific authority to direct the physical position and path of an aircraft (heading, altitude, route, etc.).
23. Morris Markey, "Roi-Namur Battle Related from the Sky," *New York Times*, February 8, 1944, 3; "Chapter II: Air Support," in *Amphibious Operations: The Marshall Islands*; Isely and Crowl, *Marines and Amphibious War*, 334.
24. "Chapter II: Air Support," 2-5–6.
25. "Chapter II: Air Support," 2-5–6; Commanding General, Fifth Amphibious Corps, *Special Report on FLINTLOCK Operations* (San Francisco: Headquarters, Fifth Amphibious Corps, 1944), MCHD, 15–16; Commander, Fifth Amphibious Corps, "Extracts from Observers' Comments on FLINTLOCK Operation" (San Francisco: Headquarters, Fifth Amphibious Corps, 1944), MCHD, 8.
26. Commander Support Aircraft, "Marshall Islands Operation–January 1944," in *Amphibious Operations: The Marshall Islands*, 2-3.
27. "Chapter I: Landing Operations," in *Amphibious Operations: The Marshall Islands*; Heinl and Crown, *The Marshalls*, 64–99.
28. Revealingly, the Marines took 165 of Roi-Namur's 500 Korean laborers as prisoners. "Chapter I: Landing Operations," in *Amphibious Operations: The Marshall Islands*, 1-16.
29. "Chapter III: Naval Gunfire," in *Amphibious Operations: The Marshall Islands*; McMillian, "Naval Gunfire at Roi-Namur," 54–55.
30. Japanese POWs quoted in Bulletin no. 17, 70-36.
31. "CO USS Minneapolis Comments" and "Commander Task Unit 53.5.2 Comments," in Secret Information Bulletin no. 17, 70-112–117.
32. P. H. Torrey, "Plans and Operations for Aircraft," in Bulletin no. 17, 70-140–141.
33. D. B. Ingerslew, "Schedule," in Bulletin no. 17, 70-153.
34. "Chapter III: Naval Gunfire," in *Amphibious Operations: The Marshall Islands*, 3-14–22.

35. This analysis stems from the author's own military experience as an air support control officer and his general knowledge of the divergence between ground and aviation training both in the U.S. military generally and the U.S. Marine Corps specifically.
36. "Chapter III: Naval Gunfire," in *Amphibious Operations: The Marshall Islands.*
37. Commander Support Aircraft, "Marshall Islands Operation–January 1944," 2-8–12.
38. "From Commander Northern Attack Force–Roi and Namur," in *Amphibious Operations: The Marshall Islands*, 3-26.
39. "Chapter I: Landing Operations," in *Amphibious Operations: The Marshall Islands*, 1-15; "Support Aircraft Recommendations," in Bulletin no. 17, 70-158.
40. "Chapter VIII: Communications," in *Amphibious Operations: The Marshall Islands.*
41. "Fire Support," in Bulletin no. 17, 70-117.
42. "Fire Support"; "Chapter I: Landing Operations," in *Amphibious Operations: The Marshall Islands.*
43. "Chapter I: Landing Operations," 1–15.
44. Commanding General, Fifth Amphibious Corps, *Special Report on FLINTLOCK*, 15; Commander, Fifth Amphibious Corps, "Extracts from Observers' Comments," 10, 15; Naval gunfire officer, *Naval Gunfire Report*, 20; "Chapter VIII: Communications," in *Amphibious Operation: The Marshall Islands.*
45. Holland Smith in "Chapter VI: Ship to Shore Movement," in *Amphibious Operations: The Marshall Islands*, 6-6.
46. Richard Conolly, "Air Support–Roi-Namur," in *Amphibious Operations: The Marshall Islands*, 2-13.
47. Headquarters of the Commander in Chief, U.S. Fleet, chapter 70, in Bulletin no. 17, 70-1.
48. Morison, *Aleutians, Gilberts, and Marshalls*, 211, 221.
49. "Chapter III: Naval Gunfire," in *Amphibious Operations: The Marshall Islands*, 3-16.
50. Alva Dopking, "Warship Fire Tore to Pieces Big Namur-Roi Blockhouses," *New York Times*, February 4, 1944, 1.

51. Ernest J. King, "First Report to the Secretary of the Navy," April 23, 1944, in *U.S. Navy at War, 1941–1945: Official Reports to the Secretary of the Navy* (Washington, DC: U.S. Navy Department, 1946), 93.
52. Dopking, "Warship Fire," 3.
53. Isely and Crowl, *Marines and Amphibious War*, 307–9; Craig L. Symonds, *World War II at Sea: A Global History* (New York: Oxford University Press, 2018), 513–14.
54. Quoted in Isely and Crowl, 302.

CHAPTER 5. MORE SHELLS, MORE PLANES, MORE HARMONY

1. Austin Long, *The Soul of Armies: Counterinsurgency Doctrine and Military Culture in the U.S. and UK* (Ithaca, NY: Cornell University Press, 2016), 19.
2. Long, 81.
3. Ernest J. King, "Second Report to the Secretary of the Navy: Covering Combat Operations 1 March 1944 to 1 March 1945," March 27, 1945, in *U.S. Navy at War, 1941–1945*, 146–47.
4. "Strategic Features of the Marianas Operation," in *Amphibious Operations: Invasion of the Marianas, June–August 1944*, December 30, 1944 (Washington, DC: Headquarters of the Commander in Chief, U.S. Navy, 1944), 1-1.
5. U.S. Department of State, *Foreign Relations of the United States Diplomatic Papers: The Conferences at Cairo and Tehran, 1943* (Washington, DC: Government Printing Office, 1943), 780.
6. Toll, *Conquering Tide*, 436–39.
7. Quoted in Toll, *Conquering Tide*, 439.
8. Isely and Crowl, *Marines and Amphibious War*, 310–11.
9. Shaw, Nalty, and Turnbladh, *History of U.S. Marine Corps Operations*, 231–46; Isely and Crowl, *Marines and Amphibious War*, 306–15.
10. "Chronology of Events Affecting Supporting Fires," in Bulletin no. 20, *Battle Experience: Supporting Operations for the Capture of the Marianas Islands*, 74-9–11.
11. James J. Fahey, *Pacific War Diary, 1942–1945: The Secret Diary of an American Sailor* (1963, repr. Boston: Houghton Mifflin, 2003), 162.

12. Fahey, *Pacific War Diary*, 166.
13. Yamauchi Takeo, "'Honorable Death' on Saipan," in *Japan at War: An Oral History*, ed. Jaruko Taya Cook and Theodore F. Cook (New York: The New Press, 1992), 283.
14. Conolly in "Commander Task Force 53 Comments," in Bulletin no. 20, *Battle Experience Supporting Operations for the Capture of the Marianas Islands (Saipan, Guam, and Tinian), June–August 1944*, December 21, 1944 (Washington, DC: Government Printing Office, 1944), 74-8.
15. Support Aircraft Commander, CTF-51, "Chapter II: Air Support," in *Amphibious Operations: Invasion of the Marianas*, 2-1.
16. "Strategic Features of the Marianas Operation," 1-1–5; "Chronology of Events Affecting Supporting Forces: Saipan," 74-9–11; Support Aircraft Commander, "Chapter II: Air Support," 2-1.
17. "Capture of Saipan," in *Amphibious Operations: Invasion of the Marianas*, 1-3–5.
18. Shaw, Nalty, and Turnbladh, *History of U.S. Marine Corps Operations*, 274–75.
19. Toll, *Conquering Tide*, 466.
20. Alexander, *Storm Landings*, 70–72; Heinrichs and Gallicchio, *Implacable Foes*, 112–21.
21. Commander Task Unit 53.5.3, "Comments," in Bulletin no. 20, 74-71.
22. William Manchester, *Goodbye, Darkness: A Memoir of the Pacific War* (Boston: Little, Brown, and Company, 1979), 267.
23. "Strategic Features of the Marianas Operation," 1-1; "Capture of Saipan," 1-5; "Chronology of Events Affecting Supporting Forces: Saipan," 74-11–12.
24. "Capture of Saipan," 1-5; "Chronology of Events Affecting Supporting Forces: Saipan," 74-12.
25. "Chronology of Events Affecting Supporting Forces: Saipan," 74-12–16.
26. Ben Bradlee, *A Good Life: Newspapering and Other Adventures* (New York: Simon and Schuster, 1995), 78.
27. Bradlee, 80.

28. "Ammunition," in Bulletin no. 20, 74-44.
29. "Chronology of Events Affecting Supporting Forces: Saipan," 74-13–16.
30. Frederic A. Stott, *Saipan under Fire* (Andover, MA: privately printed, 1945), 15.
31. "Capture of Saipan," 1-5.
32. Stott, *Saipan under Fire*, 21.
33. Takeo, "'Honorable Death' on Saipan," 288–89.
34. "Casualty List Saipan: Cumulative Daily Totals," in "Chapter V: Logistics," in *Amphibious Operations: Invasion of the Marianas*, 5-22.
35. "Enemy Forces," in Bulletin no. 20, 74-4–5.
36. Samuel Eliot Morison put the number at 1,780 prisoners, saying "less than half were Koreans." Ian Toll concludes that American forces captured just 736 military prisoners, "most of whom were Korean labor troops." See Morison, *History of United States Naval Operations in World War II*, vol. 8, *New Guinea and the Marianas: March 1944–August 1944* (Boston: Little, Brown and Company, 1953), 339, and Toll, *Conquering Tide*, 510.
37. Naval gunfire officer, "Communications," in "Northern Troops and Landing Force: Report of Marianas Operation Phase I (Saipan)," August 1944, COLL/3666, MCHD, 14.
38. Signal officer, "Naval Gunfire Support," in "Northern Troops and Landing Force," 27.
39. Naval gunfire officer, "Call Fires," in "Northern Troops and Landing Force," 8; Shaw, Nalty, and Turnbladh, *History of U.S. Marine Corps Operations*, 250.
40. "Call Fires," in Bulletin no. 20, 74-50.
41. "Chapter III: Naval Gunfire," in *Amphibious Operations: Invasion of the Marianas*.
42. "Call Fires," in Bulletin no. 20, 74-50.
43. Morison, *New Guinea and the Marianas*, 326.
44. Naval gunfire officer, "Call Fires," 8.
45. Naval gunfire officer, "Coordination with Artillery and Air Support," in "Northern Troops and Landing Force," 13.

46. Signal officer, "Signal Communications," in "Signal Officer's Report: Phase 1 (SAIPAN)," 1944, COLL/3666, MCHD, 32.
47. Naval gunfire officer, "Coordination with Artillery and Air Support," 13; Shaw, Nalty, and Turnbladh, *History of U.S. Marine Corps Operations*, 275.
48. "Maps, Charts, Photographs, and Intelligence Material," in Bulletin no. 20, 74-75–76.
49. "Ammunition," 74-44–45.
50. "Chapter II: Air Support," in *Amphibious Operations: Invasion of the Marianas*; Silverthorn interview.
51. Rear Admiral Walden Ainsworth, "Commander Task Group 53.5 Comments," in Bulletin no. 20, 74-48–49.
52. Captured enemy reports quoted in "Naval Gunfire Report," in "Northern Troops and Landing Force," 20–21.
53. Japanese POWs quoted in "Effect of Naval Gunfire," in *Amphibious Operations: Invasion of the Marianas*, 3-14.
54. Captured enemy extract quoted in "Naval Gunfire Report," 21.
55. Japanese POW quoted in "Effect of Naval Gunfire," 3-14.
56. Japanese POWs quoted in "Naval Gunfire Report," 19–20.
57. King, "Second Report to the Secretary of the Navy," 162.
58. Turner, "Planning," in *Amphibious Operations: Invasion of the Marianas*, 3-1.
59. Toll, *Conquering Tide*, 457.
60. Heinrichs and Gallicchio, *Implacable Foes*, 136–37; Herbert P. Bix, *Hirohito and the Making of Modern Japan* (New York: Harper Collins, 2000), 479–80.
61. Stott, *Saipan under Fire*, 24.

CHAPTER 6. APPROACHING THE CRESCENDO

1. Kennedy, *Engineers of Victory*, xvii.
2 Kennedy, xxv–xxvi.
3. In the U.S. Marine Corps, the designation "company grade" refers to the ranks of second lieutenant, first lieutenant, and captain, while "field grade" denotes the more senior positions of major, lieutenant colonel, and colonel.

4. "Donald M. Weller," biographical file, Historical Reference Branch, MCHD, 1; Donald McPherrin Weller, session I, interview by Benis M. Frank, April 9, 1970, Marine Corps Oral History Collection, Archives Branch, MCHD.
5. "Weller," biographical file, 1.
6. Weller interview, session I.
7. Donald M. Weller, session II, interview by Benis M. Frank, April 9, 1970, Marine Corps Oral History Collection, Archives Branch, MCHD.
8. "Weller," biographical file, 1; Weller interview, session I.
9. Weller interview, sessions I and II.
10. "Weller," biographical file, 1–2; Weller interview, session II.
11. Weller interview, session II; "Weller," biographical file, 2.
12. E. A. Craig, "Coordination of Air, Artillery, and Naval Gunfire," October 1, 1944, HAF, COLL/3634, MCHD, 1; Weller interview, session II.
13. Craig, "Coordination of Air, Artillery, and Naval Gunfire," 1.
14. Charles S. Corben, "Naval Gunfire Report," in *Headquarters Northern Troops and Landing Force: Marianas Phase I (Saipan)*, August 10, 1944, COLL/3666, MCHD, 13.
15. Corben, "Naval Gunfire Report," 13.
16. Corben, 7.
17. Corben, 7; Samuel Taxis, interview by Benis M. Frank, August 27, 1981, Marine Corps Oral History Collection, Archives Branch, MCHD.
18. Craig, "Coordination of Air, Artillery, and Naval Gunfire," 1. Unsurprisingly, contemporaneous planning for the Iwo Jima assault called for an attack with two divisions abreast and one in reserve.
19. The fire direction center managed and approved field artillery fires for a respective artillery unit. Craig, "Coordination of Air, Artillery, and Naval Gunfire"; "Annex E: Special Comments," in *Fourth Marine Division Operations Report*, August 1944, COLL/3666, MCHD; "Section III: Naval Gunfire Support," in *Final Report on Saipan Operation, Regimental Combat Team 24*, August 28, 1944, COLL/3666, MCHD, 64; Taxis interview.

20. "Section IV: Air Support," in *Final Report on Saipan Operation, Regimental Combat Team 24*, August 28, 1944, COLL/3666, MCHD; "Annex E: Special Comments," 17–18.
21. "Annex E: Special Comments," 18.
22. Craig, "Coordination of Air, Artillery, and Naval Gunfire," 1.
23. "Corps General Order 70-44: Standard Operating Procedures for Headquarters and Shore and Beach Party Elements of Joint Assault Signal Company," November 23, 1944, https://cgsc.contentdm.oclc.org/digital/collection/p4013coll8/id/4609/, 6.
24. B. F. Prewitt, "Air Operations Report–Forager," in *Headquarters Expeditionary Troops Task Force 56 Report on Marianas Operations*, September 2, 1944, COLL/3666, MCHD, 6.
25. In military parlance, harassing fire disturbs an enemy, suppressing fire temporarily degrades an enemy capability, neutralizing fire leaves a target ineffective, and destruction fire renders a target materially destroyed.
26. Craig, "Coordination of Air, Artillery, and Naval Gunfire," 1–3.
27. Craig, 3.
28. Prewitt, "Air Operations Report–Forager," 137.
29. Prewitt, 137.
30. Joseph L. Stewart, "Personal Letter to Colonel Donald M. Weller," October 2, 1944, HAF, COLL/3634, MCHD, 1.
31. Stewart, 1; Craig, "Coordination of Air, Artillery, and Naval Gunfire."
32. Task organization dictates a unit's personnel and structure.
33. Harry W. G. Vadnais, "Signal Report," in "Headquarters Northern Troops and Landing Force: Marianas Phase I (Saipan)," August 12, 1944, COLL/3666, MCHD, 31; Corben, "Naval Gunfire Report"; Donald M. Weller, "Proposed Naval Gunfire Liaison Officer Replacement Policy," October 23, 1944, HAF, COLL/3634, MCHD.
34. Corben, "Naval Gunfire Report," 12; Weller, "Proposed Naval Gunfire Liaison Officer Replacement Policy"; "Annex E: Special Comments," 21.
35. Vadnais, "Signal Report," 32.
36. Corben, "Naval Gunfire Report," 8.

37. "Fleet Marine Force Pacific Naval Gunfire Support in the Forager Operation," October 7, 1944, COLL/3666, MCHD, 136–37.
38. Donald M. Weller, "Salvo-Splash! Part II—The Development of Naval Gunfire Support in World War II," U.S. Naval Institute *Proceedings* 90, no. 9 (September 1954): 1017.
39. For Marine aviation numbers, see Robert Sherrod, "Appendix VIII: Growth of Marine Corps Aviation," in *History of Marine Corps Aviation*, 434–35.
40. "The Brood of 'Noisy Nan,' " *Time Magazine* 43, no. 24 (June 12, 1944): 71–72; Sherrod, *History of Marine Corps Aviation in World War II*, 434–35.
41. John P. Condon, *U.S. Marine Corps Aviation* (Washington, DC: Government Printing Office, 1987), 20.
42. Condon, 20–21.
43. "Brood of 'Noisy Nan,'" 72.
44. "Section IV: Air Support," 72.
45. Nimitz quoted in Isely and Crowl, *Marines and Amphibious War*, 508; Condon, *U.S. Marine Corps Aviation*, 21; Sherrod, *History of Marine Corps Aviation*, 326–27.
46. In military aviation parlance, control refers to the physical direction of an aircraft in flight (heading, altitude, route, etc.).
47. Condon, *U.S. Marine Corps Aviation*, 21; Sherrod, *History of Marine Corps Aviation*, 327–29. Despite Vandegrift's concession, the Marine Corps did not lose an aircraft wing (Sherrod wrote that the proposal was "lost in the course of subsequent developments"). The Corps did, however, decommission fifteen separate squadrons in October and November of 1944.
48. Prewitt, "Air Operations Report–Forager," 5–6.
49. "Annex E: Special Comments," 19.
50. Vadnais, "Signal Report," 31.
51. Vadnais, 31; Corben, "Naval Gunfire Report," 15; Isely and Crowl, *Marines and Amphibious War*, 332.
52. Heinl, "Naval Gunfire Training in the Pacific," 12–13; Heinl, "Minority Report on (J)ASCO," 30.

53. Even while assuming duties as V Corps naval gunfire officer, Weller remained the naval gunfire officer for Fleet Marine Force, Pacific, responsible for both operational troops and training personnel in the entire theater.
54. Weller interview, session II.
55. Weller interview, session II; Donald M. Weller, "Proposed Naval Gunfire Liaison Officer Replacement Policy."
56. Heinl, "Naval Gunfire Training in the Pacific," 14; I. E. McMillian, "Naval Gunfire at Guam," *Marine Corps Gazette* 32, no. 9 (September 1948): 53.
57. Weller, "Salvo-Splash! Part II," 1017.
58. A reverse slope target lies, from the attacker's perspective, on the far slope of a hill or mountain. The position is, naturally, more difficult to both detect and strike.
59. Weller, "Salvo-Splash! Part II," 1017; Weller interview, session II.
60. Commanding Officer, 2d Joint Assault Signal Company, "Report of Air-Ground Exercises," December 1944, HAF, COLL/3634, MCHD, 1–6.
61. Prewitt, "Air Operations Report–Forager," 8.
62. "Section III: Naval Gunfire Support," 65–66.
63. "Annex E: Special Comments," 22; Weller, "Salvo-Splash! Part II."
64. Isely and Crowl, *Marines and Amphibious War*, 434.
65. Spector, *Eagle against the Sun*, 494.
66. Isely and Crowl, *Marines and Amphibious War*, 432.
67. George W. Garand and Truman R. Stobridge, *History of U.S. Marine Corps Operations in World War II*, vol. 4, *Western Pacific Operations* (Washington, DC: Government Printing Office, 1971), 462–64.

CHAPTER 7. PINNACLE IN THE PACIFIC

1. Kumiko Kakehashi, *So Sad to Fall in Battle: An Account of War Based on General Tadamichi Kuribayashi's Letters from Iwo Jima* (New York: Presidio Press, 2007), 3–29.
2. Whitman S. Bartley, "Appendix V: Task Organization," *Iwo Jima: Amphibious Epic* (Washington, DC: Government Printing Office, 1954), 228–29.

3. Yoshitaka Horie, "Situation of Summer and Autumn 1944," enc. in *Explanation of Japanese Defense Plan and Battle of Iwo Jima* [hereafter *Explanation*], January 25, 1946, World War II Documents Collection, National Museum of the Pacific War (NMPW), Fredericksburg, TX.
4. Horie, *Explanation.*
5. Horie, "Strength, Arms, and Ammunitions," in *Explanation*; Millett, *Semper Fidelis*, 426–29.
6. Horie, "The Defense Policy of Lieutenant General Kuribayashi," in *Explanation.*
7. Dan King, *A Tomb Called Iwo Jima: Firsthand Accounts from Japanese Survivors* (North Charleston, SC: Pacific Press, 2020), 96.
8. Horie, "Defense Policy."
9. Horie, "Appendix," in *Explanation.*
10. Horie, "Defense Policy"; Horie, "Appendix"; Kakehashi, *So Sad to Fall*, 49–57; Spector, *Eagle against the Sun*, 494–95; Gatchel, *At the Water's Edge*, 148–49.
11. See Alexander, *Storm Landings*, 87; Spector, 422; Millett and Murray, *War To Be Won*, 365.
12. Quoted in Isely and Crowl, *Marines and Amphibious War*, 468.
13. Richard S. Pryor, "Radio Interview with Vice Admiral R. K. Turner and General H. M. Smith, Transcript," February 24, 1945, World War II Documents Collection, NMPW, 2.
14. Alexander, *Closing In*, 3.
15. "Chapter I: Narrative," in U.S. Fleet, Headquarters of the Commander in Chief, *Amphibious Operations: Capture of Iwo Jima, 16 February to 16 March 1945* (Washington, DC: Headquarters of the Commander in Chief, U.S. Navy, July 17, 1945), https://www.history.navy.mil/research/library/online-reading-room/title-list-alphabetically/a/amphibious-operations-capture-iwo-jima.html, 1-4–6.
16. "Ammunition Expenditure," in Bulletin no. 23, *Battle Experience: Bombardments of Iwo Jima, November 1944–January 1945. Third Fleet Operations in Support of Central Luzon Landings, including the South China Sea Sweep, 30 December 1944–23 January 1945* (Washington, DC: Headquarters of the Commander in Chief, U.S. Navy, 1945, 79-24–26.

17. "Chapter III: Air Support," in *Amphibious Operations: Capture of Iwo Jima.*
18. Isely and Crowl, *Marines and Amphibious War*, 432–40.
19. "Annex George to Operation Plan No. 1-45," in "Operations Plan, Iwo Jima, 4th Marine Division," January 14, 1945, World War II Documents Collection, NMPW, 5–6.
20. William Walter Buchanan, interview by Benis M. Frank, June 16, 1969, Marine Corps Oral History Collection, Archives Branch, MCHD.
21. Morison, *History of United States Naval Operations in World War II*, vol. 14, *Victory in the Pacific*, 1945, 34.
22. Vernon E. Megee interview, session 2, Benis M. Frank, May 17, 1967, Marine Corps Oral History Collection, Archives Branch, MCHD, 33–4; "Annex George to Operation Plan No. 1-45," 5–7.
23. "Annex George to Operation Plan No. 1-45," 5–7.
24. Raymond Henri et al., *The U.S. Marines on Iwo Jima* (1945; repr., The Infantry Journal, 2019), 20.
25. Weller interview, session 2.
26. Weller interview.
27. Paddy Griffith, *Battle Tactics of the Western Front: The British Army's Art of Attack, 1916–18* (New Haven, CT: Yale University Press, 1994), 142–43.
28. John Keegan, *The First World War* (New York: Alfred A. Knopf, 1999), 292–93; Bruce I. Gudmundsson, *On Artillery* (Westport, CT: Praeger, 1993), 70–71, 88. For their part, and despite their late entry into the conflict, the Americans' rolling barrage produced similarly dubious results in World War I. See Mark Ethan Grotelueschen, *The AEF Way of War: The American Army and Combat in World War I* (New York: Cambridge University Press, 2007), 104–5, 287–88.
29. "Naval Gunfire Support," in "Fifth Amphibious Corps Operation Plan No. 3-44: Iwo Jima Operation," January 2, 1945, COLL/3692, Archives Branch, MCHD, 6; "Chapter II: Naval Gunfire," in *Amphibious Operations: Capture of Iwo Jima*, 2-3; Buchanan interview.
30. Henri et al., *U.S. Marines on Iwo Jima*, 18.
31. Weller interview, session 2.
32. "Annex George to Operation Plan No. 1-45," 7. Emphasis in original.

33. "G-3 Special Action Report, Iwo Jima Campaign," in *Fifth Amphibious Corps Report on Iwo Jima Campaign*, March 31, 1945, COLL/3692, Archives Branch, MCHD, 10–11; "Chapter II: Naval Gunfire," 2-3; Morison, *Victory in the Pacific*, 35.
34. Henri et al., *U.S. Marines on Iwo Jima*, 21.
35. Toll, *Twilight of the Gods*, 490.
36. Akikusa quoted in King, *Tomb Called Iwo Jima*, 117.
37. Pryor, "Interview with Turner and Smith," 2; Fenn Wilson, interview by unknown, November 10, 1989, Marine Corps Oral History Collection, Archives Branch, MCHD.
38. "Chapter I: Narrative," 1-7.
39. Earl J. Stearns, *The Operation of the 27th Marine Combat Team (Fifth Marine Division) on Iwo Jima, Volcano Islands, 19 February–23 March 1945: Personal Experience of a Regimental Weapons Company Commander* (Fort Benning, GA: The Infantry School, 1948), 15.
40. "G-3 Special Action Report, Iwo Jima Campaign," 11–12; Buchanan interview.
41. Stearns, *Operation of the 27th*, 17.
42. "G-3 Special Action Report, Iwo Jima Campaign," 10–11; "Annex George to Operation Plan No. 1-45," 6–7.
43. James Orvill Raines, *Goodnight Officially: The Pacific War Letters of a Destroyer Sailor*, ed. William M. McBride (Boulder, CO: Westview Press, 1994), 240.
44. Commander, Amphibious Group Two, *Report of Iwo Jima Operation*, April 1945, COLL/3692, Archives Branch, MCHD, 2; Commanding General, Fleet Marine Force (Pacific), *Iwo Jima Naval Gunfire Support: Expeditionary Troops Report*, June 1945, COLL/3692, Archives Branch, MCHD, 27.
45. Raines, *Goodnight Officially*, 239.
46. Raines, 239.
47. The concept mirrored—almost exactly—the V Corps' previously proposed AAG (Air, Artillery, and Naval Gunfire) Center. Rather mysteriously, the V Corps dropped the AAG acronym. Nonetheless, the concept survived intact.

48. "Naval Gunfire," in *3d Marine Division Reinforced Iwo Jima Action Report*, April 30, 1945, COLL/3692, Archives Branch, MCHD, 52–54; Bartley, "Appendix V," 207–8.
49. Brian S. McFadden, "Marine Close Air Support in World War II" (master's thesis, U.S. Army Command and General Staff College, 1999), 47; "Chapter II: Joint Fire Support Command and Control," in Chairman of the Joint Chiefs of Staff, Joint Publication 3–09, *Joint Fire Support* (Washington, DC: Office of the Chairman of the Joint Chiefs of Staff, 2019).
50. "G-3 Special Action Report, Iwo Jima Campaign," 11–13; Toll, *Twilight of the Gods*, 490–93; Wilson interview.
51. Sherrod, *On to Westward*, 186.
52. "G-3 Special Action Report, Iwo Jima Campaign," 13.
53. John Bradley interview, World War II Interviews, Naval History and Heritage Command, Washington, DC.
54. For historians, the task of identifying the original "flag raisers" has proven a most onerous assignment. After several official investigations and revisions spanning more than seventy years, the Marine Corps seems to have settled on the names of the troops involved. See Breanne Robertson, ed., *Investigating Iwo: The Flag Raisings in Myth, Memory, and Esprit de Corps* (Quantico, VA: Marine Corps History Division, 2019).
55. Wilson interview; Gatchel, *At the Water's Edge*, 150.
56. Sherrod, *On to Westward*, 195.
57. Sherrod, 180.
58. Raines, *Goodnight Officially*, 242.
59. Satoru Ōmagari quoted in King, *Tomb Called Iwo Jima*, 131.
60. Close air support refers to aircraft operating in close proximity to friendly ground units, therefore requiring detailed integration with ground commanders.
61. "Transcript of Military Service Record of Brigadier General Vernon E. Megee," November 14, 1950, Megee Personal Papers, COLL/3983, Archives Branch, MCHD; "General Vernon E. Megee, 91, Dies; Was Pioneer in Combat Aviation," Megee Personal Papers, COLL/3983, Archives Branch, MCHD.

62. Vernon Megee, "Role of Aviation in the Seizure of an Advanced Base," October 1937, Megee Personal Papers, COLL/3983, Archives Branch, MCHD.
63. Megee interview, session 2, 28.
64. Megee interview, 28–29. Emphasis in original.
65. Vernon E. Megee, "Landing Force Air Support Control Unit 1, Special Action Report, Iwo Jima Campaign," March 17, 1945, COLL/3692, Archives Branch, MCHD, 2.
66. " Chapter III: Air Support," 3-3–4; Vernon E. Megee, "Coordination of Artillery, Naval Gunfire, and Air," August 13, 1946, Megee Personal Papers, COLL/3983, Archives Branch, MCHD.
67. "Maximum trajectory" or "maximum ordinate" refers to the highest point of an ordnance arch.
68. "Annex George to Operation Plan No. 1-45," 4; Megee, "Coordination of Artillery, Naval Gunfire, and Air," 4–5; "Chapter III: Naval Gunfire," in *Amphibious Operations: Invasion of the Marianas*, 3–9.
69. Megee, "Coordination of Artillery, Naval Gunfire, and Air"; "Annex George to Operation Plan No. 1-45," 4.
70. Megee, "Coordination of Artillery, Naval Gunfire and Air," 5.
71. Commander, Amphibious Group Two, quoted in "Chapter III: Air Support," 3-4.
72. Toll, *Twilight of the Gods*, 501–6.
73. Henri et al., *U.S. Marines on Iwo Jima*, 17.
74. "A. J. Kiely Tells of War on Iwo Jima," *Hartford Courant*, March 25, 1945.
75. Henri et al., *U.S. Marines on Iwo Jima*, 76.
76. "Annex Jig to Fourth Marine Division Operations Report, Iwo Jima: 4th Tank Battalion Report," May 30, 1945, https://archive.org/details/JigReport4thMarineDivisionIwoJima, 8.
77. Megee interview, session 2, 46.
78. Megee interview.
79. Megee interview, 37; Toll, *Twilight of the Gods*, 503.
80. Toll, 505–6; Holland M. Smith and Percy Finch, *Coral and Brass* (1948; repr., New York: Bantam Books, 1987), 250; "Naval Gunfire," 54.

81. Stearns, *Operation of the 27th*, 17–35; Henri et al., *U.S. Marines on Iwo Jima*; Sherrod, *On to Westward*, 186, 195.
82. Smith and Finch, *Coral and Brass*, 263.
83. Garand and Stobridge, *History of U.S. Marine Corps Operations*, 701; Gatchel, *At the Water's Edge*, 150.
84. Bartley, "Appendix V," 191–92; Toll, *Twilight of the Gods*, 515.
85. Weller interview, session 2.
86. Pryor, "Interview with Turner and Smith," 2.
87. Smith and Finch, *Coral and Brass*, 265, 226.
88. Garand and Stobridge, *History of U.S. Marine Corps Operations*, 711; Toll, *Twilight of the Gods*, 515–16; Millett, *Semper Fidelis*, 431.
89. "Corps Artillery Officer's Report," in *Appendix 4 to Annex C to VAC LANFOR Special Action Report, Iwo Jima Campaign*, March 1945, COLL/3692, Archives Branch, MCHD; Smith and Finch, *Coral and Brass*, 265.
90. Horie, "Appendix"; Naval Gunfire Training Section, "Ammunition Expenditures, Various Operations in Central Pacific Area," August 4, 1945, COLL/3692, Archives Branch, MCHD.
91. B. F. Prewitt, "Air Report," in *Fifth Amphibious Corps Report on the Iwo Jima Campaign*, May 1945, COLL/3692, Archives Branch, MCHD.
92. Stearns, *Operation of the 27th*, 39.
93. Commanding General, Fleet Marine Force, Pacific, *Iwo Jima Naval Gunfire Support: Expeditionary Troops Report*, 1945, COLL/3692, Archives Branch, MCHD, 8.
94. Kuribayashi quoted in Horie, "Value of Bombardment of American Air Forces and Vessels."
95. Horie, "Conclusion."
96. Pryor, "Interview with Turner and Smith," 2.
97. Pryor.
98. Stearns, *Operation of the 27th*, 39.

CHAPTER 8. EXAMINING SUCCESS

1. Heinrichs and Gallicchio, *Implacable Foes*, 274.
2. On postwar criticism, see Jonathan T. Baker, "Iwo Jima: The Unnecessary Battle" (master's thesis, USMC Command and Staff College, 2011),

and Robert S. Burrell, *The Ghosts of Iwo Jima* (College Station: Texas A&M University Press, 2006). The authors contend that Iwo Jima's strategic value to the Allies was low by early 1945 and that the island's military significance has been romanticized in American memory.

3. Richard B. Frank, *Downfall: The End of the Imperial Japanese Empire* (New York: Penguin Books, 1999), 118–21.
4. Millett and Murray, *War To Be Won*, 505–7.
5. Frank, *Downfall*, 77.
6. Owing to the battle's length, heavy use of artillery, high casualty rates, and deplorable weather, Okinawa saw some of the highest rates of "combat fatigue" of the entire Pacific War. For an excellent narrative account of the campaign—at sea, ashore, and in the air—see Joseph Wheelan, *Bloody Okinawa: The Last Great Battle of World War II* (New York: Hachette Books, 2020).
7. Heinrichs and Gallicchio, *Implacable Foes*, 412; Wheelan, 332, 343.
8. For exhaustive and compelling analysis of the war's final months, see Frank, *Downfall*; also, Max Hastings, *Retribution: The Battle for Japan, 1944–45* (New York: Alfred A. Knopf, 2008).
9. Gerald Gilbert, *The Evolution of Tactics* (London: Hugh Rees Limited, 1907), 183.
10. Millett and Murray, *War To Be Won*, 84–5.
11. King, *U.S. Navy at War, 1941–1945*, 171.
12. Sherrod, *On to Westward*, xi.
13. Millett, *Semper Fidelis*, 439. Emphasis in original.
14. Isely and Crowl, *Marines and Amphibious War*, 34–44.
15. USMC, *Tentative Manual for Landing Operations*, paragraphs 2-312–325.
16. McMillian, "Naval Gunfire at Roi-Namur," 51; Corps air officer, "Air Officer Report of GALVANIC Operations," in *Report by Special Staff Officers on Gilbert Islands*, January 6, 1944, COLL/3653, MCHD, 1–4.
17. Alexander, *Closing In*, 8–13.
18. Quoted in Rick Atkinson, *The British Are Coming: The War for America, Lexington to Princeton, 1775–1777* (New York: Henry Holt, 2019), 115.
19. Commander, Fifth Amphibious Corps, *Corps Training Memorandum Number 17-43: Joint Assault Signal Company*, 1943, HAF 723,

COLL/3634, MCHD; Heinl, "Most Shot-At Island in the Pacific," 397–99; Wilson interview.

20. Corps signal officer, "Analysis of Communication Reports, Galvanic Operation," in *Report by Special Staff Officers on Gilbert Islands*, January 6, 1944, COLL/3653, MCHD, 2–4; Corps naval gunfire officer, "Report on Naval Gunfire during GALVANIC," in *Report by Special Staff Officers on Gilbert Islands*, January 6, 1944, COLL/3653, MCHD, 7–8, 10, 15; Greene, "Greater Coordination," 40.
21. Amphibious Warfare School Senior Course, *Naval Gunfire Support Handbook*, 7; McMillian, "Naval Gunfire at Roi-Namur," 51; U.S. Marine Corps Schools, PHIB-11: *Amphibious Operations—Naval Gunfire Support* (Quantico, VA: Marine Barracks, Marine Corps Schools, 1945), 24; William B. Oldfield, "Our Naval Gunfire Preparation," *Marine Corps Gazette* 29, no. 7 (July 1945): 44.
22. Charles S. Corben, "Naval Gunfire Report," in *Headquarters Northern Troops and Landing Force: Marianas Phase I (Saipan)*, August 10, 1944, COLL/3666, MCHD, 8, 13; Shaw, Nalty, and Turnbladh, *History of U.S. Marine Corps Operations*, 275.
23. Heinl, "Naval Gunfire Training in the Pacific," 14; Commanding Officer, 2d Joint Assault Signal Company, "Report of Air-Ground Exercises," December 1944, HAF, COLL/3634, MCHD, 1–6.
24. Commanding General, Fleet Marine Force (Pacific), *Iwo Jima Naval Gunfire Support: Expeditionary Troops Report*, June 1945, COLL/3692, Archives Branch, MCHD, 27.
25. Commander, Amphibious Group Two, quoted in "Chapter III: Air Support," in *Amphibious Operations: Capture of Iwo Jima*, 3-4.
26. See "Chapter II: Joint Fire Support Command and Control," in Joint Publication 3–09, *Joint Fire Support.*
27. Heinl, "Naval Gunfire Training in the Pacific," 15.
28. Heinl, 11.
29. Weller interview, session II.
30. Emphasis in original. Heinl, "Naval Gunfire Support: A New Staff Function," 19–22.
31. Millett, *Semper Fidelis*, xvii.

32. R. D. Heinl Jr., "And Now the Anglico," *Marine Corps Gazette* 35, no. 1 (January 1951): 22–23.
33. National Security Act of 1947, Chapter 343, Stat. 496 (1947), https://www.intelligence.senate.gov/sites/default/files/laws/nsact1947.pdf; Heinl, "And Now the Anglico," 24; Reber, "Evolution of Amphibious Communications," 42.
34. Theo Farrell, "Introduction: Military Adaptation in War," in Russell, Osinga, and Farrell, *Military Adaptation in Afghanistan*, 1.
35. Grissom, "Future of Military Innovation Studies," 905–34.
36. On the Marine Corps' historical prioritization of flexibility and innovation, see Krulak, *First to Fight.*
37. O'Connell, *Underdogs*, 7.
38. Russell, *Innovation, Transformation, and War*, 8. Keith Bickel constructs a very similar argument in the Marines' development of "small wars" doctrine during the Banana Wars. See Bickel, *Mars Learning.*
39. Kennedy, *Engineers of Victory.*
40. R. W. Komer, *Bureaucracy Does Its Thing: Institutional Constraints on U.S.-GVN Performance in Vietnam* (Santa Monica, CA: RAND, 1972), vi.
41. Komer, vii–viii.
42. Millett and Murray, *Military Innovation in the Interwar Period*, 308. Similarly, Sharon Tosi Lacey concluded in her study of U.S. Army and Marine infantry tactics in the Pacific that American success "was the result of difficult and patient work by commanders and evolving staffs that studied and acted upon the lessons of every engagement." See Lacey, *Pacific Blitzkrieg*, xiii.
43. The V Corps' after-action report for Tarawa totaled more than 700 pages; its Iwo Jima version ran to an astounding 1,600 pages.
44. Heinl, "Minority Report on (J)ASCO"; Isely and Crowl, *Marines and Amphibious War*, 251–52.
45. Biddle, *Military Power*, 38.
46. Martin Blumenson, *The Patton Papers, 1940–1945* (Boston: Houghton Mifflin Company, 1974), 39–40.
47. Jonathan M. House, *Combined Arms Warfare in the Twentieth Century* (Lawrence: University Press of Kansas, 2001), 281.

48. Lynn Montross and Nicholas A. Canzona, *U.S. Marine Operations in Korea, 1950–1953*, vol. II, *The Inchon-Seoul Operation* (Washington, DC: Historical Branch, G-3, Headquarters U.S. Marine Corps, 1955), 67–78.
49. Montross and Canzona, 102, 202.
50. Rod Andrew Jr., *The First Fight: U.S. Marines in Operation Starlite—August 1965* (Washington, DC: Government Publishing Office, 2015), 49–51.
51. Quoted in Andrew, 50.
52. For the interwar period's example of an "officer corps" of innovators, see Millett and Murray, *Military Innovation in the Interwar Period*, 325.
53. Lynn, *Battle*, xviii.
54. David H. Berger, Message to the Marine Corps, March 8, 2022, "33rd Anniversary of FMFM-1 Warfighting," https://www.hqmc.marines.mil/cmc/News/Article/Article/2959606/33rd-anniversary-of-fmfm-1-warfighting/.

BIBLIOGRAPHY

PRIMARY SOURCES

Biographical Files. Historical Resources Branch, Marine Corps History Division, Quantico, VA.

Collection 3634 (Historical Amphibious Files)

Collection 3653 (Gilbert Islands)

Collection 3654 (Guadalcanal & Bougainville)

Collection 3660 (Marshall Islands)

Collection 3666 (Mariana Islands)

Collection 3692 (Iwo Jima)

Collection 3983 (Vernon E. Megee Personal Papers)

Jones, B. Q. *Interviews and Statements by Officers of the 1st Marine Division on the Guadalcanal Operations, December 5, 1942–January 19, 1943*. https://cgsc.contentdm.oclc.org/digital/collection/p4013coll8/id/4338/rec/1.

U.S. Fleet, Headquarters of the Commander in Chief. *Amphibious Operations: Capture of Iwo Jima, 16 February to 16 March 1945*. Washington, DC: Headquarters of the Commander in Chief, U.S. Navy, July 17, 1945, https://www.history.navy.mil/research/library/online-reading-room/title-list-alphabetically/a/amphibious-operations-capture-iwo-jima.html.

———. *Amphibious Operations: Invasion of the Marianas, June–August 1944*. Washington, DC: Headquarters of the Commander in Chief, U.S. Navy, 1944.

———. *Amphibious Operations: The Marshall Islands, January–February 1944*. Washington, DC: Headquarters of the Commander in Chief, U.S. Navy, May 20, 1944.

———. *Battle Experience: Bombardments of Iwo Jima, November 1944–January 1945. Third Fleet Operations in Support of Central Luzon Landings, including the South China Sea Sweep, 30 December 1944–23 January 1945*. Bulletin no. 23. Washington, DC: Headquarters of the Commander in Chief, U.S. Navy, 1945.

———. *Battle Experience: Supporting Operations for the Capture of the Marianas Islands (Saipan, Guam, and Tinian), June–August 1944*. Bulletin no. 20. Washington, DC: Headquarters of the Commander in Chief, U.S. Navy, December 21, 1944, https://www.history.navy.mil/content/dam/nhhc/browse-by-topic/War%20and%20Conflict/WWII-Pacific-Battles/Battle%20Experience%20-%20Marianas.pdf.

———. *Battle Experience: Supporting Operations for the Occupation of the Marshall Islands including Eniwetok, February 1944*. Bulletin no. 17. Washington, DC: Government Printing Office, 1944.

———. *Battle Experience: Solomon Islands and Alaskan Actions, January–February 1943*. Bulletin no. 6. Washington, DC: Headquarters of the Commander in Chief, U.S. Navy, 1944.

World War II Documents Collection. Nimitz Research Center, National Museum of the Pacific War, Fredericksburg, TX.

PROFESSIONAL ARTICLES

Campbell, Harold D. "Aviation in Guerrilla Warfare." *Marine Corps Gazette* 15, no. 5 (May 1931).

Emmons, Roger M. "Tarawa Bombardment." *Marine Corps Gazette* 32, no. 3 (March 1948): 42–47.

Greene, Thomas N. "Greater Coordination of Supporting Fires." *Marine Corps Gazette* 31, no. 4 (April 1947): 40–43.

Haan, William G. "A Positive System of Coast Defense (Army)." *Journal of United States Artillery* 53 (December 1920).

Heinl Jr., Robert D. "And Now the Anglico." *Marine Corps Gazette* 35, no. 1 (January 1951): 22–25.

———. "Minority Report on (J)ASCO." *Marine Corps Gazette* 31, no. 7 (July 1947): 28–32.

———. "Naval Gunfire Support: A New Staff Function." *Military Review* 26, no. 9 (December 1946): 19–26.

———. "Naval Gunfire Support in Landings." *Marine Corps Gazette* 29, no. 9 (September 1945): 40–43.

———. "Naval Gunfire Training in the Pacific." *Marine Corps Gazette* 32, no. 6 (June 1948): 10–15.

———. "The Most Shot-At Island in the Pacific." U.S. Naval Institute *Proceedings* 73, no. 4 (April 1947): 397–99.

Hunt Jr., R. C. D. "Naval Gunfire Support of Landing Troops." *Field Artillery Journal* 32, no. 4 (April 1942): 286–88.

McMillian, I. E. "Naval Gunfire at Guam." *Marine Corps Gazette* 32, no. 9 (September 1948): 52–56.

———. "Naval Gunfire at Roi-Namur." *Marine Corps Gazette* 32, no. 7 (July 1948): 50–55.

Oldfield, W. B. "Our Naval Gunfire Preparation." *Marine Corps Gazette* 29, no. 7 (July 1945): 43–59.

———. "Shore Fire Control Parties." *Marine Corps Gazette* 29, no. 11 (November 1945): 53–54.

Reber, J. J. "The Evolution of Amphibious Communications." *Marine Corps Gazette* 40, no. 11 (November 1956): 38–43.

Weller, Donald M. "Salvo-Splash! The Development of Naval Gunfire Support in World War II." U.S. Naval Institute *Proceedings* 80, no. 8 (August 1954): 845.

———. "Salvo-Splash! Part II—The Development of Naval Gunfire Support in World War II." U.S. Naval Institute *Proceedings* 90, no. 9 (September 1954).

NEWSPAPER ARTICLES

"A. J. Kiely Tells of War on Iwo Jima." *Hartford Courant*, March 25, 1945.

"Brood of 'Noisy Nan.'" *Time* 43, no. 24 (June 12, 1944).

Dopking, Alva. "Warship Fire Tore to Pieces Big Namur-Roi Blockhouses." *New York Times*, February 4, 1944.

Markey, Morris. "Roi-Namur Battle Related from the Sky." *New York Times*, February 8, 1944.

"Some Will Be Killed." *Time* 42, no. 26 (December 27, 1943): 26.

"Tarawa: The Marines Win New Glory in the Gilberts and Prove There Is No Cheap Way to Victory." *Life* 15 (December 6, 1943): 36.

MEMOIRS

Bradlee, Ben. *A Good Life: Newspapering and Other Adventures*. New York: Simon and Schuster, 1995.

Churchill, Winston S. *The Second World War*. Vol. 4, *The Hinge of Fate*. Boston: Houghton Mifflin, 1950.

Fahey, James J. *Pacific War Diary, 1942–1945: The Secret Diary of an American Sailor*. 1963. Reprint, Boston: Houghton Mifflin, 2003.

Manchester, William. *Goodbye, Darkness: A Memoir of the Pacific War*. Boston: Little, Brown and Company, 1979.

Raines, James Orvill. *Goodnight Officially: The Pacific War Letters of a Destroyer Sailor*, ed. William M. McBride. Boulder, CO: Westview Press, 1994.

Sherrod, Robert. *Tarawa: The Incredible Story of One of World War II's Bloodiest Battles*. 1944. Reprint, New York: Skyhorse Publishing, 2013.

Smith, Holland M., and Percy Finch. *Coral and Brass*. 1948. Reprint, New York: Bantam Books, 1987.

Stott, Frederic A. *Saipan under Fire*. Andover, MA: Privately Printed, 1945.

Vandegrift, A. A., and Robert B. Asprey. *Once a Marine: The Memoirs of General A. A. Vandegrift, Commandant of the U.S. Marines in World War II.* New York: Ballantine Books, 1964.

ORAL HISTORIES

Bowden, Arwin. Interview by Floyd Cox and Becky Lindig, March 9, 2000. World War II Veterans Oral History Collection, Nimitz Education and Research Center (NERC), Fredericksburg, TX.

Bradley, John. Interview by unknown. World War II Interviews. Naval History and Heritage Command, Washington, DC.

Buchanan, William Walter. Interview by Benis M. Frank, June 16, 1969. Marine Corps Oral History Collection, Archives Branch, Marine Corps History Division (MCHD).

Crowe, Henry P. Jim. Interview by Benis M. Frank, March 2, 1969. Marine Corps Oral History Collection, Archives Branch, MCHD.

Ellis, John H. Interview by Richard Misenhimer, November 26, 2002. World War II Veterans Oral History Collection, NERC, Fredericksburg, TX.

Hatch, Norman. Interview by unknown. World War II Veterans Oral History Collection, NERC, Fredericksburg, TX.

Megee, Vernon E. Interview by Benis M. Frank, May 17, 1967. Marine Corps Oral History Collection, Archives Branch, MCHD.

Silverthorn, Merwin H. Interview by Benis M. Frank, March 19, 1969. Marine Corps Oral History Collection, Archives Branch, MCHD.

Smith, Oliver Prince. Interview by Benis M. Frank, June 9, 1969. Marine Corps Oral History Collection, Archives Branch, MCHD.

Takeo, Yamauchi. "'Honorable Death' on Saipan." In *Japan at War: An Oral History*, edited by Jaruko Taya Cook and Theodore F. Cook. New York: The New Press, 1992.

Taxis, Samuel. Interview by Benis M. Frank, August 27, 1981. Marine Corps Oral History Collection, Archives Branch, MCHD.

Weller, Donald M. Interview by Benis M. Frank, April 9, 1970. Marine Corps Oral History Collection, Archives Branch, MCHD.

Wilson, Fenn. Interview by unknown, November 10, 1989. Marine Corps Oral History Collection, Archives Branch, MCHD.

U.S. GOVERNMENT PUBLICATIONS

Amphibious Warfare School Senior Course. *Naval Gunfire Support Handbook.* Quantico, VA: Marine Corps Schools, 1948–1950.

Bureau of Aeronautics, Navy Department. "NAVAER: Airplane Characteristics and Performance: Model F4F-4." Washington, DC: Naval History and Heritage Command, July 1, 1943.

———. "Standard Aircraft Characteristics NAVAER 1335D: F6F-5 Hellcat." Washington, DC: Naval History and Heritage Command, 1949.

Chairman of the Joint Chiefs of Staff. Joint Publication 3–09, *Joint Fire Support.* Washington, DC: Office of the Chairman of the Joint Chiefs of Staff, 2019.

U.S. Department of State. *Foreign Relations of the United States Diplomatic Papers: The Conferences at Cairo and Tehran, 1943*. Washington, DC: Government Printing Office, 1943.

U.S. Marine Corps. *Tentative Manual for Landing Operations*. Quantico, VA: U.S. Marine Corps Schools, 1934.

U.S. Marine Corps Schools. PHIB-11, *Amphibious Operations—Naval Gunfire Support.* Quantico, VA: Marine Barracks, Marine Corps Schools, 1945.

U.S. Navy. *Annual Report of the Secretary of the Navy for the Fiscal Year 1937*. Washington, DC: Government Printing Office, 1937.

———. *Annual Report of the Secretary of the Navy for the Fiscal Year 1939*. Washington, DC: Government Printing Office, 1939.

———. *Annual Report of the Secretary of the Navy for the Fiscal Year 1940*. Washington, DC: Government Printing Office, 1940.

———. *Annual Reports of the Navy Department for the Fiscal Year 1932*. Washington, DC: Government Printing Office, 1932.

———. *U.S. Navy at War, 1941–1945: Official Reports to the Secretary of the Navy*. Washington, DC: Department of the Navy, 1946.

SELECT SECONDARY SOURCES

Adams, Michael C. C. *The Best War Ever: America and World War II*. Baltimore: Johns Hopkins University Press, 1994.

Alexander, Joseph H. *Across the Reef: The Marine Assault of Tarawa*. Washington, DC: Marine Corps Historical Center, 1993.

———. *Closing In: Marines in the Seizure of Iwo Jima*. Washington, DC: Marine Corps Historical Center, 1994.

———. *Storm Landings: Epic Amphibious Battles in the Central Pacific*. Annapolis, MD: Naval Institute Press, 1997.

———. *Utmost Savagery: The Three Days of Tarawa*. New York: Ivy Books, 1995.

Andrew Jr., Rod. *The First Fight: U.S. Marines in Operation Starlite—August 1965*. Washington, DC: Government Publishing Office, 2015.

Baker, Jonathan T. "Iwo Jima: The Unnecessary Battle." Master's thesis, USMC Command and Staff College, 2011.

Ballendorf, Dirk Anthony, and Merrill Lewis Bartlett. *Pete Ellis: An Amphibious Warfare Prophet, 1880–1923*. Annapolis, MD: Naval Institute Press, 1997.

Barno, David, and Nora Bensahel. *Adaptation under Fire: How Militaries Change in Wartime*. New York: Oxford University Press, 2020.

Bartley, Whitman S. *Iwo Jima: Amphibious Epic*. Washington, DC: Government Printing Office, 1954.

Berger, David H. Message to the Marine Corps, March 8, 2022. "33rd Anniversary of FMFM-1 Warfighting," https://www.hqmc.marines.mil/cmc/News/Article/Article/2959606/33rd-anniversary-of-fmfm-1-warfighting/.

Bickel, Keith B. *Mars Learning: The Marine Corps' Development of Small Wars Doctrine, 1915–1940*. Boulder, CO: Westview Press, 2001.

Biddle, Stephen. *Military Power: Explaining Victory and Defeat in Modern Battle*. Princeton, NJ: Princeton University Press, 2004.

Bidwell, Shelford, and Dominick Graham. *Fire-Power: The British Army Weapons and Theories of War, 1904–1945*. 1982. Reprint, South Yorkshire: Pen and Sword Military Classics, 2004.

Bix, Herbert P. *Hirohito and the Making of Modern Japan*. New York: Harper Collins, 2000.

Black, Jeremy. *Combined Operations: A Global History of Amphibious and Airborne Warfare*. Lanham, MD: Rowman and Littlefield, 2018.

Blumenson, Martin. *The Patton Papers, 1940–1945*. Boston: Houghton Mifflin Company, 1974.

Boggs Jr., Charles W. *Marine Aviation in the Philippines*. Washington, DC: Government Printing Office, 1951.

Burrell, Robert S. *The Ghosts of Iwo Jima*. College Station: Texas A&M University Press, 2006.

Cameron, Craig M. *American Samurai: Myth, Imagination, and the Conduct of Battle in the First Marine Division, 1941–1951*. New York: Cambridge University Press, 1994.

Carafano, James Jay. *GI Ingenuity: Improvisation, Technology, and Winning World War II*. Mechanicsburg, PA: Stackpole Books, 2006.

Chapin, John C. *Breaking the Outer Ring: Marine Landings in the Marshall Islands*. Washington, DC: Marine Corps Historical Center, 1994.

Condon, John P. *U.S. Marine Corps Aviation*. Washington, DC: Government Printing Office, 1987.

Doubler, Michael D. *Closing with the Enemy: How GIs Fought the War in Europe, 1944–1945*. Lawrence: University Press of Kansas, 1994.

Dower, John W. *War without Mercy: Race and Power in the Pacific War*. New York: Pantheon Books, 1986.

Ellis, John. *Brute Force: Allied Strategy and Tactics in the Second World War*. New York: Viking, 1990.

Fahey, James C. *The Ships and Aircraft of the U.S. Fleet*. Second War Edition. New York: Gemsco, 1944.

Felker, Craig C. *Testing American Sea Power: U.S. Navy Strategic Exercises, 1923–1940*. College Station: Texas A&M University Press, 2007.

Frank, Richard B. *Downfall: The End of the Imperial Japanese Empire*. New York: Penguin Books, 1999.

———. *Guadalcanal: The Definitive Account of the Landmark Battle*. New York: Penguin Books, 1990.

———. *Tower of Skulls: A History of the Asia-Pacific War, July 1937–May 1942*. New York: W. W. Norton, 2020.

Garand, George W., and Truman R. Stobridge. *History of U.S. Marine Corps Operations in World War II*. Vol. 4, *Western Pacific Operations*. Washington, DC: Government Printing Office, 1971.

Gatchel, Theodore L. *At the Water's Edge: Defending against the Modern Amphibious Assault*. Annapolis, MD: Naval Institute Press, 1996.

Gilbert, Gerald. *The Evolution of Tactics*. London: Hugh Rees Limited, 1907.

Griffith, Paddy. *Battle Tactics of the Western Front: The British Army's Art of Attack, 1916–18*. New Haven, CT: Yale University Press, 1994.

Grissom, Adam. "The Future of Military Innovation Studies." *Journal of Strategic Studies* 29, no. 5 (October 2006): 905–34.

Grotelueschen, Mark Ethan. *The AEF Way of War: The American Army and Combat in World War I*. New York: Cambridge University Press, 2007.

Gudmundsson, Bruce I. *On Artillery*. Westport, CT: Praeger, 1993.

———. *Stormtroop Tactics: Innovation in the German Army, 1914–1918*. 1989. Reprint, Westport, CT: Praeger Publishers, 1995.

Hastings, Max. *Overlord: D-Day and the Battle for Normandy*. New York: Simon and Schuster, 1984.

Heck, Timothy, and B. A. Friedman, eds. *On Contested Shores: The Evolving Role of Amphibious Operations in the History of Warfare*. Quantico, VA: Marine Corps University Press, 2020.

Heinl Jr., Robert Debs. *Soldiers of the Sea: The United States Marine Corps, 1775–1962*. 2nd ed. Baltimore: Nautical and Aviation Publishing Company of America, 1991.

Heinl Jr., Robert Debs, and John A. Crown. *The Marshalls: Increasing the Tempo*. Quantico, VA: Historical Branch, G-3 Division, Headquarters, U.S. Marine Corps, 1954.

Heinrichs, Waldo, and Marc Gallicchio. *Implacable Foes: War in the Pacific, 1944–1945*. New York: Oxford University Press, 2017.

Henri, Raymond, et al. *The U.S. Marines on Iwo Jima*. 1945, The Infantry Journal. Repr. 2019.

Herman, Arthur. *Freedom's Forge: How American Business Produced Victory in World War II*. New York: Random House, 2013.

Hoffman, Frank G. *Mars Adapting: Military Change during War*. Annapolis, MD: Naval Institute Press, 2021.

Hone, Trent. *Learning War: The Evolution of Fighting Doctrine in the U.S. Navy, 1898–1945*. Annapolis, MD: Naval Institute Press, 2018.

Hough, Frank O., Verle E. Ludwig, and Henry I. Shaw Jr. *History of U.S. Marine Corps Operations in World War II*. Vol. 1, *Pearl Harbor to Guadalcanal*. Washington, DC: Government Printing Office, 1966.

House, Jonathan M. *Combined Arms Warfare in the Twentieth Century*. Lawrence: University Press of Kansas, 2001.

Howard, Michael. "Military Science in an Age of Peace." *RUSI Journal* 119, no. 1 (March 1974): 3–11.

Isely, Jeter A., and Philip A. Crowl. *The U.S. Marines and Amphibious War: Its Theory, and Its Practice in the Pacific*. Princeton, NJ: Princeton University Press, 1951.

Johnson, Wray R. *Biplanes at War: U.S. Marine Corps Aviation in the Small Wars Era, 1913–1934*. Lexington: University Press of Kentucky, 2019.

Kakehashi, Kumiko. *So Sad to Fall in Battle: An Account of War Based on General Tadamichi Kuribayashi's Letters from Iwo Jima*. New York: Presidio Press, 2007.

Keegan, John. *The First World War*. New York: Alfred A. Knopf, 1999.

———. *The Second World War*. New York: Penguin Books, 2005.

Kennedy, Paul. *Engineers of Victory: The Problem Solvers Who Turned the Tide in the Second World War*. New York: Random House Trade Paperbacks, 2013.

King, Dan. *A Tomb Called Iwo Jima: Firsthand Accounts from Japanese Survivors*. North Charleston, SC: Pacific Press, 2020.

Krulak, Victor H. *First to Fight: An Inside View of the U.S. Marine Corps*. Annapolis, MD: Naval Institute Press, 1984.

Lacey, Sharon Tosi. *Pacific Blitzkrieg: World War II in the Central Pacific*. Denton: University of North Texas Press, 2013.

Linn, Brian McAllister. *The Echo of Battle: The Army's Way of War*. Cambridge, MA: Harvard University Press, 2007.

Long, Austin. *The Soul of Armies: Counterinsurgency Doctrine and Military Culture in the U.S. and UK*. Ithaca, NY: Cornell University Press, 2016.

Lorelli, John A. *To Foreign Shores: U.S. Amphibious Operations in World War II*. Annapolis, MD: Naval Institute Press, 1995.

Lynn, John A. *Battle: A History of Combat and Culture, from Ancient Greece to Modern America*. Boulder, CO: Westview, 2003.

McFadden, Brian S. "Marine Close Air Support in World War II." Master's thesis, U.S. Army Command and General Staff College, 1999.

McManus, John C. *Fire and Fortitude: The U.S. Army in the Pacific War, 1941–1943*. New York: Dutton Caliber, 2019.

Merillat, Herbert Christian Laing. *The Island: A History of the First Marine Division on Guadalcanal*. Yardley, PA: Westholme, 2010.

Millett, Allan R. "Assault from the Sea: The Development of Amphibious Warfare between the Wars." In *Military Innovation in the Interwar Period*, edited by Allan R. Millett and Williamson Murray, 50–95. New York: Cambridge University Press, 1996.

———. *Semper Fidelis: The History of the United States Marine Corps*. Rev. ed. New York: The Free Press, 1991.

Millett, Allan R., and Jack Shulimson, eds. *Commandants of the Marine Corps*. Annapolis, MD: Naval Institute Press, 2004.

Millett, Allan R., and Williamson, Murray, eds. *Military Innovation in the Interwar Period*. New York: Cambridge University Press, 1996.

———*A War To Be Won: Fighting the Second World War*. Cambridge, MA: Belknap Press, 2000.

Morison, Samuel Eliot. *History of United States Naval Operations in World War II*. Vol. 1, *The Rising Sun in the Pacific: 1931–April 1942*. 1948. Reprint, Boston: Little, Brown and Company, 1968.

———. *History of United States Naval Operations in World War II*. Vol. 7, *Aleutians, Gilberts and Marshalls: June 1942–April 1944*. 1951. Reprint, Edison, NJ: Castle Books, 2001.

———. *History of United States Naval Operations in World War II*. Vol. 8, *New Guinea and the Marianas: March 1944–August 1944*. Boston: Little, Brown and Company, 1953.

———. *History of United States Naval Operations in World War II*. Vol. 14, *Victory in the Pacific: 1945*. Boston: Little, Brown and Company, 1964.

Nagl, John A. *Learning to Eat Soup with a Knife: Counterinsurgency Lessons from Malaya and Vietnam*. 2002. Reprint, Chicago: University of Chicago Press, 2005.

Nalty, Bernard C., and Danny J. Crawford. *The United States Marines on Iwo Jima: The Battle and the Flag Raisings*. Washington, DC: History and Museums Division, Headquarters, U.S. Marine Corps, 1995.

Nasca, David S. *The Emergence of American Amphibious Warfare, 1898–1945*. Annapolis, MD: Naval Institute Press, 2020.

Newcomb, Richard F. *Iwo Jima*. New York: Holt, Rinehart, and Winston, 1965.

Nolan, Cathal J. *The Allure of Battle: A History of How Wars Have Been Won and Lost*. New York: Oxford University Press, 2017.

O'Brien, Phillips Payson. *How the War Was Won: Air-Sea Power and Allied Victory in World War II*. Cambridge: Cambridge University Press, 2015.

O'Connell, Aaron B. *Underdogs: The Making of the Modern Marine Corps*. Cambridge, MA: Harvard University Press, 2012.

Powell, James S. *Learning under Fire: The 112th Cavalry Regiment in World War II*. College Station: Texas A&M University Press, 2010.

Prange, Gordon W., Donald M. Goldstein, and Katherine V. Dillon. *At Dawn We Slept: The Untold Story of Pearl Harbor*. 1981. Reprint, New York: Penguin, 2001.

Robertson, Breanne, ed. *Investigating Iwo: The Flag Raisings in Myth, Memory, and Esprit de Corps*. Quantico, VA: Marine Corps History Division, 2019.

Rothenberg, Gunther E. "From Gallipoli to Guadalcanal." In *Assault from the Sea: Essays on the History of Amphibious Warfare*, ed. Merrill L. Bartlett. Annapolis, MD: Naval Institute Press, 1983.

Rottman, Gordon L. *U.S. Marine Corps World War II Order of Battle: Ground and Air Units in the Pacific War, 1939–1945*. Westport, CT: Greenwood Press, 2002.

———. *U.S. World War II Amphibious Tactics: Army and Marine Corps, Pacific Theater*. Long Island City, NY: Osprey Publishing, 2004.

Russell, James A. *Innovation, Transformation, and War: Counterinsurgency Operations in Anbar and Ninewa, Iraq, 2005–2007*. Stanford, CA: Stanford Security Studies, 2011.

Russell, James A., Frans Osinga, and Theo Farrell, eds. *Military Adaptation in Afghanistan*. Palo Alto, CA: Stanford Security Studies, 2013.

Schrijvers, Peter. *The GI War against Japan: American Soldiers in Asia and the Pacific during World War II*. New York: New York University Press, 2005.

Shaw Jr., Henry I., Bernard C. Nalty, and Edwin T. Turnbladh. *History of U.S. Marine Corps Operations in World War II*. Vol. 3, *Central Pacific Drive*. Washington, DC: Government Printing Office, 1966.

Sherrod, Robert. *History of Marine Corps Aviation in World War II*. San Rafael, CA: Presidio Press, 1952.

———. *On to Westward: The Battles of Saipan and Iwo Jima*. 1945. Reprint, Baltimore: Nautical and Aviation Publishing Company of America, 1990.

Smith, Peter C. *Dive Bomber! Aircraft, Technology, and Tactics in World War II*. Mechanicsburg, PA: Stackpole Books, 1992.

Spector, Ronald H. *Eagle against the Sun: The American War with Japan*. New York: Vintage Books, 1985.

Symonds, Craig L. *World War II at Sea: A Global History*. New York: Oxford University Press, 2018.

Taaffe, Stephen R. *Commanding the Pacific: Marine Corps Generals in World War II*. Annapolis, MD: Naval Institute Press, 2021.

Thompson, George Raynor, and Dixie R. Harris. *The Signal Corps: The Outcome (Mid-1943 through 1945)*. Washington, DC: U.S. Army Center of Military History, 1991.

Toll, Ian W. *The Conquering Tide: War in the Pacific Islands, 1942–1944*. New York: W. W. Norton, 2016.

———. *Twilight of the Gods: War in the Western Pacific, 1944–1945*. New York: W. W. Norton, 2020.

Travers, Tim. *How the War Was Won: Command and Technology in the British Army on the Western Front, 1917–1918*. New York: Routledge, 1992.

Ulbrich, David J. *Preparing for Victory: Thomas Holcomb and the Making of the Modern Marine Corps, 1936–1943*. Annapolis, MD: Naval Institute Press, 2011.

Venzon, Anne Cipriano. *From Whaleboats to Amphibious Warfare: Lt. Gen. "Howling Mad" Smith and the U.S. Marine Corps*. Westport, CT: Praeger, 2003.

Weinberg, Gerhard L. *A World at Arms: A Global History of World War II*. New York: Cambridge University Press, 1994.

Wheelan, Joseph. *Bloody Okinawa: The Last Great Battle of World War II*. New York: Hachette Books, 2020.

Wheeler, Richard. *A Special Valor: The U.S. Marines and the Pacific War*. 1983. Reprint, Annapolis, MD: Bluejacket Books, 2006.

Younger, Stephen M. *Silver State Dreadnought: The Remarkable Story of Battleship* Nevada. Annapolis, MD: Naval Institute Press, 2018.

Zabecki, David T. *Steel Wind: Colonel Georg Bruchmüller and the Birth of Modern Artillery*. Westport, CT: Praeger, 1994.

INDEX

ABOUT THE AUTHOR

Chris Hemler spent ten years on active duty in the U.S. Marine Corps, holding posts with the 24th Marine Expeditionary Unit, 2d Marine Aircraft Wing, and U.S. Naval Academy Marine Detachment. In 2019 he was awarded the General Lemuel Shepherd Memorial Dissertation Fellowship and Rear Admiral Samuel Eliot Morison Scholarship. He holds a PhD in military history from Texas A&M University and serves as a principal advisor with Frontier Design Group.

The Naval Institute Press is the book-publishing arm of the U.S. Naval Institute, a private, nonprofit, membership society for sea service professionals and others who share an interest in naval and maritime affairs. Established in 1873 at the U.S. Naval Academy in Annapolis, Maryland, where its offices remain today, the Naval Institute has members worldwide.

Members of the Naval Institute support the education programs of the society and receive the influential monthly magazine *Proceedings* or the colorful bimonthly magazine *Naval History* and discounts on fine nautical prints and on ship and aircraft photos. They also have access to the transcripts of the Institute's Oral History Program and get discounted admission to any of the Institute-sponsored seminars offered around the country.

The Naval Institute's book-publishing program, begun in 1898 with basic guides to naval practices, has broadened its scope to include books of more general interest. Now the Naval Institute Press publishes about seventy titles each year, ranging from how-to books on boating and navigation to battle histories, biographies, ship and aircraft guides, and novels. Institute members receive significant discounts on the Press' more than eight hundred books in print.

Full-time students are eligible for special half-price membership rates. Life memberships are also available.

For more information about Naval Institute Press books that are currently available, visit www.usni.org/press/books. To learn about joining the U.S. Naval Institute, please write to:

Member Services
U.S. Naval Institute
291 Wood Road
Annapolis, MD 21402-5034
Telephone: (800) 233-8764
Fax: (410) 571-1703
Web address: www.usni.org